D1824729

Translated Texts for Historians

This series is designed to meet the needs of students of ancient and medieval history and others who wish to broaden their study by reading source material, but whose knowledge of Latin or Greek is not sufficient to allow them to do so in the original language. Many important Late Imperial and Dark Age texts are currently unavailable in translation and it is hoped that TTH will help to fill this gap and to complement the secondary literature in English which already exists. The series relates principally to the period 300-800 AD and includes Late Imperial, Greek, Byzantine and Syriac texts as well as source books illustrating a particular period or theme. Each volume is a self-contained scholarly translation with an introductory essay on the text and its author and notes on the text indicating major problems of interpretation, including textual difficulties.

The cover illustration is the drawing of an asphodel in *The Greek Herbal of Dioscorides illustrated by a Byzantine AD 512, Englished by John Goodyer AD 1655, Edited and first printed by Robert T. Gunther AD 1933*, Oxford 1934, fig. 199, p. 210, reproduced by kind permission of the Oxford University Press

A full list of published titles in the Translated Texts for Historians series is available on request. The most recently published are shown below.

For full details of Translated Texts for Historians, including prices and ordering information, please write to the following: **All countries, except the USA and Canada**: Liverpool University Press, 4 Cambridge Street, Liverpool, L69 7ZU, UK (*Tel* +44-[0]151-794 2233 *Fax* +44-[0]151-794 2235, Email J.M. Smith@liv.ac.uk, http://www.liverpool-unipress.co.uk). **USA and Canada:** University of Pennsylvania Press, 4200 Pine Street, Philadelphia, PA 19104-6097, USA (*Tel* +1-215-898-6264, *Fax* +1-215-898-0404).

Translated Texts for Historians
Volume 37

A Christian's Guide to Greek Culture

The Pseudo-Nonnus *Commentaries* **on** *Sermons* **4, 5, 39 and 43 by Gregory of Nazianzus**

Translated with an introduction and notes by
JENNIFER NIMMO SMITH

Liverpool
University
Press

First published 2001
Liverpool University Press
4 Cambridge Street
Liverpool, L69 7ZU

British Library Cataloguing-in-Publication Data
A British Library CIP Record is available.
ISBN 0-85323-917-7

Set in Times by
Koinonia, Manchester
Printed in the European Union by
Cromwell Press, Trowbridge, Wiltshire.

To my mother, the memory of my father, and, as ever, my husband

TABLE OF CONTENTS

ABBREVIATIONS

PRIMARY TEXTS

Ael.   Aelian, *N.A.* = *Nature of Animals*
        V.H. = *Historical Miscellany* (*Varia Historia*)
Aesch.   Aeschylus
Alex.   Lycophron, *Alexandra*
Anon. Prol.   *Anonymous Prolegomena to Platonic Philosophy*, ed. L.G.
        Westerink
Anth. Pal.   *Anthologia Palatina*
Apollod.   Apollodorus, *Libr.* = *Library*
            Epit. = *Epitome*
Ap. Rhod.   Apollonius Rhodius, *Argonautica*
Aristoph.   Aristophanes
Athen.   Athenaeus, *The Deipnosophists*
Call.   Callimachus
Clem. Al.   Clement of Alexandria, *Exhort.* = *Exhortation to the Greeks*
            Protrept. = *Protrepticon*
            Strom. = *Stromata*
Commentaries   *Pseudo-Nonniani in IV Orationes Gregorii Nazianzeni*
        Commentarii editi a Jennifer Nimmo Smith collationibus
        Versionum Syriacarum a Sebastian Brock Versionisque Armenicae
        a Bernard Coulie additis
D.L.   Diogenes Laertius, *Lives of the Philosophers*
D.S.   Diodorus Siculus, *Library*
Dem.   Demosthenes
Eur.   Euripides
Gr. Naz.   Gregory of Nazianzus
Hdt.   Herodotus, *Histories*
Hes.   Hesiod, *Theog.* = *Theogony*
        Works = *Works and Days*
        Sh. = *Shield of Herakles*
Hyg.   Hyginus, *Fab.* = *Fables*
        Astr. = *Astronomia*
Iambl.   Iamblichus, *Life of Pythagoras*

Il.   Homer, *Iliad*

Isocr.   Isocrates, *Or.* = *Orations*

Luc.   Lucian

Malalas   John Malalas, *The Chronicle*

Met.   Ovid, *Metamorphoses*

Od.   Homer, *Odyssey*

Olymp.   Olympiodorus, *Commentary on Plato's Phaedo*

Palaeph.   Palaephatus, *On Unbelievable Tales*

Paus.   Pausanias, *Description of Greece*

Photius   Photius, *Library*

Pind.   Pindar, *Ol.* = *Olympian Odes*
      Pyth. = *Pythian Odes*
      Nem. = *Nemean Odes*

Pl.   Plato, *Charm.* = *Charmides, or Temperance*
      Gorg. = *Gorgias*
      Ph. = *Phaedo*
      Rep. = *Republic*
      Theaet. = *Theaetatus*
      Tim. = *Timaeus*

Pliny   Pliny the Elder, *N.H.* = *Natural History*

Plut.   Plutarch

Ps-Erat.   Pseudo-Eratosthenes, *Catasterisms*

Ps-N.   Pseudo-Nonnus

Sen.   Seneca

Serv.   Servius, *on Aen.* = *Commentary on the Aeneid*
      on Ecl. = *Commentary on the Eclogues*
      on Georg. = *Commentary on the Georgics*

Socr.   Socrates, *Ecclesiastical History*

Soph.   Sophocles

Steph. Byz.   Stephanus of Byzantium, 10th cent. epitome of 6th cent.
      Ethnica

Str.   Strabo, *Geography*

Theocr.   Theocritus

Thuc.   Thucydides, *Histories*

Tzetz.   John Tzetzes, *Alex.* = *Scholia on the Alexandra of Lycophron*

Xen.   Xenophon, *Anab.* = *Anabasis*
      Apol. = *Apology of Socrates*
      Hunting = *On hunting with hounds* (*Cynegeticus*)
      Mem. = *Memorabilia*

Zen.   Zenobius, *Epitome collectionum Lucilli Tarrhaei et Didymi, Corpus Paroemiographorum Graecorum* I

THE MANUSCRIPTS OF THE *COMMENTARIES*, THEIR RECENSIONS AND THEIR *VERSIONS*

Arm.   The Armenian Version of the *Commentaries*
F   The manuscript Vat. Gr. 437
G.V.   The Georgian Versions of the *Commentaries*
L   The manuscript, British Library (Add.) 18231, AD 972
m   The abbreviated recension of the *Commentaries*
n   The longer recension of the *Commentaries*
Syr.   The Syriac Version of the *Commentaries*

OTHER

Bernardi   J. Bernardi, *CJ = Grégoire de Nazianze Discours 4–5 Contre Julien*
           43 = Grégoire de Nazianze Discours 43
Brock   S. Brock, *The Syriac Version of the Pseudo-Nonnos Mythological Scholia*
Byz.   *Byzantion*
BZ   *Byzantinische Zeitschrift*
Cameron, *Christianity*   Averil Cameron, *Christianity and the Rhetoric of Empire*
Cameron, *Procopius*   Averil Cameron, *Procopius and the Sixth Century*
CQ   *Classical Quarterly*
Demoen   C. Demoen, *Pagan and Christian Exempla in Gregory Nazianzen*
Fontenrose   J. Fontenrose, *The Delphic Oracle: its Responses and Operations*
Gantz   T. Gantz, *Early Greek Myth*
GRBS   *Greek, Roman and Byzantine Studies*
H.H.   *Homeric Hymn*
Kaster, *Guardians*   R. Kaster, *Guardians of Language. The Grammarian and Society in Late Antiquity.*
Kennedy, *Greek Rhetoric*   G.A. Kennedy, *Greek Rhetoric under Christian Emperors*
Kurmann   A. Kurmann, *Gregor von Nazianz Oratio 4 Gegen Julian Ein Kommentar*

Lampe   *A Patristic Greek Lexicon* edited by G.W.H. Lampe, Oxford, 1961
Lugaresi   L. Lugaresi, *4 = Gregorio di Nazianzo Contro Giuliano
        L'Apostata Orazione IV*
Lugaresi   *5 = Gregorio di Nazianzo La Morte di Giuliano L'Apostata
        Orazione V*
Meredith, *Cappadocians*   A. Meredith, *The Cappadocians*
Meredith, *Gr. Nys.*   A. Meredith, *Gregory of Nyssa*
'Nonnus'   'Nonnus and Pseudo-Nonnos: the poet and the commentator',
        J. Nimmo Smith, in ΦΙΛΕΛΛΗΝ, ed. C.N. Constantinides, N.M.
        Panagiotakes, E. Jeffreys and A.D. Angelou, pp. 281–299
OCD   *The Oxford Classical Dictionary*, 3rd Edition, ed. Simon
        Hornblower and Anthony Spawforth, Oxford, 1996
Parke   H.W. Parke, *The Oracles of Zeus*
PG   *Patrologia Graeca*
PL   *Patrologia Latina*
PO   *Patrologia Orientalis*
Ruether   Rosemary Radford Ruether, *Gregory of Nazianzus, Rhetor and
        Philosopher*
SC   Sources Chrétiennes
Thesaurus   *Thesaurus Pseudo-Nonni. Commentarii in IV Orationes
        Gregorii Nazianzeni, curantibus B. Coulie, J. Nimmo Smith et
        CETEDOC*
Weitzmann, *Greek Mythology*   K. Weitzmann, *Greek Mythology in
        Byzantine Art*
Weitzmann, *Age of Spirituality*   K. Weitzmann, ed., *Age of Spirituality.
        Late Antique and Early Christian Art. Third to Seventh Century*
West   M.L. West, *The Orphic Poems*
Westerink, *Anon. Prol.*   *Anonymous Prolegomena to Platonic Philosophy*,
        ed. and trans. L.G. Westerink
Westerink, *Olymp.*   L.G.Westerink, *The Greek Commentaries on Plato's
        Phaedo. 1. Olympiodorus*

ACKNOWLEDGEMENTS

I should like to thank the General Editors for commissioning this work, Mary Whitby for her constructive criticism and patience during its progress, the reader (N.B. McLynn) for his stimulating report, and The Carnegie Trust for the Universities of Scotland for their grant towards the production of the volume.

My gratitude is also due to Jill Evans and the other staff of the Inter-Library Loans Department, Main Library, George Square, Edinburgh, for their ready and efficient help over the years.

Jennifer Nimmo Smith
Edinburgh
March 2001

INTRODUCTION[1]

The Christian accounts of the Delphic reply (perhaps its final utterance) to Julian's envoy in the 360s AD are bleak:

> Tell ye the king: the carven hall has fallen in decay:
>   Apollo hath no chapel left, no prophesying bay,
> No talking spring. The stream is dry that had so much to say.[2]

The words, whether passed on as an appeal for funds for a fallen sanctuary, or an admission of decline, make clear the oracle's despair.[3] Yet the learning of which the god Apollo was the patron continued to flourish at least until the late sixth century, despite the triumph of Christianity. Within decades of the oracle's utterance, Gregory of Nazianzus (AD 330–390?) composed *Sermons* 4, 5, 39 and 43, which are remarkable for their large number of classical allusions.[4] They reflect Gregory's determination, shared by other Christians

1 This Introduction is largely based on the introduction to the edition of the Pseudo-Nonnus *Commentaries*, and the later extensions to, and discussions of, the material given in the paper, 'Why Pseudo-Nonnos: pagan learning through Christian eyes' at the Classical Association Conference held in St Andrews in April 1995; in 'Mythology and Magic in the Sixth Century AD', given to the Classical Association of Scotland (Edinburgh and SE Centre) on 6 December 1996; and in my introduction to the *Thesaurus Pseudo-Nonni*, pp. x–xi and xlix.

2 *Anthologia Palatina*, vol. III, ch. vi, no. 122, translated by Sir William Marris, *The Oxford Book of Greek Verse in Translation*, Oxford, 1938, No. 627 reprinted by kind permission of Oxford University Press.

3 The authenticity of this oracle, reported in the 10th-century *Passio Artemii*, most probably from the Arian historian Philostorgius (?AD 368–439), and also found in the 12th-century George Cedrenus, is disputed, though it is generally admired. For Parke and Wormell it is the 'last utterance at Delphi, probably given by the priests', H.W. Parke and D.E.W. Wormell, *The Delphic Oracle*, Oxford, 1956, vol. I, p. 290; for Fontenrose, it is 'quasi-historical', p. 56, and, as Query 263, 'not genuine'. T.E. George reviews the evidence and previous discussions of the case in 'Julian and the last oracle at Delphi', *GRBS* 24 (1983), pp. 355–66. He concludes that the words probably represent an authentic tradition.

4 Demoen, p. 74. The texts of Gregory's *Sermons* 4, 5 and 43 have been edited and translated into French by J. Bernardi, *Grégoire de Nazianze Discours 4–5 Contre Julien* and *Discours 42–43*, both volumes with full introductions and notes. *Sermon* 39 is, as yet, not edited in this series. There is a commentary in German on *Sermon* 4 by Alois Kurmann, and others on *Sermons* 4 and 5 by L. Lugaresi, in Italian, as noted in the bibliography. The English translations are of an earlier date and vintage, *Sermons* 4 and 5 by C.W. King, *Julian the Emperor, containing Gregory Nazianzen's two invectives and Libanius' monody*, … in 1888, and those of *Sermons* 39

both before and after him, to preserve the useful aspects of Greek[5] learning for the service of the Church in a world where a pagan system of education still held power. Less than two centuries later, the work of the unknown commentator which is translated here highlights the survival of Greek learning in these same sermons, albeit in an artless and elementary way. The commentator, in contrast to Gregory, used a basic technique of the schools to compose his work. His *Commentaries* are but 'collections and explanations' of the majority of Gregory's classical references in these sermons. They are carried out with great single-mindedness and only a token regard for the nature and eloquence of the texts. Some of his explanations are inadequate, and others confused or incorrect. All are nevertheless written in the same unpretentious, immediately identifiable and confident style. They present us with a striking insight into one Christian's attitude to the interface between Greek literature and pagan beliefs in an increasingly Christianised world.

Both types of work are thus formed, according to the ability of their authors, by the training of the schools. I shall give a brief account of the nature of this before setting both authors and their works within the context of their respective times.

EDUCATION AND EASTERN CHRISTIANITY

Although the early Christians had turned away in disgust from the 'wisdom of the world', it has long been recognised that many of the arguments they used against it were based on practices within its educational system.[6] Some

---

and 43 by C.G. Browne and J.E. Swallow, *Select Orations of Saint Gregory Nazianzen, vol. VII: A Select Library of the Nicene and Post-Nicene Fathers of the Christian Church*, 1894, pp. 352–59 and 395–422, respectively. *Sermon 43* is also translated in L.P. McCauley et al., *Funeral Orations of Gregory of Nazianzus and Ambrose*, Washington, DC, 1968.

5 I use 'Greek' rather than 'Hellenic' here, in the title and throughout the work, because it stands for both the language and the culture and beliefs expressed in that language, an aspect only found in this term in English, though present in both *Hellēn* and *Hellēnizein* in Greek. Jewish writers described Gentiles, whether Christian or pagan, as *Hellēnes*, and many Greek Christian Fathers of the East used the word of pagans whose beliefs were based on Greek mythology or philosophy (see both LSJ and Lampe s.v.). In the *Commentaries*, the commentator applies this term to Greek nationals and their pagan cults alike. The Syriac version of the *Commentaries* translates it as 'Greek' or 'pagan' according to its context.

6 Averil Cameron, for example, speaks of the 'deep ambiguity' that lies in the Apostle Paul's long rhetorical comparison between wisdom and folly at the beginning of 1 Corinthians 1.17–2.16, and 3.18–20, *Christianity*, pp. 33–35, with notes 61–70.

individual efforts at subversion of this must have existed, such as that reflected in the legendary account of the martyrdom of St Babylas of Nicomedia (AD ?304). He was denounced and martyred, with eighty-four of his pupils, for teaching them Christian hymns and psalms instead of Greek learning.[7] Still, there were, on the whole, no full-scale attempts in the East to set up a Christian system of primary education. Parents were expected to look after their children's moral and religious training in the home; they left the schools to ensure that their children made their way in the world, a way firmly linked with a thorough training in Greek learning and culture.[8] When adults decided to be baptised into the Christian faith, of course, they were expected to attend the classes of instruction organised in the churches by church leaders.

Pagan and Christian children attended the same primary schools, and boys in particular went on to the secondary schools, and then, for higher education, to the great centres of learning based in the cities of Alexandria, Antioch, Athens, Beirut, the Caesareas in Cappadocia and Palestine respectively, and Constantinople. Once children had learnt their letters and numbers at the primary stage, often from copying out and sounding the names of gods and heroes from the Homeric poems, together with copybook apophthegms, they went on to study literature and other subjects at the next. There they were set passages of Homer to begin with, learning the meanings of obsolete and difficult terms, and the 'story' behind every proper name, before going on to consider selected works of other poets, orators and dramatists.[9] These 'stories' were also used as examples, to illustrate points at issue, and to clinch an argument. The students could also be set short

7 *Inédits byzantins d'Ochrida, Candie et Moscou*, ed. F. Halkin, Subsidia hagiographica 38, Brussels, 1963, pp. 330f., discussed as Item 192 in the Prosopography (*Dubii, Falsi, Varii*) of Kaster, *Guardians*, p. 387.

8 The leading account of education both Greek and Roman from Homer to the end of classical antiquity is to be found in H.I. Marrou, *A History of Education in Antiquity*, translated from the French edition of 1948 by George Lamb, New York, 1956. M.L.W. Laistner's study of 1951, *Christianity and Pagan Culture in the Later Roman Empire, together with An English Translation of John Chrysostom's Address on Vainglory and the Right Way for Parents to Bring Up Their Children*, is also of great value, with M.L. Clarke, *Higher Education in the Ancient World*, London, 1971, and the useful survey in Neil Hopkinson, *Greek Poetry of the Imperial Period*, Cambridge, 1993, pp. 3–10. Kaster, *Guardians*, pp. 11–31, provides a salutary critique of the narrow scope and exclusivity of ancient education.

9 See *Comm.* 4.76 for Ps-N.'s description of the three works of Hesiod, 'which are studied (sc. in the schools)', a passage also discussed by M.L. West, *Hesiod. Theogony*, Oxford, 1966, p. 52.

exercises in composition, and were trained to declaim in public, producing set speeches which were often on melodramatic and unlikely themes.[10] Much emphasis was placed on learning by rote. More technical rhetorical and philosophical studies followed, with music, mathematics and medicine in higher education; there is evidence that, in the sixth century in Alexandria, at least, some kind of 'general courses' preceded more detailed teaching on specific texts.[11]

The work was carried out with many aids for both teachers and students. Commentaries were written to elucidate every type of text, first composed as separate treatises and then added, as excerpts, or notes collected from several different authors, to the margins of the texts upon which they commented; handbooks on the theory and practice of rhetoric, with collections of illustrations of specific points from the orators, had been composed since the fifth century BC. These described how speeches of different types should be composed, and the forms of language appropriate to each. By the second century AD, they included lists of exercises (*progymnasmata*) for beginners in writing short passages in varied modes – a fable, for example, or an anecdote, a narrative, the explanation of a proverb, an argument for or against any given proposition, a discussion of a commonplace, praise or blame of an individual, personification, description, a detailed argument, and a discussion of a law. Each topic was divided and subdivided, and provided with examples. There were also collections of figures of speech, with citations of classical authors. Each figure of speech in the latter was given under a separate heading, or in a separate paragraph. There is one, from the third or fourth century AD by the rhetor Tiberius, which is devoted to figures of speech from a single author, Demosthenes. It begins with an explanation of what a figure of speech is, lists the ones he intends to explain, and then explains and illustrates them. The handbooks more usually draw upon several authors, as even Tiberius does: though he concentrates mainly upon Demosthenes, he also cites from Aeschines, Thucydides, Homer, Isocrates and Euripides among others. The majority of these works have prefaces, which describe the importance and usefulness of the work to come,

---

10 For a lively collection of 4th-century examples of these in translation, with an excellent introduction and notes, see D.A. Russell, *Libanius. Imaginary Speeches. A Series of Declamations*, London, 1996.

11 Westerink, *Olymp.*, intro., p. 27 and the note to 1.§11.6 on pp. 52–53. These passages are also discussed with specific reference to the vocabulary of the *Commentaries* in the Introduction by the author to *Thesaurus Pseudo-Nonni*, pp. x–xi, and n. 8.

and are written in a clear didactic Greek.[12] Assiduous students also published the notes they had made on the lectures of famous philosophers, or wrote their own additions to their masters' works.

All this learning for devout Christians, however, was but a means to an end, the preaching and teaching of the doctrines of Christianity. Knowledge of Greek learning and thought, and practice in its philosophy and rhetoric, gave the leaders of the religious establishment credibility and an equal voice among the so-called 'pagan élite',[13] especially after Christianity received imperial approval in the fourth century. The traditional system of education was still one road to office in both Church and State. Nor were the centres of learning closed to Christian teachers and rhetors; they taught there together with pagan scholars.

Christians with such pagan learning had still to remain on guard to preserve their interpretation of Christianity from all taint of heresy. They did not always succeed. A brilliant scholar like Origen (AD ?184/5–?254/5), who had made use of his classical education to support his widowed mother and siblings as a teacher, gave this teaching up when he felt that its continued practice was incompatible with his other role as a Christian exegete. He sold his library of fine classical texts for the daily payment of a small pension for his upkeep for the rest of his life.[14] Even this did not save his teachings from dispute during his lifetime and after his death, and he and his works were finally condemned and anathematised by the Church in the

12 For the later rhetorical handbooks, see Kennedy, *Greek Rhetoric*, ch. 2, and *idem*, *A New History of Classical Rhetoric*, Princeton, 1994 (which revises and abridges *The Art of Persuasion in Greece*, *The Art of Persuasion in the Roman World*, and the previously mentioned book), ch. 3, for the earlier examples of such works. One of the most influential of these was by the pagan rhetor, Hermogenes (2nd cent. AD), *On Issues*. It explains the art of rhetoric, the importance of defining the subjects 'at issue' in the argument, and how these should be marshalled and handled (M. Heath, *Hermogenes, On Issues. Strategies of Argument in Later Greek Rhetoric*, Oxford, 1995, intro., pp. 20–24). The text of Tiberius, described by Kennedy, *Greek Rhetoric*, p. 123, is given in Spengel, *Rhetores Graeci*, iii, pp. 59–82, and edited by G. Ballaira, *Tiberii de figuris Demosthenicis*, Athens, 1968. Citations from Aeschines are found in 11.18 and 31.10, from Homer in 11.26 and 28, from Thucydides in 27.13, Isocrates in 33.11, and Euripides in 47.20.

13 The persisting influence of a 'classical education' is described most recently by Kaster, *Guardians*, pp. 27–28, and by Cameron, *Christianity*, pp. 138–40.

14 Eusebius, *H.E.* 6.3.8. Origen was not alone: other Fathers of the Church did the same. Jerome (AD 331–420) vividly describes how he felt his love of Cicero's works stood between him and God (*Select Letters,* trans. F.A. Wright, Loeb, repr. 1954, *Ep.* 22), and Augustine (AD 354–430) resigned from teaching rhetoric in Milan after his conversion to Christianity in 386 (*Confessions*, 8.6.13–9.4).

mid-sixth century.[15] His methods nevertheless inspired other Christian thinkers despite their later rejection of his thought or silence about his work.[16] Among these were Gregory of Nazianzus and Basil of Caesarea, the subject of Gregory's *Sermon* 43. Their knowledge of Origen's works is shown by their joint authorship of, or close association with, a selection of passages from his work, the *Philocalia*.[17] In one of these passages, a letter from Origen to a pupil, another Gregory,[18] Origen described how Greek

15 Origen's life and teaching is discussed by Henry Chadwick, *Early Christian Thought and the Classical Tradition, Studies in Justin, Clement and Origen*, Oxford, 1966, and H. Crouzel, *Origène*, translated as *Origen: The Life and Thought of the First Great Theologian*, by A.S. Worrall, San Francisco, 1989, among others. See E.A. Clark, *The Origenist Controversy. The Cultural Construction of an Early Christian Debate*, Princeton, 1992, for an analysis of 4th- to 6th-century discussions of his work. The 9th-century scholar Photius, twice Patriarch of Constantinople, condemns his ideas in his *Library*, a collection of notes on 280 books, in Codex 8 (Wilson, p. 30): 'Read Origen, *On first principles*, in four books, of which the first is about Father, Son and Holy Spirit. In which he utters many blasphemies ...' He also adds, about the fourth book: 'how scripture is divinely inspired; finally how one ought to read and understand the scriptures'.

16 Jaroslav Pelikan, *Christianity and Classical Culture, The Metamorphosis of Natural Theology in the Christian Encounter with Hellenism*, New Haven, 1993, pp. 6–7, 29–30, 47 and 224.

17 Whether Gregory and Basil compiled it or not: see M. Harl, in the introduction to her edition (with translation and notes), *Origène Philocalie, 1–20 Sur les Écritures* (with *La lettre à Africanus sur l'Histoire de Suzanne* by N. De Lange), SC 302, Paris, 1983, pp. 19–24. Other editors of the *Ph.*, such as É. Junod, the editor of *Philocalia 21–27* (SC 226, Paris, 1976) accept both Gregory and Basil as its authors without question (*op cit.*, pp. 11–13) as do many others, including Meredith, *Cappadocians*, p. 10, though opinions remain divided. Gregory sent a copy of it as a present to a friend, a fellow bishop, Theodore (*Ep.* 115). He describes the gift as follows: 'I have sent you a little book, the *Philocalia* of Origen, which contains selections of (passages) useful for students, as a remembrance of me and of the holy Basil.' The heading to Chapter 13 reads: 'When and for whom the knowledge of philosophy is useful for the explanation of the Holy Scriptures, with proof (taken) from the Scriptures.' The text of Origen's letter appears in full in *Grégoire le Thaumaturge, Remerciement à Origène, Lettre d' Origène à Grégoire*, ed. H. Crouzel, SC 148, Paris, 1969, pp. 185–95, and is translated into English in *St Gregory Thaumaturgus, Life and Works. Translated by Michael Slusser. The Fathers of the Church. A New Translation*, Washington, DC, 1998.

18 This Gregory has been traditionally identified as Gregory Thaumaturgus or The Wonderworker (AD 213–275), the bishop of Neocaesarea in Pontus, who studied with Origen in Caesarea in Palestine, before he became the bishop of Neocaesarea, and, according to Basil, converted many there and in the whole of Pontus, to Christianity. Among these was Macrina the Elder, Basil's grandmother, and he was greatly admired by Basil and his brother Gregory of Nyssa. His influence on them is described in Meredith, *Cappadocians*, ch. 1.2. He may also have been another Gregory, a Christian student in Alexandria. See the work by M. Slusser cited above for a useful summary of current scholarly opinion.

culture could be used for the interpretation of the Scriptures by reference to the well-known texts from Exodus about the 'spoiling of the Egyptians'.[19] He then argued that the gold taken from the Egyptians was probably melted down by the Israelites to make the Ark and other sacred objects for divine worship, adding a warning that there were dangers involved in such learning, and that the Scriptures should always be the main subject of study for Christians.[20] His warnings were not heeded by some who later fell into heresy: Gregory and Basil followed this advice themselves and passed it on to others.

GREGORY'S BACKGROUND AND EDUCATION[21]

Gregory of Nazianzus was the son of a new member of the Christian Church. His father, Gregory the Elder (AD 275–374), was originally an Hypsistarian, a member of a sect which worshipped one god and reverenced fire. He married a Christian, Nonna, and was converted to her faith at the age of fifty by her prayers and constant tears, and baptised when the bishops of the Eastern Church passed through Nazianzus on their way to the Council of Nicaea in AD 325. His family was wealthy (a wealth from which he was temporarily disinherited when he became a Christian) and he had been involved in the civil administration of Nazianzus, with some success. He was thus invited to become its bishop, less than five years after his baptism. Gregory, his first son, was born in AD 330, and dedicated even before his birth to the service of the Church by his mother. To this devout family background was added, perhaps because of his father's perception of an omission in his own upbringing, all the advantages of a classical education.[22]

19 3.22, 11.2 and 12.35–6. This passage recurs in Jerome, Augustine, *De Doctrina Christiana*, 2.40 (O. Stählin, 'Zu einem vielgebrauchten Vergleich', *Blätter für das Gymnasial-Schulwesen* 52 [1916], p. 178) and is a commonplace in later Christian writers.

20 *Philocalia* 13.3 and 13.4.

21 Full details of Gregory's life and times, of which the above is but a partial summary, can be found in P. Gallay, *La vie de S. Grégoire*, Paris, 1930, and in the Introduction to his edition of Gregory's Letters (*Briefe*, Berlin, 1969); Rosemary Radford Ruether, *Gregory of Nazianzus, Rhetor and Philosopher*, Oxford, 1969; and Jean Bernardi, *Saint Grégoire de Nazianze. Le Théologien et son Temps (330–390)*, Paris, 1995. There are shorter accounts also in F.W. Norris, L. Williams and F. Williams, *Faith gives Fullness to Reasoning, The Five Theological Orations of Gregory of Nazianzen*, Leiden, 1991; Meredith, *Cappadocians*, ch. 4; and Carolinne White, *Gregory of Nazianzus, Autobiographical Poems*, Oxford, 1996.

22 Gregory notes of his father that, though unskilled in oratory, he surpassed the teaching skills of other, more learned, preachers through his piety and orthodoxy (*Sermon* 18.16).

Gregory's younger brother, Caesarius (later St Caesarius) was also well educated and went on to become a physician in the Imperial Court in Byzantium. His sister, Gorgonia, became a devout and pious wife and mother. The family of Gregory's lifelong friend Basil, on the other hand, was of well-established Christian stock on both sides, converted to Christianity in the previous century,[23] and his father was a teacher of rhetoric in Caesarea in Cappadocia. Basil (AD 329/330–379) had several brothers and sisters: his eldest sister, Macrina, was both extremely learned and leader of a women's religious community. One of his brothers, Gregory of Nyssa, taught rhetoric before he became a bishop; another brother, Peter, became the bishop of Sebaste.

Gregory took pains to emphasise his early love of literature, though he defined it carefully as a determination 'to make bastard letters serve as assistants to the genuine ones'.[24] After he had studied in Caesarea in Cappadocia, where he possibly first met Basil, he went on to Caesarea in Palestine, to the rhetor, Thespesius, then Alexandria, and at last to Athens.[25] There Basil joined him from Constantinople.[26] Together they faced the lively and obstreperous rival parties of students who tried to drag newcomers to their own, favoured tutor. Gregory saved Basil, according to his own account in *Sermon* 43, from a noisy and humiliating initiation into student life, and defended him in a public debate against former friends. While other students went their own ways in the largely pagan city, Gregory and Basil concentrated on their studies, both religious and secular (denoted by him as those

23 See n. 18 above for Basil's paternal grandmother, Macrina the Elder, and Gregory Thaumaturgus in Neocaesarea. Basil of Caesarea, too, has been the subject of many studies: see the recent account of his life and career in Philip Rousseau, *Basil of Caesarea*, Berkeley, 1994, with its full bibliography.

24 Lines 112–114 in *Poem* 2.1.11 (in the translation by C. White cited in n. 21 above).

25 For his studies in the Caesareas of Cappadocia and Palestine, see *Sermon* 7.6. In 43.13 he again mentions the local Caesarea with reference to both his and Basil's studies. Jerome describes him as the student of the rhetor, Thespesius, in Palestine, *Of Illustrious Men*, 113, *PL* 23, 747A. Gregory makes a very brief reference to his time in Alexandria, being more concerned to explain he was so eager to go to Athens that he set out there at the beginning of winter, a dangerous time to undertake a voyage (*Poem* 2.1.11.124–130).

26 The evidence that they both studied in Antioch under the pagan rhetor Libanius, given by the 5th-century ecclesiastical historians Socrates (4.26) and Sozomen (6.17), is not supported by Gregory's description of his studies in *Poem* 2.1.11, for he mentions only Alexandria (lines 128–9) and Athens (211 onwards) after Palestine, but is accepted by some modern scholars, most notably J. Mossay, *Theologische Realenzyklopädie* 14, 165, and Meredith, *Cappadocians*, p. 21.

'from outside').[27] The latter left a deep impression on the two young men, despite the fact that both went on to high office in the Church, Basil becoming Bishop of Caesarea and Gregory briefly attaining to the See of Constantinople. They treated their knowledge of Greek culture with caution, however, with Origen's teaching in mind.[28]

Basil wrote a letter of advice, ostensibly to his nephews, and, possibly, nieces, on how to profit from Greek literature.[29] It may well have been intended for a wider circulation, and, although its actual date of composition is not known, was probably written within the last ten years of his life.[30] In a much-cited passage in this, he says: 'So, just as we bent back the thorns when we picked roses, let us, in benefiting from whatever is good in such works as these, protect ourselves from the harm (within them).'[31] This image recurs in Gregory's poetry, in a bitter meditation on the life of a teacher of rhetoric which faced him if he refused an unwanted promotion in the Church[32] – 'was I to be left penniless in charge of a penniless flock, ...

27 *Sermon* 43.21: 'Two ways were known to us, the first of greater value, the second of smaller consequence: the one leading to our sacred buildings and our teachers there, the other to the instructors "from outside". All others we left to those who would pursue them'. See Ruether for an analysis of the effect Gregory's rhetorical and philosophical studies had on his career and writings. The rhetorical aspects of these have also most recently been studied by Kennedy, *Greek Rhetoric*, pp. 215–39, and are discussed by Bernardi, *Grégoire de Nazianze*, pp. 171–74, and his education, pp. 110–18.

28 Basil, indeed, later described his studies in Athens as wasted time (with a reference to 1 Cor. 1.20, *Ep.* 223), but Gregory's affection for Athens, despite his frank acknowledgement of its paganism (*Sermon* 43.21) never wavered – 'Athens, the home of eloquence, Athens, a city to me, if to anyone, truly golden, patron of all that is excellent' (43.14).

29 *Saint Basil on the Value of Greek Literature*, ed. N.G. Wilson, London, 1975, addressed by Basil to the young ('Children'), 1.2.

30 Wilson notes that the tone of the first chapter, in which Basil refers to his (unspecified) age and his experience of life, would otherwise seem 'intolerably sententious', intro., p. 9.

31 Wilson, *Saint Basil*, 4.48–51, and 8.1–5: 'But, let us revert to my initial statement, that we should not absorb all (pagan learning) without exception, but only what is of use'. The teaching in this letter is explicitly linked to Origen by M. Naldini, 'Paideia origeniana nella "Oratio ad adulescentes" di Basilio Magno', *Vetera Christiana* 13 (1976), pp. 298–318. Rousseau, *Basil of Caesarea*, chs 2 and 3, sets the letter in the context of Basil's later attitude to classical learning. The theme of 'a rose among thorns' is used by Gregory of Nyssa as well in a letter (*Grégoire de Nysse Lettres*, ed. P. Maraval, SC 363, Paris, 1990, *Ep.* 28.1–3), where he describes his feelings when receiving a reproachful letter from a dear friend. The passage was also found in letters attributed to Basil (*Ep.* 342) and to Libanius (*Ep.* 1587), but was finally identified as originally by Gregory by P. Maas (Maraval, *Lettres*, p. 72 and n. 4).

32 *Poem* 2.1.11, lines 469–73. Basil induced him to become bishop of Sasima against his will, to maintain the influence of the orthodox church in that part of Cappadocia in AD 372.

possessing in abundance only those evils with which the cities are filled, gathering thorns without a rose to cull?' He firmly defends the advantages bestowed by pagan learning in his eulogy of Basil in *Sermon* 43.11, where he points out that, like all God's works, it is detrimental or beneficial according to the use made of it, and that Christians 'gather from them what is useful for life and enjoyment, and avoid what is dangerous'. He concludes

> so from secular education we have received principles of enquiry and speculation, while we have rejected their idolatry, terror and pit of destruction ... We must not then devalue education, because some are pleased to do so, but rather suppose such to be boorish and uneducated, desiring all to be as they themselves are, in order to hide themselves in the crowd and escape the detection of their want of culture.[33]

Even John Chrysostom (AD 340/350–407), who, having followed both Christian and pagan studies in his youth, violently attacked the evils he saw within the latter in one treatise, *Against the Enemies of Monasticism*, later agreed that pagans as well as Christians 'who were illustrious for their self-restraint' could be held up as examples to the young.[34] His account of how children should be taught Bible stories in the home, relying as his method does upon the employment of repetition, praise and identifying the pleasure engendered in the young pupil by recognition of key names and items of vocabulary, sets a high standard for educational methods of the time.[35]

---

33 *Sermon* 43.11. Both this and the preceding passage are discussed (with reference to Basil's work) in Ruether, pp. 164–65, n. 2. Her view that Gregory was not aware of his full debt to Greek thought (pp. 166–67 and 174) is opposed by F.W. Norris, 'Of Thorns and Roses: the Logic of Belief in Gregory Nazianzen', *Church History* 53 (1964), pp. 455–64. For further studies of the influence of Greek philosophy on Gregory's theological teaching, see Norris et al., *Faith gives Fullness to Reasoning*, and Pelikan, *Christianity and Classical Culture*.

34 *Against the Enemies of Monasticism* is translated by D.G. Hunter, 1988, and discussed in detail in J.N.D. Kelly, *Golden Mouth. The Story of John Chrysostom, Ascetic, Preacher, Bishop*, London, 1995, pp. 51–54, and the later *On Vain Glory and How Parents Should Bring up Children*, on pp. 85–7. See Anne-Marie Malingrey, *Sur la vaine gloire et l'éducation des enfants*, introduction, texte critique et notes, SC 188, Paris, 1972, section 79, in the translation by Laistner, *Christianity and Pagan Culture in the Later Roman Empire*, p. 118, with p. 53 for John's reference to the beneficial use of some pagan examples.

35 *Christianity and Pagan Culture in the Later Roman Empire*, sections 39–46.

THE POLITICAL AND CULTURAL CONTEXT OF
SERMONS 4, 5, 39 AND 43

Both Basil's letter and Gregory's discussion of education, though certainly
written in later life in the case of the latter, reflect the peaceful co-existence
between pagan and Christian teachers known to them in their student days.
This peace was abruptly, if briefly, interrupted in AD 362. The Emperor
Julian (who reigned from 361 to 363) had been brought up a Christian, but
had turned away from Christianity. Inspired by his studies of Greek learning
to the worship of 'Hellenism', he attempted to restore pagan rites and festivals.
A year after becoming emperor, he moved to ban Christian teachers from the
schools, unless they sacrificed to the pagan gods, the literature about which
they could not otherwise teach without hypocrisy.[36] Pagan as well as Christian teachers disagreed with the edict.[37] But while some Christian rhetors,
such as the Apollinarii, buckled down to rewriting parts of the Old and New
Testaments in epic and tragic metres, as prose historical works or as Platonic
dialogues, classical histories and tragedies, to provide texts for their students,[38]

36 For full details of Julian's life and beliefs, see J. Bidez, *La Vie de l'Empereur Julien*,
Paris, 1930; R. Browning, *The Emperor Julian*, London, 1975; P. Athanassiadi-Fowden, *Julian
and Hellenism*, Oxford, 1981; and R.B.E. Smith, *Julian's Gods*, London, 1995.

37 E.D. Hunt, 'Christians and Christianity in Ammianus Marcellinus', *CQ* 35 (I) (1985), pp.
186–200.

38 These, a father and son, were both teachers and priests, the father a presbyter and his son,
A. the Younger, later a bishop of Laodicea. The latter was later condemned for Christological
heresy (Meredith, *Gr. Nys.*, pp. 46–47). Gregory speaks of their works as 'innovations', not
inspired by the Holy Spirit, as his own poems were to be (*Ep.* 101.73). Socrates, 3.16 describes
them in detail but adds that the fact that they did not survive was not to be regretted, because the
holy Scriptures, while divinely inspired, did not teach the art of speaking, 'which enables (us)
to defend the truth against those who wish to oppose it', a verdict possibly connected with A.
the Younger's heresy (Alan Cameron, 'The Empress and the Poet: Paganism and politics in the
court of Theodosios II', *Yale Classical Studies* 27 [1982], p. 284). This view of the help the
study of pagan literature and rhetoric provides to Christians is found in another writer, however,
as noted by Wilson, *Saint Basil on the Value of Greek Literature*, intro., p. 11. Zacharias
Scholasticus (AD 465/6–after 536), a Christian from Gaza who became the bishop of Mitylene,
studied rhetoric and philosophy in Alexandria, and decided to prolong his studies there for
another year to improve his skill in public disputation with the pagans on those matters, before
moving to Beirut to study law (*Life of Severus*, *PO* 2.1, Paris, 1907, p. 46). Most of his work,
though written originally in Greek, only survives in Syriac, except for a fragment of a tract and
an account of several discussions with the pagan philosopher, Ammonius, and another scholar,
about the creation of the world (*PG* 85 1011–1144). The work is composed as a set of Socratic
dialogues, filled with literary allusions and Platonic tags, as befits his schooling. Their
arguments are analysed by P. Merlan, 'Ammonius Hermiae, Zacharias Scholasticus and
Boëthius', *GRBS* 9(2) (1968), pp. 193–203.

others protested vigorously. A Christian pamphlet, associated by some with Basil himself, attacking the emperor's beliefs, was sent to him in his lifetime, and Gregory produced *Sermons* 4 and 5 in absolute rejoicing after the latter's death.[39] In these, traditionally known as the *Invectives against Julian the Apostate*, he attacked and rejected Julian's equivalence of 'Hellenism' with religion rather than Greek culture.[40] He makes every possible use of rhetorical techniques in these works, as studies in later rhetoric have shown.[41] They are written as a pamphlet, not delivered as sermons, in the form of a comprehensive rebuke of Julian's life, actions and beliefs.[42] Gregory's harsh and intemperate language – one editor states: 'It takes but a glance at the work to note the virulence of a polemic written in vitriol'[43] – displays the depth of the former's concern at the threat he perceived Julian's action had been to the Church. In his eyes, and in his only too vivid words, Julian's restriction of 'Hellenism' to 'Hellenes' set the former in competition against athletes (Christian orators) either 'forbidden to compete or deprived of a limb'.[44]

While the usual Christian targets of adulterous, cowardly, deceitful, lascivious, murderous and obscene gods and their rites appear in full, the works spare none of Julian's admired models either, even those, such as

39 The pamphlet may have been from Basil according to Sozomen, 5.18. There are certainly letters exchanged between Julian and Basil in the latter's collected letters, *Saint Basile. Lettres*, ed. Y. Courtonne, vol. 1, Paris, 1957, 40 and 41. While these are probably not genuine, their existence attests the recognition of Basil's attitude to the emperor's action (Lugaresi 5, p. 256, with reference to Courtonne, *Lettres*, p. 94, n. 1). He was also linked by Gregory with himself as the objects of Julian's persecution (*Sermon* 5.39), and is generally assumed to have helped Gregory in the final production of *Sermons* 4 and 5 at the end of 364 (Bernardi *CJ*, pp. 36–37), or beginning of 365 (Lugaresi 4, pp. 44–45).

40 See n. 5 above for the ambiguity of the term. Gregory himself, although he does not use it frequently in these sermons (in fact it only occurs in *Sermon* 4), and condemns that special meaning in 4.5, deploys it himself elsewhere in 4 for 'pagan' (in 88, 91 and 93, as noted by Bernardi, *ad loc.*).

41 M. Guignet, *S. Grégoire de Nazianze et la Rhetorique*, Paris, 1911, gives a good overall introduction to Gregory's reliance on his training, and Kennedy discusses *Sermons* 4 and 5 in *Greek Rhetoric*, pp. 221–23.

42 *Comm.* 4. intro. Both Bernardi *CJ*, p. 15, n. 8 and Lugaresi 4, p. 14, note that the term is not completely applicable to *Sermons* 4 and 5, because they do not precisely follow the rules for an encomium, the opposite of an invective.

43 'Il suffit de feuilleter l'ouvrage pour que saute aux yeux la virulence d'une polémique écrite au vitriol', Bernardi, *CJ*, intro., p. 38. This can be added to other descriptions of the work by various writers, collected by Lugaresi 4, intro., pp. 11–14. He too notes the venom of Gregory's style, which he sees as a part of Gregory's pastoral duty, as well as a development of his personal reaction to Julian's apostasy, pp. 14–15.

44 *Sermon* 4.6.

Solon and Xenocrates, of whom little ill is usually found.[45] Gregory's use of allusion to Greek culture is positive, however, as well as negative, in line with his theme that 'literature belonged to all' in *Sermon* 4.4: 'May I be granted the learning and the eloquence of Herodotus and Thucydides, to depict the sheer evil of the man (Julian) for the ages to come ...'[46] These techniques apart, Julian's pagan heroes are balanced by Christian saints and martyrs, his philosophers by the monks.[47] The full force of biblical and divine anger is roused against him: 'the serpent, ... the Assyrian'; whose wisdom and its fruits 'shall soon be cut down like grass, and wither as the green herb'.[48] In other passages biblical texts and allusions to the Scriptures are skilfully interwoven.

Both *Sermons* 4 and 5 and *Sermon* 39, *On the Epiphany*, the first of Gregory's sermons on baptism, fitted well within the established Christian polemical tradition, in that all had extended attacks, of various degrees of subtlety, on pagan beliefs. This was the main object of the inclusion of such references in *Sermon* 39, in chapters 4–6, to contrast between the purity of the Christian sacrament, and the evil, obscene and bloodthirsty rites of the pagans. The rest of the sermon is devoted to a call to all believers to be baptised, a sacrament still in the fourth century often deferred until the hour of death.

Sermon 43, *On the death of Basil the Great*, is more literary in tone and also follows a rhetorical format, that of an encomium.[49] Gregory praises his subject, Basil, by describing and then dismissing pagan examples in favour of the Christian virtues and achievements of the latter. Basil's ancestors, for example, were greater than the ancient families of Greek mythology; some

45 *Sermon* 4.72. Solon was one of the Seven Sages (see *Comm.* 4.19 below) and Xenocrates an abstemious philosopher (*Comm.* 4.24). This unparalleled attack on Solon has led Kurmann and Lugaresi to suppose (see their accounts on 4.72) that Gregory is in fact referring to Alcmaeon here, who also visited Croesus – see the notes to *Comm.* 4 19 below. Xenocrates was known for winning a contest in drinking wine (Lugaresi *4, ad loc.*), but was otherwise admired (Bernardi *CJ, ad loc.*)

46 *Sermon* 4.92.

47 *Sermon* 4.69 lists John, Peter, Paul, James, Stephen, Luke, Andrew and Thecla before condemning (in 70) Heracles, Pelops and the others explained in *Comm.* 4.3–12, and the philosophers Socrates, Epictetus, Anaxarchus and others (*Comm.* 4.13–18), before praising the monks in *Sermon* 4.71.

48 *Sermon* 4.1, referring to Ezekiel 29.3 and Isaiah 10.12 (Bernardi *CJ*, p. 86), and 4.3, to *Psalms* 37.2 (*CJ*, p. 90).

49 *Comm.* 43.1. See both Kennedy, *Greek Rhetoric*, pp. 228–37 and Bernardi *43*, pp. 28–32, for a detailed analysis of the work in this context. Bernardi *43*, pp. 25–28, argues that the text we have now is probably a later reworking of the shorter eulogy which Gregory actually gave, on 1 January 382.

even outdid the skill of Artemis, goddess of hunting, because in their flight from persecution large numbers of deer freely offered themselves to them for meat when they were hungry.[50] Other citations and references display Gregory's learning and love of culture – his and Basil's affection for each other is described by a quotation from Pindar, as are Basil's scholarly achievements.[51] A description of the persecutions launched by the Emperor Valens is preceded by the account of Xerxes' invasion of Greece.[52] His praise of education has been noted in the section above. It is later followed, it is true, by an attack on bishops who have been undeservedly elevated without having undergone the long training he and Basil had followed:

> But a bishop is easily found, without the experience furnished by toil, having but recent repute and being sown and springing up at once, as in the fable of the giants. We manufacture holy men in a day, and we bid them to be wise, who have no training in wisdom …[53]

It has already been stated that these four stand out among Gregory's sermons, with some of his poems, as being especially rich in examples drawn from Greek culture. Christian Demoen has noted, in an important study of this aspect of Gregory's style mentioned above,[54] that seventy per cent of the pagan examples found in his prose works lie within *Sermons* 4, 5, 39 and 43, fifty per cent of these being within *Sermons* 4 and 5. He rightly relates the number of pagan literary allusions found in individual sermons to the level of education Gregory anticipated in his hearers (or readers, in the

50 *Sermon* 43.3 and 5–7.

51 *Sermon* 43.20 cites Pindar, *Ol.* 6.1–3: 'Such were our feelings for each other, when we had thus supported, as Pindar has it, our "well-built chamber with pillars of gold" as we advanced under the united influences of God's grace and our own affection'; in 43.24, Pindar's words in *Nem.* 4.69 are recast 'beyond Gadeira (for 'to the west of G.') there is no passage' to express Basil's full acquisition of human knowledge. Gregory's use of Pindar is sparing and repetitive: both images appear elsewhere, *Ol.* 6.1–3 in *Ep.* 9.1.2 and 204.5.2, and *Nem.* 4.69 in *Ep.* 173.4.3. To these and the other passages (*Fr.* 105 in *Ep.* 114, and *Nem.* 1.53, in both *Ep.* 10.12 and *Sermon* 4.100) identified by I. Opelt, 'Die Christliche Spätantike und Pindar', *Byzantinische Forschungen* 2 (1967), pp. 296–98, may be added the misquotation in *Ep.* 10.2.6 from *Ol.* 8.76. There are no references to Pindar in *Ep.* 8 and 194.

52 *Sermon* 43.45.

53 'They grow up as soon as they are sown, as the myth makes the Giants (do)', *Sermon* 43.26, explained in *Comm.* 43.17.

54 In *Pagan and Christian Exempla in Gregory Nazianzen*, Demoen gives a full description and analysis of all the pagan and biblical examples employed by Gregory in his writings, poetry and prose alike, to establish a so-called 'Hellenization of Christianity' (as the author notes on p. 23), with regard to literary allusion, both Christian and pagan, especially in *Sermons* 4 and 5. His statistics for the occurrence of pagan material are given on p. 74, as already cited.

case of *Sermons* 4 and 5).[55] The *Invectives*, thus, were a rallying-cry to the well-educated, both Christian and pagan; *Sermon* 39 was delivered in Constantinople, a 'university city'; literary references would be expected in a eulogy (of whatever length)[56] on Basil the Great, a scholar and fellow student of Gregory's, in his home city of Caesarea. Other passages of such allusion occur in similar situations: in *Sermon* 7.20, Gregory's funeral oration on his brother Caesarius (in describing his learning); in *Sermon* 25.6 and 7 in his initial praise of Maximus, a Christian philosopher; in *Sermon* 27.10, where such topics are described as being a more appropriate field of discussion for the followers of the heretic Eunomius, a one-time teacher, than the nature of God;[57] and in *Sermon* 28, in praise of the natural and divinely inspired artistry of 'irrational creatures' in comparison with that of the thinkers, artists and craftsmen of the Greeks (28.25). The last-named three, like *Sermon* 39, were preached in Constantinople. With the exception of *Sermon* 7, hardly any allusions to pagan literature appear in sermons given in Nazianzus itself, and but two in the eulogy of Gregory the Elder, which ecclesiatical dignitaries from outside the neighbourhood might have been expected to attend. In his praise of his mother in the same sermon, however, Gregory also emphasises how little attention she paid to 'Greek tales, and lyrics from plays' (18.10). His use of Old and New Testament examples is also a notable feature of his style.[58]

Gregory's deep faith and powerful eloquence thus succeeded where the Apollinarii had failed, and produced in *Sermons* 4, 5, 39 and 43 a proper use of 'bastard letters' and a 'synthesis of pagan and Christian learning'.[59]

55 See pp. 69–70, with notes 130–33, for his analysis of the possible composition of Gregory's audiences.

56 See n. 49 above.

57 Eunomius (AD 335–394) was a Cappadocian of humble origins who had learnt tachygraphy and become a teacher in Constantinople. He was later installed as the bishop of Cyzicus. He followed and developed the Arian heresy, which denied that God the Father and God the Son were of the same nature (Meredith, *Cappadocians*, pp. 63–65). Gregory attacks the word-play of his followers in this matter as the result of a poor education (Norris et al., *Faith gives Fullness to Reasoning*, pp. 104–05, on *Sermon* 27.10).

58 Demoen, pp. 134 and 216. Demoen gives a comprehensive and most useful set of lists at the end of his work: Inventory I, pp. 329–96, consists of the subjects of Gregory's allusions to biblical and pagan topics alike as they appear in all his poems, sermons and letters in their traditional order; Inventory II, pp. 397–433, gives all the topics (divided into biblical and then pagan material) in alphabetical order; and Inventory III, pp. 435–58, lists the biblical topics according to their occurrence in the LXX, the NT, and in the Apocrypha to both works.

59 See the beginning of the previous section, with n. 24, and Kennedy, *Greek Rhetoric*, p. 215, with Bernardi, *Grégoire de Nazianze*, p. 350 and Demoen, pp. 21–23.

CHRISTIANITY AND PAGAN LEARNING FROM THE FOURTH
TO THE SIXTH CENTURIES AD

Gregory's sermons, however, despite his high status as a theologian and their popularity,[60] remained a unique phenomenon in their 'Hellenisation of Christianity' as far as the frequency of their use of mythological allusion was concerned. The technique hardly appears in Basil's sermons;[61] and his brother, Gregory of Nyssa, made little use of it. A recent discussion of the latter's work, indeed, states that 'one of the peculiarities of Gregory (of Nyssa) from our point of view is the almost total absence in him of reference to, or direct citation from, his non-Christian sources'.[62] This quotation does not take account of Gregory's habit of employing pagan examples where appropriate (as, for example, in attacks upon the Eunomian heresy).[63] The publicly expressed works of both Basil and Gregory of Nyssa are otherwise clear products of their training in rhetoric.[64] Their letters, too, bear this training out; for both add references to Greek learning in letters to those whom they know, or assume, will appreciate them, as was also Gregory of Nazianzus' practice.[65]

---

60 He, alone with St John the Divine, was granted the title of 'The Theologian'. A selection of his sermons was translated into Latin by Rufinus of Aquileia (AD 345–410). Syriac and Armenian versions of them all were made at early stages in their tradition, and a selection of them, which included *Sermons* 39 and 43, were read as a part of the liturgy in the Eastern Church.

61 Demoen, p. 54.

62 Meredith, *Gr. Nys.*, p. 3.

63 For Eunomius, see n. 57 above. Gregory speaks of the Minotaur, the Cyclops, Scylla and the Chimaera in *Against Eunomius* 3.5.44 and in 7.3.3 (without the Cyclops), for example, and compares his doctrines to Homer's potion; though unlike that, which turned men's bodies to the shape of those of beasts while they kept their human souls (of the encounter of Odysseus' companions with Circe, *Od.* 11.203–43), they turned men's minds to those of beasts, 3.2.77.

64 As described by J.M. Campbell, *The Influence of the Second Sophistic on the Sermons of St. Basil the Great*, Washington, DC, 1922, and L. Méridier, *L'influence de la Seconde Sophistique sur l'œuvre de Grégoire de Nysse*, Paris, 1906, for Basil and Gregory of Nyssa, respectively.

65 In Basil's letters, for example, one to a pagan philosopher refers twice to the *Odyssey,* to Tantalus and to Fortune (*Ep.* 1); a letter to a benefactor cites examples (found also in Gregory's *Sermon* 4), to Zeno and his cloak, to Cleanthes, to Sicilian and Italian luxury, and another anecdote about Diogenes the Cynic and his rejection of a drinking cup (*Ep.* 4). The letter to Gregory of Nazianzus about his refuge in Pontus speaks of Calypso's isle, with a reference to Homer, and then of the Echinades, newly formed islands at the mouth of the river Achelous, where Alcmaeon at last escaped the Furies (*Ep.* 14); a charming rebuke to a calligrapher for slanting lines refers to Aesop's fable about the crab, and to Theseus and Ariadne (*Ep.* 334); and an appeal to the Governor of Neocaesarea for a reduction in tax for a friend's property begins with a quotation from Euripides (*Ep.* 63). This aspect of Gregory of Nyssa's letters is discussed

It is true that Christian teaching had never depended on such works of high rhetoric (in the best sense of the word) as those of Gregory, Basil, Gregory of Nyssa and others alone. With the variety of different styles of composition of the books of the New Testament as examples, and the faith in the power invested in simple fishermen to become 'fishers of men' as a guide, all kinds of works were written with increasing self-confidence by Christian authors. The rise in popularity of the saints' *Lives* in the fourth century is a case in point: they have been identified as reading matter, not for the 'simple pious' alone, but for every level of Christian society.[66]

Other writers returned to classical metres for Christian themes, whose works survived far longer than those of the Apollinarii. For example, the so-called 'Homeric Centos' recount passages from the Gospels in Homeric lines and phrases, and survive in some 30 manuscripts. They are attributed, first to an otherwise unknown bishop, Patricius; they were then worked upon by the Empress Eudocia, the newly converted daughter of a pagan philosopher from Athens, and the estranged wife of Theodosius II (reigned AD 408–450); and later by others.[67] Some other compositions by Eudocia in this 'Homeric mode' are still extant.[68] Other fifth-century Christian writings

---

in the introduction of their edition by Maraval, cited in n. 31 above, pp. 43–50, and the topics found in Gregory of Nazianzus' letters are listed in Demoen, pp. 387–90. Gregory's use of pagan literary citations in letters to his friends, both Christian and pagan, is discussed in G. Thraede, *Grundzüge griechisch-römischer Brieftopik*, Munich, 1970, p. 144.

66 Cameron, *Christianity*, pp. 141–54. Augustine's rejection of rhetoric (see n. 14 above) was inspired by hearing of the effect the *Life of St. Anthony* had on some high-ranking civil servants. Gregory of Nazianzus praised Athanasius for writing it in *Sermon* 21.5.

67 It was first published in 1502 in Venice by Aldus Manutius, in *Christiani Poetae*, II. The work was partially edited by A. Ludwich, *Eudociae Augustae, Procli Lycii, Claudiani carminum graecorum reliquiae, accedunt Blemyomachiae fragmenta*, Leipzig. 1897, and then in full by André-Louis Rey, *Patricius, Eudocie, Optimus, Côme de Jérusalem Centons Homériques (Homerocentra)*, Paris, 1998.

68 These are briefly mentioned in Socr. 7.21, and in more detail by Photius, Cod. 183, 184 (Wilson, pp. 173–76). Opposing views of the merits of both types of composition are given by A. Cameron, *Yale Classical Studies* 27, p. 279 and M.D. Usher, *Homeric Stitchings*, Lanham, MD, and Oxford, 1998. Such 'cross-overs' had long been one strand of Christian composition, not merely called forth by Julian's persecution. Methodius had written a *Symposium* in praise of Christian virginity in the early 4th century, the form of which, and much of the language, was largely derived from Plato's own *Symposium* and other works (see the translation by H. Musurillo, *St Methodius. The Symposium: A Treatise on Chastity*, London, 1958, and Cameron, *Christianity*, pp. 176–78, for the Christian context of Methodius' work). Gregory of Nazianzus himself is held to have composed the *Christus patiens*, a Christian drama, a 'cento', built up mainly of lines and phrases from Aeschylus and Euripides, edited by A. Tuilier, *Grégoire de*

continued to attack pagan beliefs, while pagan philosophers taught in the schools. Neoplatonism thrived in fifth-century Athens. The lynching of the Neoplatonist philosopher, Hypatia, in Alexandria in AD 415 by Christians, a murder condemned later by the Christian who chronicled it, did not stop the teaching there.[69] Christians nevertheless continued to convert pagan shrines and temples to Christian use, and by AD 488–9, the strife between Christian students, who were supported by local monks, and their pagan colleagues and teachers, was so fierce that Ammonius, the leading philosopher in Alexandria, had had to come to an understanding with the Patriarch to bring it to an end.[70] The understanding was condemned by his pupil, the resolute Neoplatonist Damascius, in Athens.[71]

Yet even the long epic poem in 48 books on the exploits of Dionysus[72] by Nonnus of Panopolis in Egypt (fl. AD 450–470) had a Christian parallel, whether by him or another. It paraphrased the Gospel of St John the Divine in a metre very close to that of the *Dionysiaca*.[73] From the late fifth and early

---

Nazianze. La passion du Christ, SC 149, Paris, 1969. Tuilier's arguments for its authenticity have most recently been supported in this by F. Trisoglio, *San Gregorio di Nazianzo e il Christus Patiens*, Florence, 1996. All these works display a high level of learning. Zacharias of Mitylene's 'Socratic' dialogues are mentioned in n. 38 above.

69 Socrates, 7.15. Her influence, life and thought are described in M. Dzielska, *Hypatia of Alexandria*, trans. F. Lyra, Cambridge, MA, 1995, who argues that her death was caused through fear of her influence on some Christian leaders, in political and religious struggles in Alexandria.

70 Zacharias was a witness to the conflicts during his studies in Alexandria (see n. 38 above) and describes them in detail, *Life of Severus, PO* 2.1, pp. 14–37. He considered that the Prefect of Alexandria favoured the pagans (p. 27). His account is well summarised in Athanassiadi, *Damascius*, intro., pp. 27–29. For Ammonius' decision, see Westerink, *Anon. Prol.*, intro., pp. x–xxv; Clarke, *Higher Education in the Ancient World*, pp. 103–04; and Athanassiadi, *Damascius*, pp. 30–32.

71 Damascius' opinion of Ammonius was initially high, and then correspondingly low; Athanassiadi, *Damascius*, sections 57 and 118, respectively.

72 See G. Bowersock, 'Dionysus as an epic hero', *Studies in the Dionysiaca of Nonnus*, The Cambridge Philosophical Society, 1994, Supplementary volume no. 17, pp. 156–66, in which he argues that the epic shows the influence of Christianity on pagan thought by presenting Damascius as 'a late antique epic god of salvation' (p. 162).

73 The *Dionysiaca*, in 48 books, ed. R. Keydell, Berlin, 1959, is in the course of edition in the Budé series with a French translation. There is an English translation by W.H.D. Rouse, Loeb, 1940. The attribution of the *Paraphrase* to Nonnus is disputed: see E. Livrea, *Nonno di Panopoli. Parafrasi del vangelo di S. Giovanni Canto XVIII*, Naples, 1989; B. Coulie, L.F. Sherry and CETEDOC, *Thesaurus Pseudo-Nonni quondam Panopolitani, Paraphrasis Evangelii S. Ioannis*, Brepols, 1995, intro., pp. vii–ix; L.F. Sherry, 'The *Paraphrase of St. John* attributed to Nonnus', *Byz.* 66 (1996), pp. 409–30; and D. Accorinti, *Nonno di Panopoli: Parafrasi del Vangelo di S. Giovanni: Canto XX*, Pisa: Scuole Normale Superiore, 1996.

sixth centuries onwards, the elements of Greek rhetoric began to be more generally identified in Christian writings, when examples of figures of speech and turns of phrase drawn from the Scriptures and sermons by Gregory of Nazianzus, Basil and John Chrysostom were found included in the lists of examples in rhetorical handbooks. By the mid-sixth century at least, some of Gregory's works themselves had attracted notes on their titles;[74] more notes and lengthy commentaries were composed on many of the sermons from then onwards, to explain Gregory's vocabulary and thought. One of the earliest of these fuller collections is known as the *Scholia Alexandrina*.[75] A further set of these, the *Scholia Oxoniensia*, on *Sermons* 4 and 5, is printed in *PG* 36 1206–1255***, after the *Commentaries* of Pseudo-Nonnus. Although this edition is not a full copy of its manuscript, its contents give a good impression of the learning of their compiler, who also incorporates some passages from *Comm.* 4 and 5 into its text.[76]

The sixth century also brought another harsh imperial intervention into the world of learning. After its first quarter the Emperor Justinian, in violent quest of religious conformity, began his series of stringent moves against non-Christians.[77] Greek learning could now only be taught by those who did not believe in its religious aspects, and Julian's distinction was confirmed by

74 These, on the titles to *Sermons* 1 and 2, are traditionally dated to the mid-6th century AD, as noted by Véronique Somers, *Histoire des collections complètes des Discours de Grégoire de Nazianze, Publication de l'institut orientaliste de Louvain* 48, Institut Orientaliste, Louvain-la-Neuve, 1997, p. 182.

75 I show in a description of a few of these scholia, from both printed and established collections and with reference to various manuscripts, that individual scholia on the same passage can differ from text to text, and require further investigation, either manuscript by manuscript or sermon by sermon (Nimmo Smith, 'The early scholia on the *Sermons* of Gregory of Nazianzus', *Studia Nazianzenica* I, ed. B. Coulie, Corpus Christianorum Series Graeca 41, Corpus Nazianzenum 8, Brepols, 2000, pp. 69–146).

76 These, discussed in detail by Trisoglio, 'Mentalità ed attegiamenti degli scoliasti di fronte agli scritti di S. Gregorio de Nazianzo', *II Symposium Nazianzenum*, ed. J. Mossay, Paderborn, 1981, pp. 214–19, were taken from a manuscript of Gregory's *Sermons* long identified as from Magdalen College, Oxford, as I mention in the article cited in the preceding note (pp. 78–79). References to the passages from the *Commentaries* are cited in my edition. The links between these *Scholia* and the *Scholia Alexandrina* are close, and were described in my paper, 'The *Scholia Oxoniensia* on Gregory of Nazianzus' *Invectives against Julian* (*Sermons* 4 and 5)', given at the XIII International Conference on Patristic Studies at Oxford, on 19 August 1999.

77 Cod. Just. I.5.18 §4, and Cod. Just. I.11.10. See Cameron, *Procopius*, pp. 6 and 22, with reference to the first edition of Lemerle, *Le Premier Humanisme byzantin*, Paris, 1971, pp. 68ff.; and Lemerle, *Byzantine Humanism: The First Phase, Notes and remarks on education and culture in Byzantium from its origins to the 10th century*, trans. Helen Lindsay and Ann Moffatt, Canberra, 1986, pp. 73–79.

statute. Damascius and his colleagues fled to Persia when Justinian forbad the teaching of philosophy in Athens in AD 529, while the philosophers in Alexandria continued to teach with caution.[78] Their views, it must be said, are recorded in the notes taken of their lectures by Christian students, and their successors after AD 564 were Christians themselves. The Christian scholar, John Philoponus (AD 490–567/74), who studied philosophy in Alexandria and worked there as a grammarian, wrote several commentaries on Aristotle, criticising his theories about the beginning of the world, sometimes in Christian terms. One commentary, published in AD 529, attacks Athenian Neoplatonism, and may be seen as a defence of the Alexandrian school against any similar imperial action.[79]

Attitudes to Greek culture in fields other than philosophy vary from author to author in the sixth century AD. Procopius of Caesarea (AD 500– after 562) and Agathias of Myrina (AD 532–580) still wrote about Christian matters in classical terms in their prose works, and Agathias had no compunction in admitting to the composition of poems on mythological subjects in the Preface to his *Histories*, or to publishing a collection of Hellenising epigrams by himself and other poets in the 560s.[80] Procopius is equally frank, as a Christian, in his *Secret History*. This attacks Justinian and his wife, Theodora, and their rule, in vindictive, scurrilous and superstitious terms, all in line with classical rhetorical invective.[81] The sixth-century

78 See Agathias 2.30–31, for the flight to Persia. They returned but not to Athens, as discussed by H.J. Blumenthal, *Aristotle and Neoplatonism in Late Antiquity*, London, 1996, and Athanassiadi, *Damascius*. As for the school in Alexandria, Olympiodorus succeeded Ammonius, or his successor, there and taught with relative freedom until his death in AD 564. Although he persists in Neoplatonist doctrines, he shows a positive attitude to Christian religious experiences and practices, and 'seems to have accepted Christianity at least as a creed for the uneducated' (Westerink, *Anon. Prol.*, p. xix). See Westerink, *Olymp.*, pp. 20–25, for further discussion of Olympiodorus' doctrines.

79 This attack, in AD 529, has been seen as a defence of Philoponus' own position in Alexandria as well (Westerink, *Anon. Prol.*, p. xiii). For the influence of Philoponus' philosophical commentaries, see 'John Philoponus', in *Philoponus and the Rejection of Aristotelian Science*, ed. R. Sorabji, New York, 1987, pp. 1–40, and H. Chadwick, 'Philoponus the Christian Theologian', in *Philoponus and the Rejection of Aristotelian Science*, pp. 41–56.

80 He describes the *Daphniaca* (a work in hexameters, which has not survived), as being 'adorned with certain amorous myths and other enchanting topics' (1.4). His epigrams, collected in the *Cycle*, represent the 'swan-song' of the classicising elegiac epigram (Alan Cameron, *The Greek Anthology from Meleager to Planudes*, Oxford, 1993, p. 329). He is usually accepted as a Christian, but the view is further discussed in the *Mémoire*, A. Kaldellis, 'The Historical and Religious Views of Agathias: a Reinterpretation', *Byz.* 69 (1999), pp. 206–52.

81 Cameron, *Procopius*, pp. 55–66.

Christian rhetors of Gaza wrote with such balance that the ninth-century
Photius later criticised one, Choricius, for inserting myths and Greek stories,
'slightingly, for no reason and unnecessarily' into his writings.[82] The latter
also wrote in defence of the mimes, with a wealth of classical allusions.
Romanus the Melodist (d. AD 555) rejects 'Platonisers' and the followers of
Aratus, Plato and Demosthenes (twice), Homer and Pythagoras in a series of
puns in two hymns.[83] The Christian John Lydus (AD c.490–565), a dis-
appointed functionary, turned to antiquarianism and the description of pagan
rituals and festivals. His even-handedness also drew complaint from
Photius.[84] The *Chronicle* of John Malalas (AD c.490–570) integrates pagan
myths into a Christian world history, explaining pagan gods, heroes and
philosophers as kings, nobles and 'wonder-workers'.[85] In the mid-sixth
century, Cosmas Indicopleustes, a Nestorian, wrote his *Christian Topo-
graphy* in rejection of the Christian theories of John Philoponus about the
world. He takes care to explain that he has no formal education or literary
training, but relies on the prayers of his dedicatee, Pamphilus, and divine
grace to help him in his task.[86] As a final example, Dioscorus of Aphrodito
(who died after AD 585), a well-educated lawyer in Egypt, who wrote and
transacted his business in Coptic, Greek and Latin, mingles pagan and
Christian references freely in his poems with no sense of incongruity.[87]

82 See n. 15 above for Photius' collection of notes on his reading, the *Library*. The work of
Choricius of Gaza is described in Codex 160.

83 Hymn 31, verses 15, line 5, and 16, line 2; Hymn 33, verse 16, lines 3–7.

84 M. Maas, *John Lydus and the Roman Past, Antiquarianism and Politics in the Reign of
Justinian*, London, 1990. Photius writes (Codex 180, Wilson, pp. 169–70): 'In matters of
religion he seems to have been an unbeliever. He respects and venerates Hellenic beliefs; he
also venerates our beliefs, without giving the reader any easy way of deciding whether such
veneration is genuine or hypocritical.'

85 In 'Malalas and his Contemporaries', in *Studies in John Malalas*, ed. Elizabeth Jeffreys
with Brian Croke and R. Scott, pp. 67–85. Scott discusses the different attitudes to the past
among the 6th-century Christian writers Procopius, Agathias, John Lydus, Cosmas Indicopleustes and John Malalas, among others. He notes in conclusion that 'one characteristic of the
sixth century that can be emphasised again is its confidence in attempting something new, even
where the novelty consists of reworking the old'.

86 *Cosmas Indicopleustès. Topographie chrétienne*, ed. W. Wolska-Conus, vol. 1, SC 141,
Paris, 1968, 2.1–2. Photius agrees with his lack of learning: 'His style is low and he does not
even follow ordinary syntax' and rejects his theories (Cod. 36, Wilson, pp. 31–32).

87 L. MacCoull edited his Greek poems and analysed the influences on his work in
Dioscorus of Aphrodito. His Work and his World, Berkeley, 1988. His complete work is edited
and set in context in J.-L. Fournet, *Hellénisme dans l'Egypte du VIe siècle. La Bibliothèque et
l'œuvre de Dioscore d'Aphrodito*, Cairo, 1999.

The works of all these authors show some kind of response to Greek culture, from acceptance to rejection, from the view that it was a threat, or an embellishment, a part of history, or as the only way in which to write a history, an invective or poetry. Such responses continued in other aspects of daily life. Although pagan sacrifice had been banned since AD 391, private beliefs and practices persisted, and even, in some instances, became assimilated into Christian ritual.[88] Christian saints defended their followers from pagan demons; the names of Jewish and Christian deities appear on magic charms and amulets.[89] Christian iconography flourished, adopting and adapting the conventions and symbols of earlier, pagan, Greek art. To give but a few from many possible examples in this vast subject, one may mention the adoption of the shell-motif from pagan themes to Christian in Coptic art,[90] and the well-known transference of the nimbus to depictions of Christ and the saints from pagan sun gods, emperors and figures of importance. The survival of many pagan themes in Byzantine art, whether in allegorical significance, or as abstract personification, bears witness to the continuing, if slowly declining, influence of classical culture and education.[91]

THE AUTHOR OF THE *COMMENTARIES*

While a great deal is known about Gregory of Nazianzus from his own writings, his *Life*, and many contemporary and later sources, all the information about the author of the *Commentaries* is drawn from these last alone (which do not even preserve the name of their author, as will be

---

88 Despite the ban on pagan sacrifices in 391, there is much evidence to show that dancing and singing to musical instruments became part of Christian worship (already, it must be noted, a Jewish tradition), and that the all-night celebration of festivals was transferred to the cults of Christian saints. Feasting in honour of Christian dead in graveyards continued. See MacMullen, *Christianity and Paganism in the Fourth to Eighth Centuries*, pp. 103–44.

89 Christian spells and amulets are printed by K. Preisendanz, *Papyri Graecae Magicae. Die griechischen Zauberpapyri, II*, Stuttgart, 2nd edn, 1973–4, pp. 209–32, and a 3rd- to 4th-century AD ostrakon with both a Jewish and a pagan deity from a Christian background is noted in J.G. Gager, *Curse Tablets and Binding Spells from the Ancient World*, Oxford, 1992, p. 209, no. 111. Amulets and other apotropaic devices at Anemurium in southern Turkey from the 6th and 7th centuries are mingled with pendant crosses, James Russell, 'The archaeological context of magic in the Early Byzantine Period', in *Byzantine Magic*, ed. Henry Maguire, Cambridge, MA, 1995, pp. 35–50.

90 Nahim Selim Atalla, *Coptic Art*, vol. II, Cairo, 1989, pp. 10–34.

91 R. Brilliant, 'Mythology', in Weitzmann, *Age of Spirituality*, pp. 126–31.

described below). This information may be summarised as follows.[92]

The writer is thought to have come from the Eastern Mediterranean, because he refers directly to Tyre (*Comm.* 4.66) and Antioch (*Comm.* 5.16), but explains the situation of cities and geographical features in Asia Minor (Ancyra, that is, Ankara, in Galatia, *Comm.* 43.6; Patara in Lycia, *Comm.* 4.50), Greece (Mts Athos and Ossa, which are set, wrongly, in Thessaly, 43.12; Delphi in Phocis, 5.15; and Dodona in Epirus, 5.14, among others) and Catana in Sicily (4.46). His wonder at the zoomorphic statuettes in Alexandria (another city which needs no further introduction) in 5.28, befits a visitor.

He is obviously a Christian, and condemns pagan practices and myths. Gregory is always referred to with respect, as 'the holy Gregory', 'the holy man, Gregory', and the 'holy teacher', though no other Christian writings are mentioned. The descriptions of the views of current interpreters of Socrates, Plato and Epicurus (in *Comm.* 4.22, 23 and 27), however, give both sides of each argument. The author happily follows Gregory's explanation of the Isles of the Blest as the Christian Paradise (5.8) and sees the Mysteries at Eleusis as a pagan parallel to the Christian rite of baptism (4.68).

Pagan rites are not dead in the *Commentaries*, nor are the mimes (5.19). The worship of Rhea is 'up to the present' carried on in remote parts of Caria, where the celebrants slash themselves with knives to the sound of flutes (39.2), and pagan statuettes are still to be found in Alexandria, as mentioned above. These factors, combined with linguistic observations, induced the nineteenth- and twentieth-century scholars who first wrote an account of the tradition of the *Commentaries* to set it in the early sixth century AD. Their views, though based upon a confused and incomplete text, and of necessity with little knowledge of its Syriac and Armenian versions, are sound. A recent study of the language of the *Commentaries* confirms its place among other sixth-century works.[93]

Though the *Commentaries* have provided grounds for the above assumptions about the author, they have (as stated above) kept silent about his name. In the tenth century a contemporaneous addition 'of the Abbot Nonnus' was made to the title of *Commentary* 39 in a manuscript of all four *Commentaries*. *Commentaries* 4, 5 and a part of 43, indeed, were first printed, in

---

92 This evidence was gathered by earlier scholars and is given, with full attributions in the *Commentaries*, intro., section II.

93 See the account of the language of the *Commentaries*, given in the introduction, *Thesaurus Pseudo-Nonni*, to which the reader is referred for full examples.

a Latin translation under that name in 1569.[94] The Abbot was then linked with Nonnus of Panopolis, who was at that time assumed to be the author of both the *Dionysiaca* and the *Paraphrase of the Gospel of St John the Divine*, in that both showed a similar combination of pagan learning and Christian thought. The acerbic scholar Richard Bentley rejected this identification of Nonnus with the Abbot Nonnus in no uncertain terms in the seventeenth century, as I have, in my turn, more recently.[95] The title Pseudo-Nonnus was adopted by twentieth-century scholars to make the position of the author of the *Commentaries* completely clear, and thus carried on in later publications of parts of the work, of its Syriac and Georgian versions and its edition.[96]

THE *COMMENTARIES* AND GREEK AND CHRISTIAN CULTURE

Sixth-century Christian authors – even Romanus the Melodist who attacked Greek philosophers, poets and writers, Cosmas Indicopleustes, who rejected Greek culture, and John Malalas who euhemerised its gods, heroes and philosophers – wrote with great confidence in their chosen style. A similar confidence is present in the *Commentaries*. The language, as has been described elsewhere, is not literary as such, though it retains some linguistic refinements with a correct use of cases and tenses. Despite a wide and

94 They were placed in a collection of all Gregory's works, *Divi Gregorii Nazianzeni cognomento Theologi omnia opera quae quidem exstant, nova translatione donata*, Paris, in a posthumous publication of Jacques de Billy.

95 For the references to Bentley, see the edition, pp. 4–5, with n. 16. The attribution to Nonnus, again proposed by D. Accorinti, 'Sull' autore degli scoli mitologici alle orazioni di Gregorio di Nazianzo', *Byz.* 60 (1992), pp. 5–24, is discussed in Nimmo Smith, 'Nonnus and Pseudo-Nonnos: The Poet and the Commentator', in ΦΙΛΕΛΛΗΝ: *Studies in Honour of Robert Browning*, ed. Costas N. Constantinides, Nikolaos M. Panagiotakes, Elizabeth Jeffreys and Athanasios D. Angelou, pp. 281–99. I compare all the topics in *Comm.* 5 with similar ones in the *Dionysiaca*, where they occur, and find no significant parallels between them.

96 The name was first used by Th. Sinko, 'De expositione Pseudo-Nonniana historiarum quae in orationibus Gregorii Nazianzeni commemorantur', *Charisteria C. Morawski oblata*, Cracow, 1922, p. 131; and then by K. Weitzmann, in his discussion of the miniatures in certain manuscripts which illustrate passages in the Ps-N. *Commentaries*, *Greek Mythology*, p. 3; then by S.P. Brock; J. Declerck, in his thesis, 'Pseudo-Nonni Historiae Mythologicae. Tekstkritische uitgave met inleidung et index nominum', Ghent, 1975, and in his articles on the *Commentaries*, cited in the bibliography below; and in the edition of the Georgian Version. This last, which comprises translations of *Commentaries* 39, 43 and 4, with a reconstruction of *Commentary* 5, was edited by T. Otkhmezuri, *The Georgian Translations of the Pseudo-Nonnos Mythological Scholia*, with an English summary and Georgian–Greek Lexicon, Tbilisi, 1989. The actual texts of the Syriac, Armenian and Georgian Versions of the *Commentaries* do not mention the name of their author.

learned vocabulary, combined as it is with a limited number of particles and conjunctions, and much repetition of articles and demonstratives, it remains awkward and heavy to translate. Its repetition, however, of subjects and objects, of verbs in different tenses and of different parts of the same or related verbs, gives great clarity to its narratives.

How the narratives relate to their subject matter, and what guidance they give as to their author's motives in composing the works, must now be examined. The scholarly status of the author was not discussed in the previous section, because it is, of necessity, closely involved with the very nature of the *Commentaries*, as shall now be explained.

The *Commentaries*, first of all, through their titles and sub-titles (almost all of the latter of which contain the word *historia*, or 'story')[97] have obvious connections with the teaching of the secondary schools. There the recognition of allusions to Greek culture and their use in argument was a building block, as it were, of the system. Each *Commentary*, indeed, consists of numbered paragraphs, of which each title refers to the text which the paragraph identifies. There are 97 'stories' in *Comm.* 4, 35 in *Comm.* 5, 24 in *Comm.* 39 and 18 in *Comm.* 43. Stories in the later part of 4, in 5, 39 and 43 refer back to the earlier part of 4, or to 4 and 5 together. Those in *Comm.* 4 give the first accounts of topics which recur in later commentaries, and hence treat them at greater length. While *Sermon* 39 repeats many allusions to pagan worship which Gregory has attacked before in *Sermons* 4 and 5, Pseudo-Nonnus still manages to vary his text (although my notes to the text will understandably be abbreviated).

Commentary 4 begins with a brief explanation of the words, *stēliteutikos logos*, in the title of *Sermon* 4. They define the work as a 'pillar-posting'[98] speech (a reference to the punishment of traitors in classical Athens: their name, family and crime were inscribed on tablets of bronze or stone for all to see, ratifying their loss of citizenship, and exposure to death at any man's hand), and its difference from the rhetorical type of an invective.[99] The author concludes, 'so much then for the theme (of the speech), and, as for the stories, we shall describe them in the briefest terms we can'. These start almost halfway through *Sermon* 4, omitting the references to Porus and Alexander (41), and to Plato, Chrysippus, the Peripatetic School and the

97 Stories 1 and 4 in *Comm.* 39 alone give only a quotation from *Sermon* 39 in their titles. Others include a quotation or rephrasing of the words or topic involved.

98 I am very grateful to Dr McLynn for suggesting this translation for *stēliteutikos* in his report.

99 See the note to *Comm.* 4 intro. below.

Stoa (43). Later allusions to Herodotus and Thucydides (92), to Pindar (100), Hermes and the Telchines (101) and Pythagoras (102) are also left out. A striking omission is that of moly, in 106.[100] These apart, Gregory's topics are followed in order to the end of the sermon.

There are a few omissions in *Comm.* 5 (Capricorn, in 5, for example, is not mentioned, nor Hadrian and Trajan in 8, nor the hurling of the ox's hoof at Odysseus in 39) and in *Comm.* 43 (Niobe in 9, Xerxes in 45, Crates and Diogenes in 60). *Sermon* 43 is identified as an encomium by Pseudo-Nonnus to explain why Gregory mentions the Pelopidae and other ancient heroic families. *Sermon* 39's references are all grouped together in chapters 4–6, and are thus readily identified.

The stories include learned quotations from Homer and Plato, and have references to Aristophanes, Herodotus, Hesiod, the orator Lycurgus and Xenophon. Information from Gregory's words themselves (as I have endeavoured to show in both my edition and the present work by giving full quotations of the text upon which he comments) is distilled and explained in a clearer manner, possibly also reminiscent of the beginners' rhetorical exercises in the schools. Thus, proverbs and sayings are explained and brief mentions of fables and anecdotes fully expanded.

Passages in the *Commentaries* are also often provided with material which is not supplied by Gregory's text. Some elements of this are found in mythological handbooks, such as the *Library* of Apollodorus, composed in the first or second century, which contains many Greek myths arranged in chronological order from the creation of mankind to the Dorian invasion, and the collection of star myths, the *Catasterisms* of Pseudo-Eratosthenes, which is of similar date.[101] Pseudo-Nonnus also knows versions of myths found in the Roman astronomer and mythographer Hyginus, an otherwise unattested second-century AD writer, who transmitted earlier Greek sources. The fourth-century commentary on Vergil's *Aeneid, Eclogues* and *Georgics* by the Roman scholar Servius has information known to him, but most probably drawn from common Greek sources, as in the case of Hyginus. The scholia on Aristophanes, Demosthenes, Euripides, Pindar and Plato, the original nuclei of which date back to Hellenistic scholarship, hold material of which he often provides a simpler or less complete account. His anecdotes about philosophers can be paralleled by some information in Diogenes

---

100 See the note on *Comm.* 4.60.

101 Both works are later compositions wrongly attributed to the earlier, well-known scholars, respectively Apollodorus (c.180–120 BC) and Eratosthenes (285–194 BC).

Laertius' *Lives of the Philosophers*, and may have some input from the 'general courses' taught in Alexandria as an introduction to more specialised studies of philosophy.[102] His is the first written source known to us to present the story about the Cercopes in *Comm.* 4.39, which is otherwise only found depicted in early Greek art, from the sixth century BC onwards.

The amount of this information, combined with Pseudo-Nonnus' knowledge of educational techniques (the collection and identification of stories, rhetorical terms and exercises, the reference to the works of Hesiod, which 'are studied' in *Comm.* 4.76, his knowledge of contemporary philosophical teaching, as noted above) may make it possible, as some have proposed, that Gregory's *Sermons* had become part of the secondary schools' curriculum, and that the *Commentaries* are an aid for or a reflection of that teaching.[103] They might even be seen as an earlier parallel to the *Epimerismi* of George Choeroboscus, the late eighth- to early ninth-century grammarian, who wrote these treatises on the grammatical structure of the Psalms as well as commentaries and scholia on earlier grammarians.[104]

This is, in my opinion, to place too much weight on the evidence the *Commentaries* provide. They indeed display an impressive amount of carefully marshalled and consistently presented information about the stories. Hardly a reason, on the other hand, is given for the inclusion of the stories themselves after the first brief mentions of them in the Introductions to *Comm.* 4 and 43 described above. In the comments at the end of *Comm.* 4.61, for example, the author states, 'The holy teacher mocks at them', of Gregory's reference to the 'divine language' of the gods; or at the end of 77, 'The holy Gregory, then, mocks and ridicules them because the former (verse) is shameful, and that about Zeus, unclean.' His style is idiosyncratic, accessible, anecdotal and reflects popular turns of phrase. It is a world away from the dry scholarly language of the rhetorical handbooks and Choeroboscus' works.

---

102 Discussed above in the section on Education and the Eastern Church, with n. 11.

103 N.G. Wilson, 'The Church and Classical Studies in Byzantium', *Antike und Abendland*, 16 (1970), p. 70; Kennedy, *Greek Rhetoric*, p. 238.

104 For the date of the writer, see W. Böhler and C. Theodoridis, 'Johannes von Damaskios *terminus post quem* für Choiroboskos', *BZ* 69 (1976), pp. 397–401. The *Epimerismi* were edited by T. Gaisford, *Epimerismi in Psalmos*, in *Georgii Choerobosci dictata*, Oxford, 1842, and the scholia on Theodosius of Alexandria can be found in *Grammatici Graeci*, ed. A. Hilgard, vol. 4.1, Teubner, 1894, repr. Olms, 1965. His work was much used in the schools from the 10th century onwards.

In addition, the author is sometimes embarrassed by the amount of information at his disposal. In *Comm.* 4.26, for example, he describes two different accounts of a 'dweller in a tub', one being Diogenes and the other Sotades, and ends by deciding that Diogenes was the only person to whom the story referred: 'In my opinion, the story about the banter (of Diogenes) and the tub is a single one.' He adds the information about Polyxena (*Comm.* 4.8), after a double reference to the death of Iphigeneia in *Sermon* 4.70. The same treatment is applied to an extended description of the whipping of the Laconian ephebes at the altar of Artemis in Sparta, which is divided into story 11 (on that topic) and story 12 (on her worship among the Taurians). In *Comm.* 5.33 the punishment of Prometheus is extrapolated from the second reference to Tityus' punishment in *Sermon* 5.38.

Nor does every item of information in the *Commentaries* match its well-organised presentation (though this is not to say that each lacks an interest of its own). Some of the references to Homer show only a restricted knowledge of their context, as the explanation of the *kestos* as a little basket, rather than an embroidered girdle, makes clear in *Comm.* 4.81.[105] Homeric citations (in *Sermon* 43.12 and 16) are applied to the wrong heroes.[106] The point of another is entirely missed (*Comm.* 4.97). Several allusions in the text are not identified, as has already been said. There is also confusion between some Cynic and Stoic philosophers, about the name of the tyrant who tortured Anaxarchus, on whether it was Theseus or Pirithous who was dragged up from Hades, and about exactly which Alcmaeonid saved Athens from the tyrants.[107] Some inaccuracy, to be sure, is not unusual even among the learned, relying as they did so much on memory. Gregory, for example, gives the name of Cyrus for that of Darius as the king who captured Babylon through the brave ingenuity of Zopyrus (*Sermon* 5.11), and is not precise about the name of a Pythagorean philosopher (*Sermon* 4.70).

The fact remains that the detail of some well-known myths is completely lost, as in the cases of the death of Heracles and the story of Bellerophon, among others.[108] Other facts provided by the *Commentaries* cannot be identified elsewhere, such as the death of Cerberus at Heracles' hands

---

105 I am grateful to N.B. McLynn for his suggestion that it could have been inspired by Gr.'s reference to the collection of letters he sent his grand-nephew, Nicobulus, as a '*himas*', but one 'of words' – *logikos*, not 'of loves', *erotikos* (*Ep.* 32).

106 Ps-N. gives Diomedes (*Comm.* 43.16) for Hector or Paris.

107 For the philosophers, see the notes on *Comm.* 4.15, 24, 29, and 32, and for Pirithous, *Comm.* 4.39. The Molionidae are discussed in *Comm.* 43.12, and the Alcmaeonidae in *Comm.* 43.1.

108 See *Comm.* 4.3 for Heracles and *Comm.* 43.8 for Bellerophon.

(*Comm.* 4.51 and 76) and Orestes' descent to Hades with Pylades, unless it is to be explained by a pun (*Comm.* 43.11).

The author rewrites texts he cannot explain, such as the reference to ship-building among the Athenians, *Comm.* 4.68: 'I think he is speaking about the art of sea-fighting. For the Athenians were notable sea-fighters'; or to castration in the rites of the Phrygians, *Sermon* 4.5, and among the gods, *Sermon* 5.30. He ignores the mention of the oracle in *Comm.* 4.74, and the load-bearing capacity of the arrow of Abaris in *Comm.* 43.7.

These wide variations between the different levels of information present in the *Commentaries* have led some to speculate that Pseudo-Nonnus compiled the *Commentaries* from another, more learned, scholar's notes on a text of the *Sermons*. I have argued elsewhere that such an annotated text might well have stirred his memories of his earlier education and encouraged him to extend and rework these notes for his own satisfaction.[109] Does this view fit the work as we have it?

I continue to believe that it does. The *Commentaries* present a consistent, if limited, interpretation of one aspect of Gregory's rhetorical technique, and reveal much about their author's tastes and interests. He is proud to admit to the knowledge which he has and the research which he has done (in looking at the information in Aristaenetus' work, for example, when he finds that Herodotus could provide none, in *Comm.* 5.27, and in searching to no avail for a 'speaking statue of Apollo', *Comm.* 5.17), and is always ready to provide an explanation, as for Hera's hatred of the unborn child of Zeus and Aphrodite in 5.29. Pseudo-Nonnus rationalises myths which he does not understand – Abaris' arrow, the *kestos*, Orestes and Pylades, as noted above. He conflates and sets in order the various myths on a single subject, such as Proteus (*Comm.* 4.2), the Cyclopes (4.65) and the reasons for the death of Dionysus Zagreus in *Comm.* 5.30. A similar desire for clarity is shown in his liking for etymologies: for a 'pillar-posting' oration (*Comm.* 4. Introd.), the derivation of Cynic, with the mention of 'land-dogs' (4.25), of the different meanings of *stasis* (4.32), of Pan (4.40) of the Bull-eater (4.41), of the Cyclopes (4.65), of 'worship' (4.69), and many others, some of which, it must be added, are not known elsewhere.[110] He show a wry appreciation of the fates of the seers Trophonius and Agamedes (4.1), the philosopher who prayed to the sun (4.31) and Midas (43.6), adapts the name of an astronomer in 5.1, and adds violet to the colours poor Io (whose name has similarities

---

109 In the introduction to my edition, p. 8.
110 Such as those in *Comm.* 43.14 for Elysium.

with *ion*, a violet) turned into when in the form of a cow (39.20). His tolerant attitude to some pagan parallels to Christian practices is noted above, which leads him, in fact, to ignore Gregory's condemnation of the Mysteries at Eleusis in *Sermons* 4.108 and 39.4, as 'a shameful mystery' and 'deservedly kept in silence', respectively. He is too interested in displaying what he knows about them and about the rules the initiates had to follow to pay attention to the text. Again, he shows some belief in good and evil demons in *Comm.* 4.70, though both are elsewhere rejected by Gregory (*Sermon* 27.8). He likes to balance Gregory's attacks on the philosophers with his own knowledge of contemporary views. The more salacious details of the myths and pagan practices recur in his stories, and he tells and retells them with enthusiasm – the adultery, dancing, drunkenness, immorality, obscenity and mutilation.[111] No fact is spared in the descriptions of Zeus' love affairs or Hephaestus' vain pursuit of Athena, in *Comm.* 4.91, for example, and 5.24 and 22. He admits that anger is not strange to him (or quarrels – 'we ask for anger to be stirred within us in wars', *Comm.* 4.92).

Pseudo-Nonnus has then, like Gregory, a lively interest in Greek learning, but a darker fascination than he with the dangers it holds, which he makes no attempt to hide. His work shows a strong belief in its continuing validity, for himself at least, even in a Christian world.

THE LATER HISTORY OF THE *COMMENTARIES*, THEIR TEXT, TRADITION AND VERSIONS

The Christian world itself continued to find his work of interest, attached as it was so closely to Gregory's works. It survives in at least 160 manuscripts in whole or part, most of which also contain the sermons, or at least other collections of commentaries on Gregory's text, or other works.[112] The *Commentaries* were even valued enough to be provided with illustrations,

111 Dancing in the rites of Dionysus, *Comm.* 4.38, 5.19, drunkenness, *Comm.* 39.4, the wearing of the phallus, *Comm.* 4.38 and 5.4, flute music (long condemned by Plato and Aristotle) and self-mutilation in *Comm.* 4.5 and *Comm.* 39.2 (with immorality), singing, *Comm.* 5.27 (followed by immorality).

112 The main manuscripts of the *Commentaries* are classified by date and content in the introduction to the *Commentaries*, pp. 15–19. More have been added to the 150 known to me in 1990 by the *Repertorium Nazianzenum*, published in six volumes by F. Schoningh, Paderborn from 1981–1998. Volumes 1, 3 and 4 were edited by Justin Mossay alone, Volume 2 with the help of X. Lequeux, Volume 5 with L. Hoffmann, and Volume 6 with B. Coulie. This provides a vast and invaluable list of the Greek manuscripts of Gregory's sermons, other theological works and commentaries.

possibly in the tenth century AD, as the history of Gregory's manuscripts shows. Two later examples of these illustrated manuscripts (though only of *Comm.* 43 and 39) are still to be found.[113] Some very late manuscripts are devoted to their text alone. Like Gregory's sermons, the work was translated into Syriac, Armenian and Georgian.

Although the earliest Greek witness dates only from the late ninth century AD, the revised Syriac version of its text (completed in AD 623/4) provided important evidence as to its nature and early history.[114] It has been possible to use this Syriac translation to identify an early stage of the Greek text in two Greek manuscripts, and to trace its history in later manuscripts and editions. The Greek tradition divided into two families at an early stage, after the work had been translated into Syriac, although the Syriac version then had interpolations of its own. One Greek family (*n*) then suffered other additions and was translated into Armenian; the text of the other (*m*) was drastically abbreviated to avoid repetition, when *Commentaries* 39 and 43 were placed before *Commentaries* 4 and 5.[115] While Greek scribes contin-ued to make their own changes and additions to separate manuscripts, from which later copies were derived, exemplars from both families were then translated by different Georgian scholars in different styles from the tenth century AD onwards.[116] Traces of the influence of the *Commentaries* survive in later Georgian literature.[117] It should be noted that much of the Georgian Version of *Commentary* 5 was preserved in a late eighteenth- to early

113 Weitzmann, *Greek Mythology*, pp. 6–92. He describes miniatures from certain 11th-century mss. of Gr.'s sermons which can only be explained by reference to the passages from the *Commentaries* upon them, and the illustrated manuscripts of the *Commentaries* themselves (in Jerusalem, the 11th-century ms. Taphou 14 and in the Vatican, the 12th-century Vat. gr. 1947), although the evidence from the illustrations to *Sermons* 4 and 5 in the mss. of the sermons indicate that the commentaries on those sermons had also, at one time, been illustrated. For the date of the illustrations, see pp. 87–92.

114 Brock, pp. 3–4, discusses the date of the revised version, and the contents of the first, which consist of about a third of *Comm.* 4, on pp. 18–21.

115 See the *Commentaries*, intro., pp. 9–57, for the details of these relationships.

116 The Version is described in n. 96 above. The article by its editor and the author, '*The Georgian Versions* of the *Pseudo-Nonnos Mythological Commentaries* and their Greek originals', *Le Muséon* 106 (1993), pp. 289–308, describes their text in relation to the Greek tradition.

117 See B. Coulie, 'Les versions orientales des commentaires mythologiques du Pseudo Nonnos', in *La diffusione dell' eredità classica nell' età tardoantica e medievale, Il "Romanzo di Alessandro" e altri scritti*, ed. R.B. Finazzi and A. Valvo, Alessandria (Italy), 1998, pp. 113–23, for a recent review of the later history of the *Commentaries* in Armenian and Georgian literature, and the identification of a passage from *Comm.* 4.26 in Pseudo-Callisthenes 1.27 (version C).

nineteenth-century mythological lexicon.[118]

In addition to the vagaries of its textual transmission described above, the *Commentaries* were largely taken over by Cosmas of Jerusalem in the eighth century AD and used, with his other material, in his commentary on Gregory's poetry. The title of this work begins, as the titles of the Pseudo-Nonnus *Commentaries* do, with the words: 'A collection and explanation of the stories which the holy Gregory mentioned in...' [119] While he is ready to correct *Comm.* 43.16's mention of Diomedes, in the identification of the Homeric hero whose keenness for battle was compared to the desire of a stalled horse for the open plain ('Homer speaks in this verse of Alexander/ Paris. I do not know why one of the earlier historians [sc. writers of *historiae*] applied it to Diomedes')[120] he obviously finds the work of use. He also adds the few stories from Gregory's rhetorical works (consisting of a selection from *Commentaries* 39, 43, 4 and 5) which he notes had not recurred in Gregory's poetry (and been incorporated by him in his commentary) at its end: 'so that nothing should be left unclear for those who are studying this book'.[121]

Basil Minimus, a tenth-century commentator on Gregory's sermons, speaks with better information than Pseudo-Nonnus does on the myths they both describe, and, losing patience with the account of them, refers the reader elsewhere for fuller details.[122] Nicetas of Heraclea (AD ? 1050 – died after 1117) and the twelfth-century Elias of Crete made much use of the *Commentaries* in their commentaries on Gregory's sermons, but the Greek texts of these works have not, as yet, been edited.

118 *G.V.*, pp. 53–56.

119 Cosmas' Commentary on Gregory's poetry (reprinted in Migne, *PG* 38, from the original edition of the single manuscript of its text by A. Mai, *Spicilegium Romanum*, II, xv, Rome, 1839) reworks much of the *Commentaries*. His work is sometimes quoted as the origin of material which first appeared in the *Commentaries*, although many of these passages have long been identified in previous discussions both of the *Commentaries* and of his own work (see F. Lefherz, 'Studien zu Gregor von Nazianz. Mythologie, Ueberlieferung, Scholiasten', Diss. Phil, Bonn, 1958, pp. 150–54 , and F. Trisoglio, 'Mentalità ed attegiamenti degli scoliasti ...', *II Symposium Nazianzenum*, pp. 207–14). The *Commentaries* give full references to Cosmas' commentary in their edition. The edition of Gregory's poem, *On Virtue* (*Poem* 1.2.10) by C. Crimi and M. Kertsch, *Sulla virtù*, Pisa, 1995, adds the section from Cosmas' commentary on the poem as an appendix to the work.

120 *PG* 38 614.

121 *PG* 38 619.

122 See Trisoglio, 'Mentalità ed attegiamenti...', p. 230 and n. 74. He cites a possible reference to them in *PG* 36 1105 D: 'You will find the rest of the stories given more fully elsewhere, and it is superfluous to continue to waste more time on them'.

The compilers of the *Souda*, a popular lexicon of Greek culture, also drew upon the *Commentaries* in the mid- to late eleventh century AD.[123] The twelfth-century poet and scholar, John Tzetzes, knew a manuscript of the tradition *n* of this work, adding a few items of information from it to his *Commentary upon the Alexandra of Lycophron*.[124] It was widely admired and much copied in the sixteenth century by Andreas Darmarios, and first published then in a Latin translation, with Gregory's sermons. One copyist of the time, Constantius Palaeocappa, was so taken by the work that he included much of it, from a manuscript or manuscripts in a sub-group of *n*, in a spurious find, the *Violarium*, which he attributed to another Empress Eudocia (who lived in the eleventh century AD). This listed accounts of figures from classical mythology in alphabetical order and was very popular. It was first printed in 1781.[125] Its contents, however, were found to derive from early printed editions of such works as the *Souda*, and it was exposed as a fake in the late nineteenth century.[126] The first Greek edition of the *Commentaries* was made (of 4 and 5, alone, with *Sermons* 4 and 5, and the *Scholia Oxoniensia* from the Magdalen manuscript) from contemporary copies of early manuscripts from different parts of the Greek tradition, and printed by Richard Montagu at Henry Saville's press at Eton in 1610.[127] Its text was reprinted by J.-P. Migne in the *Patrologia Graeca*, volume 36, from 1858 onwards.[128]

---

123 The lack of a critical edition of the *Commentaries* until 1992 led to difficulties in identifying passages from them in the past, as mentioned by A. Adler, the editor of the *Souda*, in her introduction, p. xviii. She nevertheless identifies many passages from the *Commentaries*, denoted the Scholia on Gregory Nazianzenus, in her edition. The Greek edition of the *Commentaries* makes full reference to the dependence of both Cosmas and the *Souda* on its text in the *apparatus criticus*.

124 See the notes to *Comm.* 4.50 and 43.8 for the material in *n*.

125 By Villoison, in Venice, and then by Flach, in the Teubner series, in 1880.

126 See K. Krumbacher, *Geschichte der byzantinischen Literatur*, 1897, pp. 542 and 579, for an account of Palaeocappa, whose use of the *Commentaries* is described in my thesis, 'Studies on the Mythological Commentaries attributed to a certain Nonnos on four Sermons by Gregory of Nazianzus with a representative text and apparatus criticus of the Commentaries on Sermons 4 and 5', PhD thesis, Edinburgh, 1983, pp. 428–32.

127 *S.Gregorii Nazianzeni in Julianum invectivae duae cum scholiis Graecis nunc primum editis*. See the *Commentaries*, intro., p. 2, n. for the other early editions of the text.

128 *PG* 36 985–1065, in parallel columns with the Greek text of *Comm.* 4 and 5 (with a reprint of Jacques de Billy's early Latin translation, made from different mss., and described in n. 94 above); *Comm.* 43 appears in part and *Comm.* 39 in full, from col. 1057–1080. A full description of the earlier editions of the Greek text is given in the introduction to the *Commentaries*, sections I and III.

This translation is presented in the hope that modern readers too will find interest in a little-known account of an unknown individual's contribution to the protean resilience of Greek culture in a changing world, with its confident application of a pagan technique of exegesis to Christian sermons.

THE NATURE AND CONTENTS OF THE TRANSLATION

The translation is based on the Greek text of my edition of the *Commentaries*: *Pseudo-Nonniani in IV Orationes Gregorii Nazianzeni Commentarii a Jennifer Nimmo Smith editi, Collationibus Versionum Syriacarum a Sebastian Brock Versionisque Armenicae a Bernard Coulie additis*, Corpus Christianorum Series Graeca 27, Corpus Nazianzenum 2, Brepols, 1992.

I have retained the simple and repetitious style of the Greek for the sake of accuracy, but added a full quotation of the passage from the appropriate sermon before each story. I have also kept to Pseudo-Nonnus' phraseology and spelling of proper names, even when they differ from Gregory's text. Elizabeth Balmer very kindly allowed me to see her translation of Gregory's *Sermons* 4 and 5, which has been of great help.[129] Other, earlier translations of the latter sermons and of *Sermons* 39 and 43 have been consulted. A brief commentary is then appended (in which significant additions to, and alterations of, the text of the *Commentaries* from the families *n* and *m* are included)[130] to show how Pseudo-Nonnus' information fits in with the more usual accounts of the topic under discussion.

129 Elizabeth Mary-Rose Balmer, 'Gregory of Nazianzus. Orations IV and V. A Translation and Commentary', MLitt, Bristol, 1995.

130 These notes expand and translate the Latin commentary in the edition of the *Commentaries* for the help of readers without a knowledge of the language and possibly unfamiliar with the sources. Textual variants are given in full in the *apparatus criticus* to the Greek edition of the *Commentaries*.

COMMENTARY ON SERMON 4

COLLECTION AND EXPLANATION OF THE STORIES WHICH ST GREGORY MENTIONED IN THE *FIRST 'PILLAR-POSTED'*[1] *ORATION AGAINST JULIAN*

INTRODUCTION[2]

The oration that is 'pillar-posted' (*stēliteutikos*) is an invective against what Julian has done. But a 'pillar-posting' (oration) differs from an invective because an invective proceeds through the divisions of an encomium, such as birth, upbringing, deeds, comparison, while a 'pillar-posting' does so by the deeds alone, and, it may be, by comparison. A 'pillar-posting' is so called by transference from a pillar (*stēlē*). A pillar is a rectangular piece of stone or bronze upon which is engraved the outrageous act of the one who is the object of the 'pillar-posting'.[3]

Thus, the Athenians inscribed (the name of) Arthmius of Zelea on a pillar, he who tried to corrupt the Greeks by bribes to yield more readily to the Persian (King), depriving both him and all his family of civic rights, and granting anyone who wished the permission to kill him, engraving the

---

1 This adjective (*stēliteutikos*) appears first in the 4th century AD, in a letter of Basil the Great (*Ep.* 223.3), and in all the mss. of these sermons. The practice is of very long standing, as noted below.

2 The passage is untitled in the mss. of the *Commentaries*.

3 A *stēlē* was originally a block of stone, and hence a tombstone, or a monument of the types described above or a boundary marker or pillar (as in *Comm.* 5.35 below). The adjective, *stēlites*, found in Isocrates (5/4th cent. BC) and Demosthenes (384–322 BC), is explained in this way by Pollux in the 2nd century AD (LSJ s.v.).

In descriptions of the science of rhetoric, speeches were divided into three types, judicial, deliberative and epideictic. A 'pillar-posted' oration falls into the third category, which includes 'speeches in praise or blame'. Gr. rejects the term 'invective' for his words because he feels it cannot deal adequately with Julian's crimes in *Sermon* 4.79 (Kurmann, *ad tit.*). Ps.-N. defines it as a sub-type of an invective. His subdivision is not found elsewhere, and these sermons do, in fact, employ all the divisions he describes as being specific to an invective (Kennedy, *Greek Rhetoric*, pp. 221–22).

reason for the censure of Arthmius on the stele as well, 'because', they say, 'he brought gold from the Medes into the Peloponnese'.[4]

One should know that often the good services of benefactors were also inscribed on pillars, just as the good service of Leucon, the governor of the Bosphorus, was inscribed in Athens.[5]

So much then for the theme (of the oration), and, as for the stories, we shall describe them in the briefest terms we can.

1

Leave these playthings to the people like Empedocles among them and Aristaeus and to some Empedotimus and Trophonius and the crowd of unfortunates like them, the one who deified himself in the Sicilian craters, as he supposed, and having taken himself away from us to a loftier destiny, was betrayed by his own sandal when it was spat out by the flames, and was shown to be, not a god after (being) a man, but a conceited and unphilosophical man after his death, who lacked even common sense, while the others, inspired by the same folly and love of self, were then exposed, and gained as much honour for their deception as scorn for its exposure. (*Sermon* 4.59)

The first story is this: Leave these playthings to the people like Empedocles among them and Aristaeus and Empedotimus and Trophonius.

This Empedocles was a Sicilian by race, a Pythagorean by philosophy. In his desire to win the vainglory of one who had been turned into a god and carried up into heaven, he threw himself into the fire which issues from Mt Etna. This fire is called 'the "mixing-bowls" of Hephaestus'. He then was destroyed by the fire, but God, who wished to reveal his vanity, caused his sandal to be ejected, undamaged, from the fire. It was thus known that he had not been carried up into heaven but had been burnt to ashes, as he deserved

---

4 Demosthenes records this decree against Arthmius in *Philippics* 3.41–45. The latter was a guest-friend of the Athenians, and his state, Zelea (a city in the Troad), was a part of their empire. He may have taken the bribe from the Persian general Megabazus, who was sent to Sparta with money in 455 BC (Thuc. 1.109) to encourage the Spartans to invade Attica.

5 Leucon's kingdom, which controlled the grain trade from the hinterland north of the Black Sea, included the Cimmerian Bosphorus (after which it was named). Leucon supplied the Athenians with grain during the Social War in 357 BC, for which both he and his sons were granted Athenian citizenship (as described by Dem. *Against Leptines* 35–36).

to be, because of his vanity.[6]

Trophonius, Empedotimus and Aristaeus were from Boeotia, from the city of Lebadia, and were seers by profession. As these also wished to gain vain glory and to prove that they had been carried up into heaven, they cast themselves into certain subterranean caverns with the intention of dying without their remains being discovered. They did indeed die; but they were known to have died there because an oracle appeared at the spot. There is a proverb, too, which says 'You have consulted at the oracle of Trophonius'. It is said about pallid people who never laugh. For everyone who went down to that oracle came back up gloomy and pallid for evermore. This, then, was a refutation of these very people, proving that they had grown pale and died without ever laughing under the ground. Trophonius and his brother Agamedes were thought worthy of giving oracles because they had founded the temple of Apollo at Delphi from their own resources.[7]

6 Empedocles (c.493–c.433 BC) was an early Greek philosopher, statesman, orator and poet from Acragas in Sicily. He combined far-reaching and important theories on the elements of the physical world with Orphic doctrines on the immortality of the soul, and was held to be a disciple of Pythagoras (see story 1 below) or of one of his followers. There are conflicting accounts of E.'s death in D.L. 8.68–69; Christian authors, as here, prefer the one that makes him out to be a charlatan. D.L.'s source notes (*loc. cit.*) that his sandals were made of bronze. Hephaestus was the god of fire, and linked with the volcanic activity in Sicily and the Lipari Isles. The word crater is derived from the Greek *krater*, a large bowl in which wine was diluted with water before it was served – a 'mixing bowl', and hence also a cup-shaped opening and the mouth of a volcano (*Schol.* on Soph. *Oedipus at Colonus* 1593). See Peter Kingsley, *Ancient Philosophy, Mystery and Magic. Empedocles and the Pythagorean Tradition*, Oxford, 1995, for a detailed investigation into the full implications of the life and death of Empedocles, of which this passage retains the slightest remnants. The impiety of this death is stressed by Gregory in *Epitaph* 69.1 and *Poem* 2.2.7.281–90.

7 Aristaeus of Proconnesus (fl. c.580 BC) dropped dead in a fuller's shop in Proconnesus, but when preparations were made to collect his corpse, it was found to have disappeared, and he was reported to have been, at about the time of his death, in conversation with a stranger on the way to Cyzicus. He reappeared seven years later (as noted by Hdt. 413–14). He is not known to Ps-N. Empedotimus may be identified with a certain Hermotimus of Clazomenae, a Pythagorean, whose soul would leave his body and wander from place to place and return with news of distant events. His enemies finally burnt his body (see Pliny *N.H.* 7.174, and E. Rohde, *Psyche*, trans. W.B. Hillis, London, 1925, p. 331, n. 112). Trophonius alone was from Boeotia, and founded an oracle there in a cave which is described by Paus. 9.37 and 39. Visits to the oracle involved terrifying confrontations with snakes (Aristoph. *Clouds* 508, and the *scholia ad loc.*), which was probably the reason for the proverb, found in Zen. 3.61, for which Ps-N. seems to provide his own explanation. The temple of Apollo at Delphi in Northern Greece was a renowned oracle in the ancient world, and there is early mention of the involvement of Agamedes and Trophonius with it (*H.H.* 3.295f.). See A. Schachter, *Cults of Boiotia*, London, 1994, for Trophonius and his cult. All three names (with that of Heracles) are again listed by Gregory as examples of impious deaths in *Epitaph* 70.1–3, and in *Poem* 2.2.7.286–90 (Kurmann, *ad loc.*)

2

For I'll pass over Proteus, the Egyptian sophist of the myth ... (*Sermon* 4.62)

Second is the story about Proteus.

This Proteus was a Thracian by race; he had Molus and Telegonus as sons. These were acting as robbers when Heracles came upon them and killed them, as he went on his travels in search of the cattle of Geryon. So, when this Proteus fell into despair at the loss of his children and threw himself into the sea, the gods pitied him and made him immortal. He became a sea-demon and went and inhabited the island of Pharia. He is also said to live with the seals. He also took Helen when Alexander came from Greece and gave him the phantom of Helen. Later, however, when Menelaus learnt after the Trojan war that Helen was in Egypt and came to Proteus, he gave her to him.

This Proteus is said to change his shape before those who came across him, and sometimes to appear in one form and sometimes in another.[8]

3

... you (Julian) who admire the funeral pyre of Heracles, which was caused by misfortune and ill-treatment of women, (*Sermon* 4.70)

Third is the story about Heracles and the pyre.

---

8 Proteus was the name of a minor sea-god with the gift of prophecy, who dwelt on the island of Pharos, off the coast of Egypt. He would only speak to those who held him fast despite his changing shape (*Od.* 4.384–417). Gregory uses the myth of other deceitful opponents (*Poems* 2.1.11.808, 2.1.12.728, and of Satan, 2.1.83.10, as listed by Bernardi *CJ*). There was also a son of Poseidon of that name whose sons (Polygonus and Telegonus) were killed by Heracles in Chalcidice (*Alex.* 115–26, a difficult poem, possibly written in the 2nd century BC, in the style of the Hellenistic poet, Lycophron, and Apollod. *Libr.* 2.5.9). The monster, Geryon, whose cattle Heracles stole (Apollod. *Libr.* 2.5.10), lived in the furthest West.

The rescue of Helen by Proteus, king of Egypt, is told in Hdt. 2.112–19, and his substitution of a phantom for her is recounted by Lycophron (*Alex.* 119, 128–30) and Servius (*on Aen.* 1.651 and 2.592). Servius even calls him 'the sea god who rules Egypt' (*on Aen.* 12.262). Both Ps-N. and Servius (*on Georg.* 4.387) make him Greek, not Egyptian. Alexander (or Paris) was a prince of Troy who preferred Aphrodite to Athena and Hera in the contest of beauty between them. Aphrodite then gave him Helen, the most beautiful woman in the world, to wife, although she was already married to Menelaus, king of Sparta. According to Euripides (*Helen* 582ff.), it was Zeus who took her from Paris and sent her to Proteus, and Hera who made a phantom in her likeness to accompany Alexander to Troy. Menelaus rescued her from Egypt after Proteus' death.

A long story is current about Heracles, that he was the son of Zeus and Alcmene, and a hero, and that he carried out the twelve labours.[9] The present story about the pyre in this passage is this.

This Heracles had a wife called Deianeira, whom he took from Oeneus, after competing for her in love with the river Achelous, and by whom he had Hyllus. While he was taking this Deianeira off and carrying her away to his native land, Nessus, one of the Centaurs, caught sight of her, fell in love with her and wanted to have sexual intercourse with her by a certain river. When Heracles learned this, he shot Nessus dead. As Nessus died he gave Deianeira some of his blood, deceiving her and suggesting, 'This blood will serve you as a love-charm for Heracles, so that', he says, 'if you should learn that he loves another, smear his garment with some of this blood, and you will change him to desire for you.' So Deianeira kept this blood. So, when Heracles fell in love with Iole, the daughter of Eurytus, and captured her and sent her by Lichas as a prisoner of war to Deianeira, Deianeira was stirred to reflection and to jealousy, and, because she wished to change his love back towards herself, she smeared the tunic of Heracles with the blood of Nessus and gave it to Heracles to put on. The blood, however, was fatal to humans. When Heracles put it on, the tunic caught fire from underneath and burnt into him.[10] As he burnt he threw himself into a nearby river and made the water hot. From then on as a result of this Thermopylae came into being, between Thessaly and Phocis.[11]

9 The twelve labours of Heracles, son of Zeus and Alcmene, the wife of Amphitryon, are described in Apollod. *Libr.* 2.4.8–5.12. The account of his choice of a life of virtue (and toil) rather than one of vice by Prodicus of Ceos (fl. 5th cent. BC), surviving in Xen. *Mem.* 2.1.21–34, and also cited by Basil the Great, *On the value of Greek Literature*, 5.55–77, made him greatly admired by pagan thinkers. Gr. mentions him often, in *Poems* 2.1.11.975, 2.1.32.20–21, 2.1.34.72, 2.1.88.5, 2.2.7.286–90, *Ep.* 52.2, 156.1, *Epigr.* 88.1–2 and *Epitaph* 70.1–3 (Demoen, Inv. II, s.n.).

10 This follows the account given in Sophocles, *Women of Trachis*, to line 771, but then omits the rest of the story of Heracles' self-appointed death on a funeral pyre, set alight, at his own command, by his son. For Gr.'s other reference to his death on the pyre, see n. 6 above. He mentions the 'flesh-devouring garment' in *Poem* 2.15.87–88.

11 Ps-N. combines the later account found also in Hyginus that Heracles threw himself into a nearby river in an attempt to stop the robe burning him (though the water only increased its effect, *Fab.* 36) with the presence of the hot springs at Thermopylae (Hdt. 7.176, 201; Soph. *Women of T.* 634). Athena created these springs for Heracles once when he was weary (*Schol.* on Aristoph. *Clouds* 1050). Thermopylae means 'Hot Gates'.

4

> ... and the butchery of Pelops, a kindness to guests or rather to the gods, as a result of which his descendants are distinguished by an ivory shoulder, (*Sermon* 4.70)

Fourth is the story about the butchery of Pelops. It is this.

Tantalus was king of Phrygia. He had a son, Pelops. This Tantalus once entertained the gods as his guests. So taking his son, Pelops, Tantalus slaughtered him, cut him up and stewed him, and served him up as a feast to the gods. Demeter put out her hand and took from this flesh and ate a piece from the shoulder. The other gods in pity for Tantalus and astonishment that he had thought so little of his son, put the pieces of flesh together, and restored Pelops to life. But the piece of flesh which Demeter had eaten from the shoulder was missing. So by adding a bit of ivory to the shoulder, they rendered Pelops complete. Thus from that time onwards the whole race of the Pelopids was marked out by this, for all had a piece of ivory in their shoulders.[12]

5

> ... and the castrations of the Phrygians, beguiled by the sound of the double flute and outraged after the flute playing, (*Sermon* 4.70)

Fifth is the story of the cutting of the Phrygians.[13] This is as follows.

In Phrygia they used to honour Rhea, the mother of the gods, above every god. So when the Phrygians carried out her rites, they would cut themselves with knives, not wishing to kill themselves, but only to draw blood. And they would do this while charmed by the music of double flutes, so that they

---

12 Tantalus was a son of Zeus and King of Phrygia (*Od*.11.532). The story of Pelops and his ivory shoulder is referred to in Pindar, *Ol*.1.27 and 37–38. The scholiast gives the story twice in much more detail, and adds Thetis (a sea-goddess who was to be the mother of Achilles) as an alternative to Demeter, the goddess of corn (who is also mentioned in Hyg. *Fab.* 83, and Servius *on Aen.* 4.603, as the god who ate Pelops' flesh). John Tzetzes, like Gr., notes that the ivory shoulder is a distinguishing mark for Pelops' descendants (*Alex.* 152–53, in which he made some use of Ps-N.'s work). The latter mentions it again in *Sermon* 39.5 and *Ep.* 38.1 (Kurmann, *ad loc.*, considers Gr. drew the reference directly from Pindar, *Ol.* 1.40).

13 The Greek *ektomai*, used in the singular by Ps-N. for Gr.'s plural, can mean both 'cutting' and 'castration'. *Syr.* translates the word as 'incisions'. Ps-N. does not understand the word as 'castration'.

could bear to strike themselves.[14] After the blows they would go on to impure acts of sexual intercourse, with women, I mean, not with men.

6

… and the torments of Mithras … (*Sermon* 4.70)

Sixth is the story about Mithras.

Mithras, then, is considered by the Persians to be the sun, and they sacrifice to him and perform certain rites in his honour. No one can therefore be initiated in his mysteries without first passing through the stages of the torments. There are stages in the torments, there being eighty of them, having a lower grade and an ascent. For first they suffer the lighter torments, then the more drastic, and then the even more drastic. Then, after going through all the torments in this way, the initiand is initiated. The torments consist of passing through fire, through cold, through hunger and thirst, through much journeying by land, through travel by sea and, in a word, through all such matters as these.[15]

7

… and the slaughter of strangers among the Taurians, (*Sermon* 4.70)

Seventh is the story about the slaughter of strangers among the Taurians. It is this.

The Taurians are a people who live in Scythia. Iphigeneia, the daughter of

14 The priests of Rhea, the Galli, whose cult in Phrygia worshipped her as Cybele or the Great Mother, used to castrate themselves during her rites (Catullus, *Atthis*; Luc. *Syr. D.* 15), as well as slash themselves (Propertius 2.22A.15–6) as they do in this passage, all to the sound of flutes, long described as stirring the emotions to a frenzy. Also mentioned in *Sermons* 4.103, 39.4 and in *Poem* 2.2.7.262 (Bernardi, Kurmann, *ad loc.*), and discussed by Ps.-N. in *Comm.* 4.59 and 39.2 below.

15 The information given by Ps.-N. here, in story 47 and in *Comm.* 39.18 below about Roman Mithraic ritual is rejected by F. Cumont, *Die Mysterien des Mithra*, Leipzig, 1923, p. 148, but Burkert, *Ancient Mystery Cults*, pp. 102–03, considers it may retain some traces of the rites. Those who worshipped Mithras certainly went through some kind of initiation process with ordeals and achieved different degrees of seniority in the cult (Jerome, *Ep.* 107.2.2); Burkert, *Ancient Mystery Cults*, pp. 98–99. The Persian deity Mithra, who was associated with the sun, was adopted by the Roman cult in the 2nd century AD. The latter's rites, however, had little connection with the Iranian religion (see de Jong, *Traditions of the Magi: Zoroastrianism in Greek and Latin Literature*, pp. 284–85, with n. 135). Gr. refers to Mithras elsewhere, in *Sermon* 4.89, 39.7 and *Poem* 2.2.7.266.

Agamemnon, was brought among them by Artemis, when she was on the point of being sacrificed on behalf of the Greeks at Aulis, when the goddess gave (them) a deer to sacrifice in her place. So while this Iphigeneia was among the Taurians, she ordered them to sacrifice those who visited the country to Artemis, so that she should not be recognised by them for who she was. And this is the slaughter of strangers to which the holy Gregory refers.[16]

But later, when Orestes was terrified by the Erinyes and came to the Taurians, and was arrested because he was a stranger and destined for slaughter, and was taken to Iphigeneia, as the priestess, he was recognised by his ivory shoulder and spared from sacrifice. Then Orestes thus took his own sister, that is, I mean, Iphigeneia, and took her to Greece.[17]

8

... and the sacrifice of the royal maiden on the way to Troy, (*Sermon* 4.70)

Eighth is the story, 'the sacrifice of the royal maiden at Troy'.[18] It is the one about Polyxena.

16 See Hdt. 4.103, where the goddess to whom the sacrifices are made is said to be Iphigeneia herself. Ps-N. expands Gr.'s reference to the Taurians with the well-established account of Artemis' rescue of Iphigeneia at Aulis. Agamemnon, one of the leaders of the Greek expedition against Troy to regain Helen, had insulted Artemis, goddess of hunting, and she then held back the Greek fleet at Aulis by adverse winds until he sacrificed his daughter to her. In classical times, Scythia, the territory of nomad tribes who originally came from Central Asia, lay in the hinterland to the north of the Black Sea, and the Taurians lived in what is now the Crimea. By the 4th century AD, however, the Scythians lived in the province of Scythia Minor, on the coast of the Black Sea, and in the Crimea, dispersed among the local populations. The term 'Scythian' was used in Byzantine literature for any northern nomadic tribe, such as the Huns, Cotrigurs, etc. Gr. often mentions this cult: *Sermons* 4.103, 112, 14.19, 39.4, 43.8, and *Poem* 2.2.7.275 (Bernardi, *ad loc.*), and Ps.-N. comments on it again in *Comm.* 4.57 and 94, 39.7 and 43.3.

17 Orestes, Iphigeneia's brother, killed his mother to avenge her murder of Agamemnon, and was then pursued by the Erinyes (or Furies), who punish those who harm their parents (or break oaths). Ps-N. omits the reason for his visit to the Taurians (that is, to carry off an ancient statue of Artemis from there to Greece, and thus appease the Erinyes) and adds the theme of the 'ivory shoulder' of the descendants of Pelops (see 4, above) to explain his recognition by Iphigeneia. This last is not one of the tokens used in the recognition scenes between Orestes and his sisters in any of the tragedies by Aeschylus, Sophocles or Euripides which survive, and may be a rationalisation by Ps-N. of the facts at his disposal.

18 Gr. is probably referring to the sacrifice of Iphigeneia here, 'on the way to Troy' (see Elias of Crete's *Commentary*, col. 325; Bernardi *CJ, ad loc.*; and Kurmann and Lugaresi *4, ad loc.*). Although the Greek, *epi tēn Troian*, can equally well be translated as 'at Troy', Ps-N. may be relying upon another's (mistaken) marginal note, as discussed above, p. xliii.

Polyxena is the daughter of Priam; hoping to marry her, Achilles entered Troy, and was shot at by Paris from ambush in the temple of Apollo and died. So, later, when his (Achilles') son Pyrrhus had grown up he appeared to him in a dream (saying that) he should sacrifice Polyxena, because of whom he had perished. Pyrrhus, being in Troy, and seizing her after the victory, slew her on the tomb of Achilles, his father.[19]

9

... and the blood of Menoeceus on behalf of Thebes, (*Sermon* 4.70)

Ninth is the story about Menoeceus.

Menoeceus is the son of Creon, king of Thebes. So, when his native land, Thebes, was attacked in war by the seven generals, Tiresias, being a seer, prophesied that the war would cease at once and they would have the victory, if one of the royal family of the earth-born ones, who had sprung from the teeth of the dragon, were to offer himself for slaughter. When Menoeceus learnt this, wishing to relieve the siege of the city, he gave himself up for slaughter against the will of his father, Creon.[20]

19 As Ps-N. has already described the fate of Iphigeneia in the previous reference to the Taurians, he now adds the account of Polyxena's death. His version of the death of Achilles is first found in Servius (*on Aen.* 6.57), though earlier descriptions, especially those in Homer (*Il.* 21.277f., 22.358–60, namely that he was killed openly at the Scaean gate, but again by Paris and Apollo, the god of archery), differ. Ps-N. follows the *Fall of Troy* of Quintus Smyrnaeus, an epic poet of the 3rd century AD, in making Achilles appear to Pyrrhus alone (14.180–222), rather than the earlier story in Eur. *Hecabe* 35–41, where he appears to all the Greeks.

20 This is a greatly simplified account of an episode (Eur. *Phoenician Women* 911–1018; Hyg. *Fab.* 68) in the Theban cycle of myths. Gr. refers to it again in *Poem* 1.2.10, 678–79 (Kurmann, *ad loc.*). Creon became king of Thebes once his sister Jocasta had killed herself and her husband and son, Oedipus, had gone into exile with his children by her. One of their sons, Polynices, took refuge with Adrastus, king of Argos, who married him to his daughter, and then attempted to restore him to the throne of Thebes at the head of an army led by them both with five other leaders (the seven generals). Tiresias was a renowned Theban seer, for whose blindness various gods were blamed, most famously Hera. Zeus then gave him the gift of prophecy (Apollod. *Libr.* 3.6.7). Cadmus, the founder and first king of Thebes, took the teeth of the dragon he killed at the spring of Ares in Boeotia, and sowed them in the ground. They sprang up as armed men (Apollod. *Libr.* 3.4.1–2). The royal house of Thebes was held to be descended from these (Eur. *Phoenician W.* 940–44). Gr. refers to Menoeceus again in *Poem* 1.2.10.678–79.

10

... and that (blood) later of the daughters of Scedasus at Leuctra, (*Sermon* 4.70)

Tenth is the story concerning the daughters of Scedasus. It is this.

After the Lacedaemonians had overwhelmingly defeated the Athenians in the Peloponnesian war they wanted to make war on their allies also. But, once they had started out against the Thebans, before they drew near the city, and while they were at Leuctra (this was also a city of Thebes), they came to blows and lost, while Epaminondas, the Thebans' general, was successful.[21]

The disaster happened to the Lacedaemonians at Leuctra for the following reason. Scedasus, a Leuctrian, had three daughters. Long ago some of the Lacedaemonians were hospitably entertained by them, and then raped the girls. So, since the Lacedaemonians were afraid that they would reveal the outrage to their father, they killed them. But when Scedasus returned to his city of Leuctra and learnt of the happening, he cursed all Lacedaemonians with defeat beside his daughters' very tomb. And this is why the defeat overtook the Lacedaemonians at Leuctra.[22]

11

... (you, Julian) who praise the Laconian youths lacerated by whips ... (*Sermon* 4.70)

Eleventh is the story about the Laconian youths. It is this.

Since the Lacedaemonians wished their citizens and children to be steadfast and brave, they trained them with severe whippings, and a prize was

---

21 The battle of Leuctra, 371 BC, put an end to the Spartan attempts to become dominant outside the Peloponnese which had continued with some success since the end of the Peloponnesian war in 404 BC. For Epaminondas, see story 19 below.

22 Xenophon first mentions such an episode at Leuctra, in *Hellenica* 6.4.7, where he tells of an oracle foretelling a Lacedaemonian defeat at the tomb of girls who had killed themselves after being raped by some Lacedaemonians. D.S. calls them the daughters of Scedasus and Leuctrus (15.54.3), but Plutarch (*Pelopidas* 20), the daughters of Scedasus alone. They are named Hippo and Molpia by Paus. 9.13.6–7. Xen., D.S. and Paus. agree that they killed themselves, but Plut. gives two versions of their death, by suicide as above (*Pel.* 20), and at the hands of their attackers (*Love Stories* 3.4.5).

awarded to him who was the most enduring.[23]

12

> ... and the blood on the altar that was pleasing to a pure and virgin goddess, (*Sermon* 4.70)

Twelfth is the story 'the blood on the altar'. It is the one about Artemis.

Since the goddess was herself a virgin and chaste, she rejoiced to be honoured with the blood from the slaughter of strangers.[24]

13

> ... (you, Julian) who extol the hemlock of Socrates ... (*Sermon* 4.70)

Thirteenth is the story about the hemlock of Socrates. It is this.

Socrates was an Athenian by race, and a philosopher by education. Anytus and Meletus accused him of introducing new divinities into the state. He was accordingly condemned to die by drinking hemlock, on the grounds of corrupting the young. He drank it and died.[25]

---

23 This and story 12 below are part of a single allusion in Gr. to the worship of Artemis Orthia in Sparta, where boys were whipped before her altar (Xen. *Constitution of the Lacedaemonians* 2.9; Plut. *Ancient Customs of the Spartans* 239C; and Paus. 3.16.10), which is also described in story 58 and *Comm.* 39.8 below (on *Sermon* 4.103, and in 39.4 respectively). Ps-N.'s accounts are far shorter than these, make no mention of Artemis Orthia as they do, and this is the only one to mention the giving of a prize. It is probably drawn from a later more general summary of the topic in which the key term, 'severe scourging', *diamastigōsis* (the name of the festival in Plut., *loc. cit.*) appears, found in the plural in the text above. Ps-N. subdivides Gr.'s lemma, and adds the sacrifice of strangers to Artemis among the Taurians as a separate story in 12 below. Such, and similar, forms of worship of Artemis were long connected (as in Eur. *Iphigeneia among the Taurians* 1446–1461; Paus. 3.16.7–10; Hyg. *Fab.* 261.18–23), though they were distinct in origin. The Spartans were well known for the harsh regime they imposed upon their children (Aristotle, *Politics* 8.4.1). Gr. also mentions the scourging in *Poem* 2.2.7.272 (Bernardi, *ad loc.*).

24 See the note above, for the subdivision of Gr.'s lemma. Ps-N. adds more information than is required, because he, or the annotator he followed (see n. 18 above), did not recognise the double reference in Gr.'s text.

25 Socrates (469–399 BC) was in fact tried and found guilty on both counts (Plato, *Apology* 24b). A draught of hemlock was the usual death penalty in Athens, and Socrates' last hours are described by Plato (c.429–347 BC) in the *Phaedo*. Gr. refers to the death of Socrates, together with those of Menoeceus, Epictetus, Anaxarchus and Cleombrotus, below in *Poem* 1.2.10.678–93, and, in *Ep.* 32, to Socrates, Anaxarchus and Epictetus (Bernardi, *ad loc.*). In the former reference he sees their deaths as inevitable, but freely accepted, but praises them in the latter.

14

... and the leg of Epictetus ... (*Sermon* 4.70)

Fourteenth is the story about the leg of Epictetus.

Epictetus was a philosopher. His leg was bound by a tyrant of Macedon. But later, the tyrant wanted to set him free. So he asked him the following question: 'Do you want me to set you free, Epictetus?' The other replied: 'Why? Am I bound?' as if his soul, indeed, were not bound. It is said therefore that it is the soul and not the body which matters in a human being.[26]

15

... and the sack of Anaxarchus, all of whose philosophy was enforced rather than freely undertaken, (*Sermon* 4.70)

Fifteenth is the story about Anaxarchus. It is this.

Anaxarchus was a philosopher. This man, when arrested by Archelaus the tyrant and thrown into a mortar, was pounded by a wooden pestle. To be pounded (*ptissesthai*) is to be beaten like husked barley (*dikēn ptisanēs*), and hence (the word for) husked barley (*ptisanē*) (is derived) from to be pounded (*ptissesthai*). While he was being brayed he said this: 'Pound, pound the sack of Anaxarchus, for you are not pounding Anaxarchus', saying in riddling words that a philosopher, as he thought, paid no attention to the body.[27]

26 Epictetus of Hierapolis was a Stoic philosopher (AD 55–135), who was once a slave of one of the Emperor Nero's freedmen. The Stoics taught that virtue was the only good, and that their followers should not allow external circumstances to affect them. This anecdote is inspired by a passage in his lectures (collected by Fl. Arrianus, cos. AD 103, in *Discourses of Epictetus* 1.18.17 – 'But the tyrant will bind–' What? Your leg. 'But he will cut–' What? Your neck. 'What will he neither bind nor cut off?' Your moral purpose) and is not historical, although it is treated by Gr. (here and in *Letter* 32.10) and by Origen (*Against Celsus* 7.53) as though it were, though neither author gives the tyrant (or in Origen's case Epictetus' master), a name. See also Gr. *Epigr.* 4.1.3. One group of manuscripts (*n*) states the tyrant is 'of Lacedaemon'. It is an early corruption (found also in *Syr.*), possibly derived from a misreading of 'Macedon'.

27 Anaxarchus (4th cent. BC) came from Abdera and was a follower of Democritus (fl. 420 BC), who taught that the whole universe was composed of atoms in perpetual movement in a void. As every thing and event in the world was caused by the chance coming together of these atoms, afflictions should be viewed with equanimity. Anaxarchus accompanied Alexander the Great in his conquest of the known world, and made an enemy of Nicocreon, the tyrant of Cyprus, who had him pounded to death with iron pestles in a mortar after Alexander's death (D.L. 9.59). His death, as noted above is mentioned again by Gr. in *Poems* 1.2.10.688–91, 2.1.17.60, *Ep.* 32.8–9, and *Epigr.* 4.2–4 (Demoen, Inv. II, s.n.).

16

> ... and the leap of Cleombrotus of Ambracia, the philosophy taught by the dialogue 'Concerning the soul', (*Sermon* 4.70)

Sixteenth is the story 'the leap of Cleombrotus'. It is this.

Cleombrotus was an Ambraciot by race (this is a city of Old Epirus). When he came across the *Phaedo*, Plato's dialogue about the soul, and learnt that separation from the body was better for the soul, he threw himself from the city-wall and died, so that his soul, as he thought, in departing should be separated from his body.[28]

17

> ... and the Pythagorean prohibition of beans, (*Sermon* 4.70)

Seventeenth is the story about the Pythagorean beans. It is this.

The Pythagoreans are a sect of philosophers (who derived) from Pythagoras the Samian. These learnt the precepts of the philosophy by means of riddles.[29] This riddle, too, was handed down among the rest, 'Do not eat beans.' This is, 'Do not take bribes in betrayal of justice.' For long ago in Athens the jurors used beans instead of counters for judgements in the law-courts. So he says that one should not eat of the beans from the law-court.[30]

---

28 The Cleombrotus mentioned in Plato's *Phaedo* 59c as a friend of Socrates may have been this philosopher whose suicide was described by the Alexandrian poet Callimachus (c.305–c.240 BC), *Epigram* 24. His death became a stock example for suicide (see Lucian, *Lover of Lies* 1; Agathias *Epigram* 60; *Greek Anthology* 11.354.17–18; Cicero, *Tusculan Disputations* 1.34.84; Augustine, *City of God* 1.22; and Gr. *Poem* 1.2.10.680–83). Plato, the friend and follower of Socrates, described and developed his thought in his writings. The *Phaedo* is represented by Plato as reporting the conversation about the immortality of the soul held by Socrates with his friends on the day he died (see story 13 above) in 399 BC. Socrates argues that the souls of those who have sought after knowledge pass on through death to eternal happiness, *Ph.*114c.

29 Pythagoras, a famous Presocratic philosopher, emigrated from Samos to Croton in South Italy in 531 BC, where he founded a religious society. His belief in the doctrine of the transmigration of souls, and that the soul reached purity by study, had a great effect on Plato and later philosophers. His precepts, which were also called 'a secret code' (*sumbola*) were deliberately obscure, to hide their meaning from all but his disciples.

30 For a list of Pythagoras' precepts and their explanations, see D.L. 8.17 and 34 and Iamblichus, 60, 106 (with 260, although this is an argument against P., as implying that he supported tyranny). Both state that beans should be avoided because (among other reasons) they were used in elections. Ps-N. links the prohibition to the Athenian *dikastai* (judges) with

18

... and the contempt for death shown by Theano, or by any other of those
who have been initiated in or who have professed the doctrines of 'that man'.
(*Sermon* 4.70)

Eighteenth is the story about the death of Theano the Pythagorean. It is this.

This woman was arrested by a tyrant to make her betray the secrets of her
native land. She, having bitten out her tongue, spat it into the face of the
tyrant, being determined not to speak out, even under duress, as the organ of
her speech was removed.[31]

19

... you, who copy people like Epaminondas and Scipio in endurance ...
(*Sermon* 4.71)

Nineteenth is the story about Epaminondas and Scipio. It is this.

Epaminondas was a Theban by race, a very great general, who held command in the war at Leuctra, and was a student of Philolaus the Pythagorean.
This man showed much self-restraint in war, and over food and sex and all
kinds of pleasure, which is why he raised very great trophies over the
Lacedaemonians.[32]

---

information also found in the *Scholia* on Aristophanes, *Knights* 41, which explains why
Athenian citizens are called 'bean-eaters' (either because they ate beans to stay awake in court,
or used them as voting counters). They were said to 'live on beans', because their votes could be
bought (Aristoph. *Knights*). Gr. knows of his preference for a 'bloodless sacrifice' (*Ep.*198.1,
Demoen, Inv. II, s.n.).

31 Theano was the name of Pythagoras' ('that man's') wife, or of a pupil of his (D.L. 8.42).
Gr. is either referring to an episode in her life of which no record has come down to us, or is
genuinely mistaken about it or is contemptuously ('or by any other of those ...') giving her
name for that of Timycha, another Pythagorean, as discussed by Kurmann, p. 279. She refused
in this way to tell the tyrant, Dionysius II of Syracuse, why Pythagoreans would not tread on
beans (Iambl. 31). It is cited as an argument in favour of suicide by the Stoics in Olymp.
1.§8.26. Such an account is also given of Anaxarchus (mentioned in story 15 above) though not
with reference to beans (D.L. 9.59), and of the *hetaira* Leaina, the confidant of the tyrannicide
Aristogeiton, Plutarch, *On Talkativeness* 8 and Pliny, *N.H.* 34.72. Gr. speaks of the Pythagoreans in *Sermons* 4.102 (which is not commented upon by Ps-N.), 27.10 and 41.2.

32 For the battle of Leuctra, see story 10 above. Epaminondas led the Thebans to victory
there, and then invaded the Peloponnese and established the independence of Messenia, a state
previously subject to Sparta, in 369 BC. He died of wounds after the battle of Mantinea in 362.
Epaminondas became a stock example of a great general in later writers, both Greek and

Scipio, too, was himself a general of the Romans, who was similar to Epaminondas in his way of life and character. He himself, too, won the highest distinction in the war against the Carthaginians, he who took the title from the victory over the race and was called Scipio Africanus.[33] The Carthaginians are Africans.

20

... (Do you see these men without resources and a home, almost without flesh and blood, who in this way draw nigh to God, those) with unwashed feet who sleep upon the ground, as your Homer has it, to honour some evil spirit or other by the fiction ... (*Sermon* 4.71)

Twentieth is the story about those with unwashed feet and who sleep upon the ground. It is this.

According to Homer the poet, the Selli are a Dodonaean people. The priests of the oak used to be selected from these. There was an oracle of Zeus in this oak-tree, which was called the Dodonaean Oak. So these priests, since they were hallowed servants of a god, neither washed nor slept upon a bed, but on the ground, as the poet says in this verse:

and around you the Selli dwell,
interpreters with unwashed feet, who sleep upon the ground.[34]

21

... These (the ascetic practices of Christian monks) are more valuable than the insatiability of Solon, the sage and lawgiver, whom Croesus tested with the Lydian gold ... (*Sermon* 4.72)

Roman, and is noted by Pausanias as one of the famous men of Greece (8.52.4). His teacher was Lysis of Tarentum (Paus. 9.13.1), not Philolaus, another well-known Pythagorean philosopher of that time who taught in Thebes (Pl. *Phaedo* 61d). See story 17 above for the Pythagoreans.

33 Publius Cornelius Scipio Africanus the Elder (236–184/3 BC) who drove the Carthaginians out of Spain and defeated Hannibal in Africa, was also noted for the nobility of his character (see his treatment of Hannibal, Plutarch, *Life of Flaminius*, *ad fin.*)

34 The 'Speaking Oak' of Dodona in Northern Greece was an ancient and famous oracle of Zeus (Homer, *Od.* 14.327–28 = 19.296–97; Parke, *The Oracles of Zeus*, pp. 1–163). This quotation about the Selli occurs in *Il.* 16.234–35. Later accounts of the oracle speak of priestesses, as in Hdt. 2.54–55; Paus. 10.12.10; and Ps-N. in *Comm.* 5.14 and 39.12 below. Callimachus, *Hymn* 4.285 speaks of the 'Pelasgians of Dodona, who couch upon the ground' as attendants of the cauldron oracle in the same place (see the notes on *Comm.* 5.14 below).

Twenty-first is the story about the insatiability of Solon. It is this.

Solon was a legislator of the Athenians. When this man was invited to frame the laws, he in return demanded an oath from the citizens that they should wait for ten years and respect the laws he had established, and then, if they did not please them, they could at that point annul them. He did this to accustom them meantime to adhere for a short time to his precepts. For he knew that once they had a taste of his legislature, they would hold to it fixedly for the future. So, after Solon had received the oath of the Athenians and legislated for them, he left Athens, as he had to spend the ten years abroad. On his travels round the cities, accordingly, he came to Lydia, as well, to the court of king Croesus. On his arrival, Croesus, who wanted to stir his admiration, sent him to his treasure-chambers, showing him that Croesus was rich in gold. And, when Solon came back from the treasure chambers, Croesus asked him whom he thought to be the happiest of all people, expecting, no doubt, that he would name him before all. But Solon replied, 'Tellus the Athenian'. For Solon did not define wealth or conspicuous display as happiness, but an untroubled life and a death of distinction.[35]

So now he calls Solon 'insatiable', as one who yearns to see more wealth than the gold of Lydia. Wealth, indeed, is a kind of happiness to do with external factors. The account (*logos*) recognises three kinds of happiness, an untroubled spirit, bodily health and an abundant provision of worldly goods.[36] Solon, therefore, should have added, 'If your soul is most noble, wealth also will suffice you for happiness in external matters.'

---

35 Solon the Athenian reformed the Athenian constitution in the 7th century BC by first cancelling all debts of the poorer citizens to the nobles, which had forced the former into slavery, and then dividing the whole citizen body into four classes, each of which, depending on its means, had some part to play in the government of the state. He also abolished most of the savage legislation of Draco, and was universally admired as one of the 'Seven Sages' of Greece. Gr.'s attack on him here is deliberate, and not a mistake for Alcmaeon, another Greek who visited Croesus, and was also admitted to his treasures (see Bernardi *CJ*, Kurmann and Lugaresi *4*, *ad loc.*, for full discussions). Ps-N. gives only the first part of Solon's well-known visit to Croesus (Hdt. 1.29–31). Gr. mentions him again in *Poem* 1.2.10.41.

36 This summary definition of happiness is derived from Aristotle, *Nicomachean Ethics* 10.9, and was attacked by the Christians, as in Gr. Naz. *Ep.* 32.6, for including external with spiritual factors in such a state.

22

... and of Socrates' love of beauty – for I am ashamed to say 'love of boys',
though he disguised it well in his conceits ... (*Sermon* 4.72)

Twenty-second is the story about Socrates' love of beauty.

Socrates, who was a philosopher, frequented the Agora and persuaded young
men to (study) philosophy, and especially those whom he thought most
fitted for philosophy, that is, the very handsome young men. For they say
that good-looking people are also naturally clever. There was, accordingly, a
opinion among the Athenians that Socrates was a paederast because he
conversed with good-looking men.[37] Plato is also found both in the
Theaetetus and everywhere else quoting Socrates (as saying) 'Theaetetus is
beautiful' and 'Charmides is beautiful'. Plato, however, contradicts the impression in his accounts that Socrates was suspected of being that sort of
person, by the following rebuttals, so to speak, that, 'You are beautiful, not
in appearance, but in soul.'[38] He was also suspected of consorting in
shameful love with Alcibiades. Those who speak about Socrates say that he
consorted with everyone, in love that was not carnal, but spiritual.[39]

37 The death of Socrates is described in story 13 above, and Plato discussed in stories 16
above and 23. There were early accusations against Socrates' sexuality (but as the boyfriend of
Archelaus the physicist, rather than as a paederast himself; Aristoxenus [b. 370 BC] *Fr.* 52, as
found in D.L. 2.19 – see the discussion in J.Geffken, 'Antiplatonica', *Hermes* 64 [1929], pp.
87–109). See K. Dover, *Greek Homosexuality*, London, 1978, for the implications of such
accusations in classical Athens, which continued until the Roman Empire and Late Antiquity (*A
History of Private Life*, I. *From Pagan Rome to Byzantium*, ed. Paul Veyne, trans. A. Gold-
hammer, Cambridge, MA, 1987, pp. 204 and 243). Any sexual liaison between men was wrong
according to Jewish and Christian precepts (LXX, Lev. 18.22) and legislated against by the
Christian Emperors Theodosius I in the 4th century AD and Justinian I in the 6th. The Agora
(market place) was the civic centre of Athens, and a general meeting place for its (male)
citizens. Gr. makes the same accusation in *Poem* 1.2.10.41.

38 Ps-N. uses the rare Greek word *anterōtēsis* for 'rebuttal' here, although its real sense is 'a
question asked in return for another in rebuttal'. It is used correctly by the 5th century AD
ecclesiastical historian Socrates (Lampe, s.v.).

39 See G.R.F. Ferrari, 'Platonic Love', in *The Cambridge Companion to Plato*, Cambridge,
1992, pp. 248–76 for a detailed discussion of Socratic and Platonic theories about love.
Theaetetus and Charmides were members of Socrates' circle. Charmides was certainly
renowned for his beauty (Pl. *Charm.* 154a–155e), but Theaetetus was ugly (he was held to
resemble Socrates, Pl. *Theaet.* 143e). Both Plato and Xenophon (c.430–355 BC) were careful to
emphasise the spiritual quality of Socrates' affection for his friends (Plato, *Symposium* 219 b–
c; Xen. *Mem.* 4.1.2), though later writers took a different view (Lucian, 2nd cent. AD,
Philosophies for Sale 15; Ps.-Lucian, *Amores* 54; and Gr., again, in *Poem* 1.2.10.286–90, as
noted in Kurmann, *ad loc.*).

23

... and Plato's greed in Sicily, because of which he was sold, and bought back, not by one of his followers or even by a Greek ... (*Sermon* 4.72)

Twenty-third is the story about Plato's greed. It is this.

When Plato the philosopher heard that Dionysius, the tyrant of Sicily, was of a noble nature, he sailed to him. The present-day interpreters of Plato say that he sailed for two reasons, both to make enquiry into the fire which issued from Etna, and to persuade Dionysius to become a philosopher. The blessed Gregory, however, says that the reason Plato went away to Sicily was because of the lavishness of Dionysius' banquets. He offers as proof the fact that he was sold. He really was sold, having been given by Dionysius to Pollis, the Lacedaemonian admiral who was there at that time. Then, when Pollis went to Aegina, he sold him to Anniceris for 50 minae.[40]

---

40 Like the *Anonymous Prolegomena to Platonic Philosophy* 4.11–12, the notes of an anonymous student on the introductory lectures to the study of Plato in 6th-century AD Alexandria, Ps-N. reduces Plato's three visits to Sicily to one. He also combines the reasons for his visits, the first being to see Mt Etna (D.L. 3.18) in 367 BC. There he met and angered the tyrant of Syracuse, Dionysius I (D.L. 18–19; D.S. 15.7) and ended up in slavery in Aegina, from which he was rescued by Anniceris the Cyrenaic philosopher (Aegina was then at war with Athens). Sicily was known for its luxury and fine cuisine (Pl. *Rep.* 404d; *Gorg.* 518b; *Ep.* 7.326), and Diogenes the Cynic (see story 26 below) accused him of going there for that reason (D.L. 6.25). The Alexandrian philosopher Olympiodorus (L.G. Westerink, *Commentary on the first Alcibiades of Plato*, Amsterdam, 1956, repr. 1965, 2.94) defended Plato against this charge. Plato was also accused of wishing to flatter Dionysius II (Luc. *Dialogues of the Dead* 20.5; *The Parasite* 34; D.L. 6.58), to whom his second visit to Sicily was made, in the hope of influencing him towards philosophy (Pl. *Ep.* 7.328–29). Neither this visit nor the third had any such result. For the importance of Plato's visits to Sicily and *Ep.* 7, which may or may not be by him, see J.E. Raven, *Plato's Thought in the Making*, Cambridge, 1965, pp. 19–26. The authenticity of *Letter* 7 is doubted by T.H. Irwin, 'Plato: the Intellectual Background', in *The Cambridge Companion to Plato*, Cambridge, 1992, p. 33, n. 8, but accepted by T. Penner, 'Socrates and the Early Dialogues', in *The Cambridge Companion to Plato*, p. 130.

Recension *m* adds: 'Many of the early Stoic philosophers also say that Plato went off to Dionysius out of greed, with whom the blessed Gr. rather agrees than with Plato's more recent interpreters. Xenophon, too, in the *Letter to Aischines*, says that Pl. went to Sicily to Dionysius out of gluttony.' See *Epistolographi Graeci*, ed. R. Hercher, Paris, 1873, p. 788, for this letter, which was one of a collection of imaginary letters, composed by a 2nd-century AD sophist, and purported to be from Xenophon to the orator Aischines. His greed and his rescue are mentioned by Gr. again in *Poem* 1.2.10.313–18 (Kurmann, *ad loc.*, Demoen, pp. 423–24, s.n.).

24

... and the epicurism of Xenocrates ... (*Sermon* 4.72)

Twenty-fourth is the story about the epicurism of Xenocrates. It is this.

Xenocrates and Aristotle were Plato's students who succeeded him in his school of philosophy. Xenocrates established the Stoic school, while Aristotle did the same for the Peripatetic.[41] Xenocrates is said to have been so self-controlled that even when revelling he was not stirred to lust because, they say, he had to such an extent ordered his passions to submit to his reason. The blessed Gregory therefore accuses him of being a glutton and an epicure and of not drawing the line at eating anything, as a philosopher (should).[42]

25

... and the banter of Diogenes ... (*Sermon* 4.72)

Twenty-fifth is the story about the banter of Diogenes. It is this.

41 Xenocrates of Chalcedon was head of the Academy, the philosophical school established by Plato, from 339–314 BC. He succeeded Speusippus, who was the direct successor to Plato, and maintained Platonic teachings. It was Zeno of Citium (335–263 BC) who established the Stoic school in Athens, in the Stoa Poikile. Aristotle of Stagira (384–322 BC), discussed in story 34 below, left the Academy after being a pupil of Plato's, and set up his own school, the Peripatetic, as noted above.

The recension *m* replaces this sentence as follows: 'Xenocrates was said to be a Stoic, taking the name from where he spent his time; Aristotle was called a Peripatetic, because he walked around (*dia to peripatois kechrēsthai*) during his teaching. They were the originators of different philosophical sects.' A *stoa* was a portico or covered colonnade; *peripatos*, 'a walking about' could also mean a 'place for walking about', a 'covered walk' or a 'hall'. It was first used of the Academy, and thence of Aristotle and his teaching. The philosopher Ammonius, discussed above in the Introduction, with n. 70, attributes the initial practice of lecturing while walking about to Plato, *Commentary on Aristotle's Categories*, ed. A. Busse, Berlin, 1895, 3.8.

42 Gr. elsewhere praises Xenocrates' lack of response to a prostitute (*Poem*.1.2.10.778–86, Kurmann, *ad loc.*), said to be Phryne or Laïs (D.L. 4.6–7). The philosopher Zeno was also noted for his self-control, and is described as disconcerting a noted gourmet by seizing a large fish from him before the latter could eat it (D.L. 7.19). As the Greek word *opsophagia* used above can mean 'a diet of fish' as well as 'epicurism', and this passage has long caused difficulty in Gr.'s tradition (see Kurmann and Lugaresi *4*, *ad loc.*), Gr. may be confusing the names of the two philosophers here. Kurmann notes that Xenocrates once won a drinking competition (Athen. 437B). A part of the tradition of *n* adds 'For philosophy is the mastery of virtue and self restraint over food', an addition also found in the *G.V.*

Diogenes the Cynic was a philosopher. He was called the Cynic by transference from dogs (*kunes*) on land.[43] For, just as these dogs have a kind of protective and discriminating ability (for they discriminate between their owners and strangers, and protect their owners) so he too imitated their discrimination and protectiveness. He both protected the tenets of philosophy, and discriminated between those that were useful to philosophy and those which were not. So this Diogenes, being such a person, was, as might be expected, very free in his speech. He accordingly cross-examined both rulers and people of importance and, in fact, everyone, about virtue. And, in his cross-examining, he did so very wittily and in jest. So this is what blessed Gregory is referring to, when he says that Diogenes was rather a jester and a deceiver than a philosopher. Banter is deceit carried out with wit.[44]

26

> ...who dwelt in a barrel, by which (banter) he made strangers give way to tyrants from tragedy, cheap bread to sesame cakes ... (*Sermon* 4.72)

Twenty-sixth is the story about the dweller in the tub. It is this, which can be interpreted in many ways; for this is also about Diogenes.

It is said, then, that this man lived in a tub in the evenings in winter because of the cold, but came out by day because of the sun. So, once, when he was warming himself, Alexander the Macedonian stood over him, by his shadow preventing him from warming himself, and saying, 'Say, Diogenes, what you would like me to grant you?' He replied, 'Grant me this, stand a little away from me so I can get warm.'[45]

43 *Kuōn* can also mean a dog-fish or shark (LSJ s.v.), a point apparently made by the Eunomians about nomenclature and attacked by Gregory in *Sermon* 29.14, in discussions about the nature of Christ.

44 Diogenes lived from c.400–325 BC, and practised the Cynic philosophy in Athens, after being a pupil of Antisthenes, the founder of the sect (D.L. 6.21). Both are mentioned ironically with the Cynics (as barking dogs) by Gr. in *Poem* 2.1.11.1030–32, and the Cynics alone are both attacked and praised in *Sermon* 25.6 and blamed in 27.9. Diogenes believed that happiness was achieved by fulfilling one's natural desires in the most economical way, and in public. This shameless behaviour led to his being called a dog (*kuōn*), for which other explanations, such as the following (from Pl. *Rep.* 376a, with D.L. 6.60) are given. See D.L. 6.40, 46, and 55 for other explanations. He was famous for the wittiness of his rebukes to every kind of pretension. The last sentence is omitted by *m*. Gr. notes his sharpness in *Ep.* 98.1.

45 This is a well-known example of Diogenes' practice of philosophy (D.L. 6.23 and 38) and simplicity of life. The Greek word *pithos* usually refers to a wide-mouthed, tall earthenware

So, it is either this story or the one which took place in the time of the Ptolemies. The one which took place in the time of the Ptolemies is this.

Sotates, a certain Alexandrian philosopher, stood in a certain place picking lice from himself in the sun. Ptolemy saw this man from above from a vantage point and descended to take him into the palace. But Sotates saw him and went under a part of a tub which was lying there, and hid from Ptolemy. Certain people later abused this man as unlucky. Others say that Ptolemy himself uttered this iambic line:

> I prefer a drop of luck to a tub of wits,

hinting that the tub was full of wits because of Sotates.[46] But after all, because he was unlucky, the abundance of wits was of no profit to him.

The above, then, is the story, while the sentence is arranged like this: 'And the banter of Diogenes, ... by which he makes strangers give way', so it is the case that Diogenes made those who cast a shadow over him retreat through his banter (he says making those who came up to him retreat 'before tyrants' instead of 'before tyrannical words'). So, either the story about the banter and the tub is a single one, and the two parts of the sentence should be taken together, or, there are two stories and it is necessary to construe the 'banter of Diogenes' as separate from or additional to 'by which'.[47] As for their describing bold words as 'tyrants', the divine man Gregory himself says, 'as if from tragedy'.[48] For writers of tragedy especially made use of this form of trope.

---

jar (between five and six feet high) which was used for storage of wine and grain, but can also refer to a wooden container for wine (LSJ). It is traditionally translated as 'tub' with reference to Diogenes. Gr. speaks of the tub again in *Sermon* 43.60 and *Poem* 1.2.10.218.

46 This episode apparently took place during the reign of Ptolemy II Philadelphus (283–246 BC). Sotates was probably Sotades of Maroneia who attacked Ptolemy in his verses (called Sotadeans) for marrying his own sister, Arsinoë I. Ptolemy had him placed in a leaden jar (*pithos*) and drowned at sea (Athen. 14.621, and G.A. Gerhard, *Phoinix von Kolophon*, Leipzig, 1909, pp. 243–44). The line of verse comes from Menander (*Sententiae,* ed. A. Meineke, *Fragmenta Comicorum Graecorum* 4, Berlin, 1841, repr. 1970, no. 240), who knew Ptolemy I, but died in 293/89 BC.

47 Another example of the difficulty Ps-N. (or the annotator he followed) finds in taking Gr.'s phrases in separation rather than as a whole. See stories 7 and 8, 11 and 12 above, and *Comm.* 5.32 and 33 below for similar excursions.

48 Gregory is referring to Eur. *Phoen.* 40, 'Stranger, make way for tyrants!', a quotation used by Diogenes when removing a cake from a plate of olives, D.L. 6.55 (see Bernardi *CJ*, Kurmann and Lugaresi *4, ad loc.*). Ps-N. obviously has no knowledge of the anecdote.

The phrase, 'cheap loaves before sesame cakes' is a parody for him. Such a type of phrase (as 'they disparaged cheap loaves in favour of sweeter bread') is used by tragedy-writers, and the more by comedy-writers.[49] The holy Gregory, then, is ridiculing him by using the parody, because, he says, through the pleasantness of his banter in speaking out he disparaged those who came across him, as he cross-examined them.

In my opinion, I hold that the story about banter and the tub is a single one.

27

> ... and the philosophy of Epicurus, which ordained no good beyond pleasure ... (*Sermon* 4.72)

Twenty-seventh is the story about Epicurus.

Epicurus was a philosopher who held the opinion that God had no providential care for the affairs of this world. He also defined pleasure as the end of all good. Present-day interpreters of the philosophers, however, say that the pleasure he defined as an end was not the impure one, but the condition which was most suited to nature.[50] But the philosophers condemn him, both because he denied the existence of Providence and because he established pleasure as his ultimate principle and not goodness, the first and only principle.[51] And this is God.

---

49 Another phrase used by Diogenes (Stobaeus, *Florilegium*, ed. C. Wachsmuth and O. Hense, Berlin, 1894, 3.17.15) in a similar context. Gregory refers to it twice, in attacks on the epicurism of Diogenes, in *Poems* 1.2.10, 276–81, and in *Sermon* 25.7. Aristophanes (c.460/450–c.386 BC) parodied many lines and scenes from the plays of Euripides and others in his comedies, which are identified in the *Scholia* on the plays.

50 Epicurus taught philosophy in Athens from 307/6 BC until his death in 270 BC. His school was called 'The Garden'. He based his teaching on the Atomist theories of Democritus (D.L. 9.44–45, and see the notes on story 15 above). Ps-N. confuses E.'s belief that the single guiding principle in one's life should be the pursuit of pleasure, which is achieved by living in complete conformity with moderate, natural desires, with monotheism. The Epicureans believed that many gods existed, but that they lived a calm and happy eternal life, untroubled by concern for mankind.

51 This was the usual long-standing criticism of Epicureanism, both pagan and Christian. See *Anon. Prol.* 9.8/9, also found in Gr. *Sermons* 25.6, 27.9 and 28.8. He praises him, however, in *Poem* 1.20.10.787–92, and in *Sermon* 7.20 knowledge of his doctrines is a sign of learning.

28

> 'Great is Crates, in your opinion: for it was a deed really worthy of a philosopher to give his wealth up to be a sheep pasture and one that is paralleled among our philosophers – but the parade he made by the public announcement of the emancipation was more appropriate for a lover of fame than a lover of philosophy.' (*Sermon* 4.72)

Twenty-eighth is the story about Crates. It is this.

Crates was a Theban from Boeotia by race. As he wished to practise the Cynic philosophy, he took his possessions and cast them away to the people, with the following announcement: 'Crates liberates what Crates owns, to prevent what Crates owns from owning Crates.' And he allowed his estate to become pastures for sheep.[52]

29

> Great was he who, when his ship was caught in a storm and all his goods cast overboard, gave thanks to Fortune for taking all away but his threadbare cloak! (*Sermon* 4.72)

Twenty-ninth is the story about the man who spoke about the threadbare cloak. It is this.

Again a Cynic philosopher, either Antisthenes or Zeno (for it applies to either), was on a voyage when a storm arose and the ship was wrecked, and he, gratefully accepting his future poverty, cried out to Fortune: 'Well done, Fortune, I thank you, because you have reduced my wealth to a threadbare cloak.'[53] It was thus clear that some of his wealth was in the ship's cargo.

52 Crates was a Cynic philosopher (365–285 BC), a disciple of Diogenes (see stories 25 and 26 above), who persuaded him to give his lands up in this way, and also to 'throw his money into the sea' (D.L. 6.87, and Gr. *Poems* 1.2.10.236–43, 1.2.11.671–73 and 2.1.12.596–97 – Demoen, p. 422). Gr. also speaks of him in *Sermon* 43.60, though Ps-N. does not comment on that passage (see the Introduction, p. xl, above). *Krates* is the Greek for 'Owner', as well as a name, and the verb *kratein* means 'to own' or 'to control'. It was usual for slaves to be set free by a public announcement.

The recension *n*, with *Arm.*, adds the following, to explain the use of the word *mēlobota* for 'sheep pastures': 'A sheep pasture (*mēloboton*) is a place where sheep (*probata*) are set free to graze. For sheep are also called *mēla*, hence shepherds are *mēlonomoi* and a sheepskin is a *mēlōtē*.' *Mēlon* was the term used by Homer for a sheep. Gr. states that his brother lived a simpler life than Crates in *Sermon* 7.10.

53 Antisthenes founded the Cynic philosophy. He also taught Zeno (see story 24 above), who founded the Stoic sect, the teachings of which are confused with those of the Cynics by

30

> Great was Antisthenes, because he, when a violent and insolent man hit him in the face, wrote the perpetrator's name on his forehead, just like an artist's signature, though perhaps (he did this) to accuse him the more keenly. (*Sermon* 4.72)

Thirtieth is the story about Antisthenes. This is very clear from the context itself.

For this Antisthenes was a Cynic philosopher, who, when struck and hit on the face, took a placard and wrote the (name of the) one who had hit him on the placard, and fixed it to his forehead and walked about like that.[54]

31

> You also praise a man who lived a little before our time, who stood the whole day praying to the sun, perhaps waiting till the sun was nearer the earth to cut short his prayer which he brought to a close at sunset, (*Sermon* 4.72)

Thirty-first is the story concerning the philosopher who stood all day in the sun. It is this.

When Rome was once attacked by barbarians in the time of the Emperor, the philosopher stood and prayed all day under the sun. And fire fell from the heaven and burnt up the barbarians and the philosopher himself.[55]

Ps-N. Gr. also tells the anecdote of Crates, *Poem* 1.2.10.236, Kurmann, *ad loc.* It is related of Zeno (D.L. 7.4–5), while other remarks are made by, or about, Antisthenes in connection with voyages (D.L. 6.6) or cloaks (D.L. 8 and 13). Philosophers habitually wore threadbare clothes to show their disdain for, or lack of, worldly goods. Gr. speaks of him as a boaster in *Sermon* 25.7.

54 This tale is told of Diogenes (D.L. 6.33) and Crates (D.L. 6.89), who were both Cynic philosophers, and of Zeno, the Stoic (Plut. 2.87A et al.; Kurmann, *ad loc.*).

55 Bernardi (*CJ, ad loc.*) explains this reference as an allusion to the states of ecstasy into which some Neoplatonic philosophers were said to fall in their prayers. Others (Kurmann, Lugaresi et al., *ad loc.*) see it as twofold inverted reference to Socrates' night-long stance in prayer in Potidaea, which he ended at dawn with a prayer to the sun, discussed in the following story. Ps-N. refers to an otherwise unknown episode connected with a siege of Rome. The name of an emperor may have fallen out of his text. Sozomen describes how the Prefect of Rome summoned Etruscans (the earliest inhabitants of Tuscany, who were conquered by the Romans, but respected by them for their learning and ancient religion) to him, when Alaric first besieged Rome in 408 AD, and how they promised to drive the Visigoths away with thunder and lightning, 9.6. No mention is made of whether their efforts, if they came about, had any success.

32

and the stance (*stasis*) of the man, who at Potidaea, in winter, remained obstinately in contemplation all through the night so that he had no feeling of the frost because of his ecstatic state (*ekstasis*) … (*Sermon* 4.72)

Thirty-second is the story concerning Potidaea.

Potidaea is a city situated in Thrace. In this Potidaea a Potidaean philosopher stood praying all night in the winter. He was so spiritually uplifted, he (Gregory) says, that he did not perceive the winter cold. He describes as 'ecstasy' the philosopher's ability to stand outside himself, and, as I said, become spiritually uplifted. Then the *stasis* he mentions is not civil strife but the fact that he stood upright while he was praying.[56]

33

… or Homer's love of learning about the Arcadian riddle, (*Sermon* 4.72)

Thirty-third is the story about the Arcadian riddle. It is this.

When Homer the poet was in Arcadia (this is a region of the Peloponnese) he met some fishermen who were picking lice off themselves, and asked them the following question: 'Men from Arcadia, fisher-folk, have we anything?' This is what the question meant – Arcadians, fishermen by trade, have we caught anything? The fishermen answered with this line: 'What we caught, we left behind, what we did not catch, we carry with us.' The line had the following meaning – As for the lice we caught, we killed them at once, but as for those we could not catch, we carry them in our clothes. Homer did not, as they say, understand this line, and, after remaining there a little time, he died of grief. They say, too, that an oracle had been given to Homer, which said that he would die whenever a riddle was put to him which he could not solve.[57]

---

56 Gr. here refers to a description of Socrates' hardiness in praying all night in the cold when on campaign in Thrace, which he ended at dawn, as mentioned above, with a greeting to the sun as it rose (Pl. *Symposium* 220 c–d; D.L. 2.23); this is not recognised by Ps-N. *Stasis* is the Greek for 'civil strife' as well as for a 'stance' or 'standing' and 'position' in general.

57 Arcadia is a landlocked region in the Peloponnese, to which Ps-N. has moved this scene, which was more usually set in the island of Ios, one of the Cyclades (Homer, *Life* 4.17–22). John Tzetzes also follows him in this (*Chiliades* 13.656–65). 'Riddle' is used to translate the Greek word, *zētēma*, 'an enquiry' or 'proposition'. Gr. thinks highly of Homer's inspiration and ability: see *Poems* 1.2.10.42, and 396–406, 2.1.41.15–16, 2.2.7.242; *Ep.* 54.1 and 71.5 (Demoen, Inv. II, s.n.).

34

> … and Aristotle's philosophy and the close attention he paid to the shifting currents of the Euripus, because of which (referring also to the Arcadian riddle) they (that is, A. and Homer) died, (*Sermon* 4.72)

Thirty-fourth is the story which is about Aristotle and the Euripus. It is this.

Aristotle the philosopher was a student of Plato's. Even though he especially devoted himself to the physiological aspect of philosophy, he was eager to explain the causes and the natures of everything under the heavenly bodies, such as the earth, the sea, the lower and upper air, animals, plants, rain, snow, earthquakes, comets, in a word, everything. So once he had searched out the nature of everything he also wanted to explain the nature of the Euripus. But when he was unable to comprehend it, he threw himself into this part of the sea, with this cry: 'Since Aristotle can't take in the Euripus, let the Euripus take Aristotle!' This is how Aristotle died.[58]

The Euripus is a part of the sea between the island of Boeotia[59] and Attica, which turns seven times a day. It turns by the water in this part ebbing and as it were being swallowed up, and by belching out and filling up of water again as it was. This happens, as I said, seven times a day.

The verb 'they died' is used of both, instead of saying 'Homer and Aristotle', the one because of the Arcadian riddle and the other because of the Euripus.

35

> … and the well of Cleanthes (*Sermon* 4.72)

Thirty-fifth is the story about the well of Cleanthes. It is this.

---

58 See story 24 above for Aristotle whose great interest in nature and natural phenomena is rightly noted by Ps-N. (D.L. 5.32). He died in Chalcis of natural causes in 322 BC (D.L. 5.10). The above account of his death is first found in Ps. Justin (3rd/5th cent. AD), *Exhortation to the Gentiles* 33 (*Cohortatio ad gentiles*, ed. J.C.T. Otto, in *Corpus apologetarum Christianorum saeculi secundi*, Vol. 3, Mauke, 1879, repr. Wiesbaden, 1971) and is also given by the 6th-century AD historian Procopius of Caesarea, 8.6.20. Gr. identifies his work as a sign of Greek learning in *Sermons* 7.20 and 23.12, and *Poems* 1.2.10.47–49 and 2.1.12.304. In *Sermons* 27.10 and 32.25, he attacks him as a rhetorician, and admires his self-control in *Poem* 1.2.25.261–70 (Demoen, p. 421).

59 Ps-N. means the island of Euboea, as he correctly states in story 62 below. Boeotia lies to the north of Attica. Strabo (64/3 BC–AD 21) describes the currents of the Euripus, 9.2.8.

Cleanthes was himself also one of the Cynic philosophers. He stationed himself in a well and used to draw water for those who passed by, and, for giving them to drink, took bread from them and ate it. This man was also admired by the philosophers for being enduring.[60]

36

... and the strap of Anaxagoras, (*Sermon* 4.72)

Thirty-sixth is the story about the strap of Anaxagoras. It is this.[61]

37

... and the dejection of Heraclitus. (*Sermon* 4.72)

Thirty-seventh is the story about the dejection of Heraclitus. It is this.

Although Heraclitus and Democritus did not live at the same time, they were natural philosophers who mocked alike at the constant changes of the world, the latter by laughing and the former by weeping. For Democritus laughed continuously at human affairs, while Heraclitus wept. Democritus was an Abderitan, and Heraclitus an Ephesian.[62]

60 See D.L. 7.168. Cleanthes (331–232 BC) was in fact a Stoic and succeeded Zeno as head of his school in Athens. Gr. knows him as a Stoic, *Sermon* 7.20.

61 The surviving Syriac text for this is as follows: 'Anaxagoras was a Pythagorean philosopher who habitually practised silence. Now they (sc. the Pythagoreans) had a rule not to strike anyone, only to rebuke by a word – a word being as it were a substitute for a blow to a sensitive person. This Anaxagoras, therefore, because he did not wish to speak, used to wear a strap, and if he wanted to rebuke someone, he would just show him the strap, and thus he would make anyone in the wrong realise, by pointing to the strap.'

Some of the Greek mss. add a cross-reference here ('see above', or 'see 15 above') and leave a space of a few lines. There are various explanations of the phrase, either that the 'strap' was a work by the philosopher Anaxagoras, which was so difficult to understand that it 'tied its readers in knots' (given first by Elias of Crete, in his commentary on *Sermon* 4, *ad loc.*), or that one of his doctrines, that all things had tiny fragments of every other substance within them, and each was only differentiated from the rest by the component which prevailed within it (so that everything was tied together?) was called the 'Strap'. The latter theory is proposed as an addition in a contemporary hand in a 10th-century ms. of the *Commentaries* (*L*) and first noted by Brock (intro. p. 24). The origins of the Syriac account are unknown, although the disciples of Pythagoras were trained to keep silence (Iambl. 68) and to correct each other tactfully (Iambl. 231). Knowledge of his doctrines was a sign of learning in Gr. *Sermon* 7.20.

62 These two philosophers, Heraclitus (fl. 504–500 BC) and the later Democritus (see n. 27 above), both taught that the whole universe suffered continuous change, Heraclitus under a

38

We shall not change their names,[63] for we could not change them to anything more ridiculous than what they are – the 'phalli' and 'ithyphalli'. (*Sermon* 4.77)

Thirty-eighth is the story about the phalli. It is this.

When the Greeks held a festival to Dionysus, they used to honour him with phalli. A phallus is a model of a man's penis made of red leather. They used to put this on themselves, either round their necks or between their thighs, and would dance, honouring Dionysus in this manner. They carry out this honour to Dionysus for the following reason. Dionysus was born from Semele, the daughter of Cadmus. When she had been killed by the thunderbolt, she was searched for by Dionysus. The young man, Polyhymnus as he was called, met Dionysus as he was roaming around in his search, and promised to show his mother to him, if he could commit paederasty with him. Dionysus promised this. Polyhymnus told him that Semele was in Lerna. Then Dionysus went into the sea to cross over to Lerna, and Polyhymnus followed him. And Dionysus, as a god, was preserved, but Polyhymnus drowned. Dionysus, in grief that his lover had died, hewed a wooden phallus out of fig wood in his honour, and always kept it, in memory, as I said, of Polyhymnus.[64]

---

ruling principle of order and measure and Democritus as the result of pure chance. Their reactions to the world were contrasted as stock examples by Seneca the orator and philosopher who became the Emperor Nero's tutor and trusted minister from AD 54–62 (*On Peace of Mind*, trans. J.W. Basore, vol. II, *Moral Essays*, Loeb, 1932, 15.2), and Juvenal the satirist, whose works were published AD 100–127 (*Satire* 10.28–30, in the translation by G.G. Ramsay, *Juvenal and Persius*, Loeb, 1918). Heraclitus was noted for his melancholy (Ael. *V.H.* 8.13; D.L. 9.6), while Democritus had a cheerful disposition (Sen. *On Anger* 2.10 [*Moral Essays*, vol. I]; Ael. *V.H.* 4.20). Gr. mentions both in *Sermon* 7.20 as examples of Greek learning and speaks of two sages who reacted in this way (one by weeping, the other by laughing) before the vanity of human wishes (*Poem* 1.2.15.79–80), and of a laughing sage in *Sermon* 42.22 (Demoen, p. 422).

63 Gr. now attacks Julian for changing the name of 'Christian' to 'Galilean', *Sermon* 4.76 – see story 43 below.

64 The story of Dionysus and Prosymnus (named Polyhymnus by Ps-N.) is told in more scurrilous detail by Clement of Alexandria (born c. AD 150) in *Exhort.* 2.34. Gr. mentions Prosymnus and the worship of Dionysus in *Sermon* 5.32 (see *Comm.* 5.19), 39.4 (*Comm.* 39.6) and *Poem* 2.2.7.276–77. Paus. 2.37.5 tells of an annual night festival to do with the descent of Dionysus into Hades by a lake near Lerna in Argos in his search for Semele. Though the testimonies to this date only from Plutarch (1st–2nd century AD), the site is of ancient religious significance (Burkert, *Greek Religion*, pp.12–15, with n. 41). See Gantz, p. 477, for other sites where Semele was brought up from Hades.

It is for this reason that they honour Dionysus with phalli. They are all phalli, but the ithyphalli are the ones they tie upright to their thighs.

39

… their 'Black-buttocked' and their 'Buttockless'… (*Sermon* 4.77)

Thirty-ninth is the story about the Black-buttocked and the Buttockless. They are different stories, and the one about the Buttockless is this.

When Pirithous went down into Hades to carry away Persephone, the wife of Pluto, he was tied up below to some rocks. So, when Heracles came down and wanted to take Pirithous, he pulled him away, but his buttocks stuck to the rocks. Pirithous was accordingly called the 'Buttockless'.[65]

The one about the 'Black-buttocked' is this. There were two brothers called the 'Cercopes' (literally, 'man-monkeys') who demonstrated every kind of injustice on earth, taking their nick-name from the shrewdness of their deeds. For one of them was called Passalus, and the other Aclemon, as Dius the commentator says. When their mother, Memnonis by name, saw them committing many atrocities on earth, she said to them: 'Don't meet the Black-buttocked One!' Once, when Heracles was lying under a tree and had propped his weapons against the plant, these drew near and wanted to lay hands on the weapons. But Heracles at once noticed, seized them and carried them off, tied head-downwards to a piece of wood. Then they remembered their mother's injunction, as they hung and saw Heracles' buttocks black with the thickness of hair. Their conversation about this to each other made

---

Comic actors wore leather phalli (*Schol.* on Aristoph. *Clouds* 538), and large model ones were carried in processions in honour of Dionysus, the god of wine (Hdt. 2.48, 49; Aristoph. *Acharnians* 243). Ithyphallic figures were depicted in all kinds of media (vases, statues, mosaics) throughout antiquity, as fertility symbols. They are still mentioned as a part of the worship of Dionysus by the antiquarian John Lydus in the 6th century AD in his book on the ancient traditions to do with the calendar, the days of the week and pagan festivals (*De mensibus*, ed. R. Wünsch, Leipzig, 1898, repr. Stuttgart, 1967, 4.51), and traces of them may linger on in the Turkish comic shadow theatre, as I discuss in 'Nonnus', p. 296, with notes 25, 26 and 27, mentioned below in the notes to *Comm.* 5.19. For the death of Semele, see *Comm.* 5.20 and 39.4.

65 Pirithous, the son of Zeus and a mortal, was a Lapith and a close friend of Theseus, the Attic hero. Theseus accompanied Pirithous on this enterprise (*Od.* 11.631). Theseus was the one whom Heracles rescued in this way (the *Schol.* on Aristoph. *Knights* 1368 explains that this was why the Athenians had lean buttocks) according to Apollod. *Libr.* 2.5.12 and *Epit.* 1.23, and not Pirithous; but Hyg. *Fab.* 79.3 states that Heracles rescued them both. See Gantz, pp. 291–95, for early representations of the myth.

Heracles roar with laughter. He at once released them from their bonds and let them go.[66]

40

> ... and the Goat-footed One and the Revered Pan, the one god (derived) from all the wooers, taking the insult he deserved as his name. (*Sermon* 4.77)

Fortieth is the story about the Revered Pan. It is this.

Penelope was the wife of Odysseus. While he was wandering around on his wanderings after the Trojan war, many came to woo Penelope. She put them off from day to day, however, because she was unwilling to marry anyone because she was waiting for Odysseus. So they all banded together and had sexual intercourse with her, and she became pregnant, and bore Pan. That is why he was called Pan (the Greek word for 'all') because they had all begotten him.[67] They (sc. The Greeks) made him into a god. This is Pan, the goat-footed one.

41

> If they want, we shall leave them their Bull-eater ... (*Sermon* 4.77)

Forty-first in the story about the Bull-eater. It is this.

Heracles is he who is called Bull-Eater. He is called it for the following reason. Heracles was passing through the land of Dryopis, carrying with him his son, Hyllus. Then when Hyllus felt hungry and asked for food, Heracles

66 For the Cercopes and Heracles, see D.S. 4.31.7; Apollod. *Libr.* 2.6.3. They had several different pairs of names (*Schol.* on Luc. *Alexander the False Prophet* 4). The commentator Dius is not known, but might well be a scholiast. Hairy buttocks were taken as a sign of manliness, to be expected in a hero like Heracles, Zen. 5.10. The scene of him carrying the Cercopes was popular in Greek Art from the 6th century BC, although this passage is the first full written account of the episode (Gantz, pp. 441–42).

67 Pan, the goat-footed, was the son of Hermes and a nymph (*H.H.* 19.33–37), or of Hermes and Penelope (Hdt. 2.145 Apollod. *Epit.* 7.38; Hyg. *Fab.* 224.4). Various scholia also make Pan the son of Penelope and all the suitors (Tzetz. *Alex.* 772, from the historian, Duris [360–240 BC], tyrant of Samos, with Servius, *on Aen.* 2.44 and the *Schol.* on Theocr. 1.3, Kurmann, *ad loc.*). A second hand in an ms. in *m* and the recension *n* add the other version of Pan's parentage, namely, that he was the son of Penelope and Hermes (in the form of a goat). Gr. describes the lewd behaviour of Pan in *Poem* 1.2.10.851–56. *Comm.* 5.29 comments on *Sermon* 5.32, where Pan is again mentioned.

asked a certain ploughman called Thiodamas for bread. Not only did he not give him any, but he was abusive as well. Then Heracles took and killed one of the plough-oxen, and feasted upon it both he and his son together. For this reason he was called the Bull-eater, because he had feasted on all of the bull.[68] This was the cause of Heracles' war against the Dryopes. For once Thiodamas went back into the city and said: 'An enemy has entered the country' (referring to Heracles), they came out against him. And Heracles was victorious over them all.[69]

42

> … and their Three-Evening-One, to give them even more pleasure, he who was both so begotten and was such a splendid begetter himself in the case of the fifty daughters of Thestius as he performed his thirteenth labour in a single night, to earn the title of god by such activities. (*Sermon* 4.77)

Forty-second is the story about the Three-Evening-One. It is this.

It is said that Heracles was conceived and born within three evenings, and these are the sort of stories they tell about him. Likewise they also say that this Heracles had sexual intercourse in one night with all the daughters of Thestius, and that they all conceived from him, with the result that they (sc. the Greeks) both deified him and called this his thirteenth labour.[70]

---

68 This is one of the titles of Heracles, Gregory's next target. He was worshipped in Lindos (see story 56 below) under that name. Gr. speaks of it again in 103, 122 and *Poem* 2.2.7.278 (Kurmann). Ps-N. adds the story of Heracles, Thiodamas and the Dryopes (Call. *Aetia* I.24–5; Apollod. *Libr.* 2.7.11) to this, as described by R. Pfeiffer, *Kallimachosstudien: Untersuchungen zur Arsinoe und zu den Aitia des Kallimachos*, Munich, 1922, p. 87 (Bernardi *CJ* et al. *ad loc.*). The Dryopes were Pelasgians (a pre-Hellenic people), whose homeland, according to Hdt. 8.31, lay between Malis and Phocis; elsewhere he notes Dryopis as a staging post on their migration south (1.56).

69 Recension *m* adds 'and he took Hylas, the son of Thiodamas, prisoner', while an ms. in *n*: 'and Heracles himself took the son of Thiodamas prisoner and departed.'

70 See story 3 above for the parentage of Heracles and his twelve labours. This epithet, *Triesperos*, is first found in Lyc. *Alex.* 33. Ps-N. distorts the story of Zeus' prolongation of the night he spent with Alcmene into three nights (D.S. 4.9.2; Apollod. *Libr.* 2.4.8; *Schol.* on *Il.* 14.324) to include his birth. Thestius, king of Thespiae near Thebes, had fifty daughters and wanted them all to have children by Heracles; the latter slept with all but one of them in one night, Paus. 9.27.6–7. In other versions of the story, the king is called Thespius, and Heracles sleeps with the girls over fifty nights (D.S. 4.29.2–3; Apollod. *Libr.* 4.11). The feat was known as his thirteenth labour (*Anth. Pal.* 16.92.13).

43

> For what would stop us from mocking him, the Emperor of the Romans, and of the world, as he thinks, deluded as he is by his evil spirits, in our turn on equal terms, and calling him 'Idolian', 'Pisaean', 'Adonaean' and 'Bull-Burner' ...? (*Sermon* 4.77)

Forty-third is the story concerning the calling of Julian the 'Idolian' and the 'Bull-Burner'. It is this.

Since Julian changed the name of the Christians to Galileans,[71] the holy Gregory now wishes to deride him and to say that 'We too can call Julian names after those associated with him.' So he says: 'Let us call him "Idolian" because he is an idolater, and "Pisaean" because he honours Zeus in Pisa.' Zeus is honoured in the city of Pisa (Pisa is a city in Elis).[72] So he says we must call Julian 'Pisaean' just like Zeus, and 'Adonaean' because of Adonis. Julian is said to have revered Adonis. This Adonis was loved by Aphrodite, though he was a mortal. He was killed by Ares because Ares was his rival in love of Aphrodite. He says that Julian should be called 'Bull-Burner' because he sacrificed whole bulls and burnt them for the gods.[73]

44

> That was a most evil and unprincipled action of his, however, when, having failed to win us over openly and being ashamed to constrain us like a tyrant, he, by hiding a fox in a lion's skin, or, if you prefer it, a most unjust man in the mask of Minos – how could I describe it more appropriately – constrained us by gentleness. (*Sermon* 4.79)

Forty-fourth is the story about the fox. It is this.

---

71 Julian often used this term in abuse of the Christians (see Bernardi *CJ* on 4.74 and 76).

72 There was a famous temple to Zeus in Olympia, near the site of the ancient town of Pisa (Hdt. 2.7).

73 Adonis was a beautiful youth, son of a legendary king of Cyprus by his own daughter (see Appendix, story 39 below) whose short-lived union with Aphrodite was celebrated and whose untimely death ritually mourned every year in women's festivals in Alexandria, Cyprus, the Near East and Greece. Ares, the god of war, was another of Aphrodite's lovers (see stories 86 and 96 below), and he was said to have killed Adonis in the guise of the boar (Serv. *on Ecl.* 10.18), the animal to which earlier writers (Panyasis, in Apollod. *Libr.* 3.14.4; Luc. *Syrian Goddess* 6; Hyg. *Fab.* 248) attributed his death. Julian arrived at Antioch on the day of this festival (Kurmann, Lugaresi 4, *ad loc.*). See both editors also for evidence for the number of sacrifices of bulls he had performed.

The fox is called 'the crafty one' (*Kerdō*).[74] Hence both evil and deceit are (called) 'crafty' (*kerdalē*). For this animal the fox is deceitful and evil.

Minos was considered to be a just man, as being the son of Zeus.[75] What the holy Gregory is saying is this, that Julian concealed his own evil under a feigned character, being an unjust person in the guise of a just one.

45

> So he sat in glory, in a glorious celebration against religion and with much pride in his tricks, a Melampus, I think, or Proteus, being and becoming all things and readily altering his appearance: but as for what was happening around him … (*Sermon* 4.82)

Forty-fifth is the story concerning Melampus and Proteus. It is this.

This Proteus is the one from Thrace, whose sons Heracles killed. He, then, was also a seer, and became a sea-deity and lived on Pharos; this was why Pharos was called the island of Proteus. He used to change his shape before those who encountered him to avoid their requests for oracles and prophecies.

Melampus too was likewise a seer and a priest in charge of mysteries. He revealed the sacred rites in Egypt to the Greeks, and the Greeks imitated them. He was also one of those who changed their shape, as a seer. For these seers have such great power, they say, that they can change their shape to whatever they wish to avoid being recognised by those who talk to them.[76]

74 The cunning of the fox was proverbial. See Aristoph. *Knights* 1067–68: 'beware of the hound-fox, lest he deceive thee … the tricky marauder'; Ael. *N.A.* 6.64: 'The fox is a rascally creature, which is why the poets are fond of calling it "crafty (*kerdalē*)"'. Gr. uses the proverb (Zen 1.93) again in *Poem* 2.1.17.31–33 (Kurmann, *ad loc.*).

75 *Il*.13.450. He was the son of Zeus by Europa, whom Zeus carried off to Crete in the guise of a bull. He ruled Crete wisely and after his death was made a judge of the dead in Hades (as described in *Comm.* 43.14). The recension *m* omits the rest of the story. See *Comm.* 43.14 on *Sermon* 43.23 for Minos and Rhadamanthus.

76 For Proteus, see story 2 above. Ps-N. rightly distinguishes between him and Melampus at first, for Melampus, given the power of understanding the speech of birds, was a renowned prophet (Apollod. *Libr.* 1.9.11), and was said to have introduced the rites of Dionysus from Egypt to the Greeks (Hdt. 2.149; Clement, *Exhort.* 2.13.5). See Bernardi *CJ*, Kurmann and Lugaresi 4, *ad loc.* as to whether Gr. meant to imply that he changed his shape like Proteus. Gr. mentions both together again in *Poem* 2.1.12.728–31.

46

> But just like the fire of Etna, as the account goes, which floods up from
> below and is kept back by force in the depths of Mt Etna (whether it be some-
> thing else or the panting of a tormented giant) and for some time rumbles
> terribly and spews smoke, a warning of evil to come, from its crest, but if it
> suffers a sudden uncontrollable increase, it bursts forth from the depths,
> rushing upwards and pouring over the lips of its craters, to ravage the sur-
> rounding land too with its treacherous and fearful flow, so he ... (*Sermon* 4.85)

Forty-sixth is the story about the fire of Etna. It is this.

Sicily is a very large island situated by Italy. In it is the city Catana, as it is
called. And above Catana is a mountain out of which much fire continuously
issues. The mountain is called Etna, and also called 'the "mixing-bowls" of
Hephaestus'.[77] This fire occurs when it overflows so much that it sweeps on
like a river and flows like water with the fiery matter which issues with it.
There is also something divine about this fire. For it is said that once a father
and his son found themselves on this mountain, and suddenly the fire flowed
out like a river, and they could not get past. The child took his father and
lifted him up. The fire was shamed by the action of the son and checked its
flow. And the son and the father passed by unharmed.[78]

47

> He (Mark of Arethusa, an elderly Christian priest) was dragged through the
> city squares, rolled into gutters, dragged by the hair of every part of his body,
> torment mixed with insult by those who deservedly suffer this in (the rites)
> of Mithras. (*Sermon* 4.89)

Forty-seventh is the story 'the torment in (the rites) of Mithras'. It is this.[79]

The Persians think that Mithras is the sun, and they make many sacrifices to
him and they are initiated into certain of his rites. No one can be initiated
into the rites of Mithras without passing through all the torments and proving

---

77 See story 1 above for this name.

78 Ps-N. adds the (adapted) story of the Pious Men of Catana, described in Lycurgus, *Against
Leocrates* 23.95 (translated by J.O. Burtt, in *Minor Attic Orators* II, 1854) and Paus.10.28.4 to
the account of Mt Etna. According to the sources, two young men left their treasures to save
their parents and fled carrying them away from an eruption and flow of lava, which stopped in
shame to let them all pass through to safety.

79 The recension *m* refers back to story 6 here and omits the rest.

himself to be free from passion and holy. There are said to be eighty torments, through which he who is to be initiated must pass, grade by grade, by
first swimming through much water for many days, for example, then by
throwing himself into fire, then by living in a desert and fasting, and other
such things, until, as we said, he should pass through the eighty torments.[80]

48

Of such a nature and so managed were the affairs of the Arethusians (those
who so tortured the priest), that the cruelty of Echetus and Phalaris was
slight in comparison with their savagery ... (*Sermon* 4.91)

Forty-eighth is the story 'the cruelty of Echetus and Phalaris'. It is this.

Echetus was tyrant of Epirus. This man was extremely cruel and devised all
kinds of punishments and instruments of torture. Those who wished people
to be punished unsparingly sent them to him, as the poet says about him,

To Echetus the king, harmful to all mankind.[81]

Phalaris is the same sort of person, and he was an inventor of new types
of instruments of torture. He was a Sicilian by race. He, in gratifying the
tyrant Dionysius, a most cruel and vengeful man, devised a brazen bull into
which one was to put those who were being punished and then kindle a fire,
so that, as those within were burnt and cried out, the noise emerged through
the mouth of the bull, and the bull appeared to bellow as it burned. When
Dionysius saw his inhumanity, he threw the man himself into the bull and
burnt him to death.[82]

---

80 See story 6 above. The recension *n* adds 'and, if he lives, there is *sphakela* (a reference to
the middle finger ?) on his tomb'.

81 Homer (*Od.* 18.84–87, 21.307–09) names Echetus as a cruel king in Epirus. Later writers
recount his harsh treatment of his daughter and her lover (Ap. Rhod. 4.1093).

82 Ps-N. takes the name Phalaris (the tyrant of Acragas in Sicily from c.570/65–554/49 BC)
to be that of the inventor of the brazen bull (as in Timaeus in Polyb. 12.25), and combines it with
the other version of the story, which names the inventor as Perilaus, who was then said to have
been burnt in his own invention by Phalaris (Call. *Aetia* II. Fr. 47, ed. Pfeiffer; *Schol.* on Pind.
Pyth. I.185); cf. Bernardi *CJ* et al. *ad loc.* Gr. mentions the bull of Phalaris in *Ep.* 32.7. Ps-N.
then adds Dionysius (which he knew from story 23 above to be the name of a tyrant in Sicily)
to his account.

One ms. in the recension *m* continues with the information about Perilaus: 'As Phalaris says
in his letter, he cast a certain Perilaus, a torturer by occupation, who had intended to gratify him
by a new kind of punishment, into the same brazen instrument of torture and kindled the pyre
beneath it, and had killed the creator of the new torment as its first and only victim, who

49

No one ever said the hydra was gentle because it had nine heads instead of one, if the myth is to be believed ... (*Sermon* 4.94)

Forty-ninth is the story about the Hydra. It is this.

There is a myth that a monster with fifty heads existed near Lerna (though others [say] it had nine) and that the heads were of snakes. Heracles came upon this monster with his servant Hyllus and killed it. This, too, is told in the myth, that, when one of its heads was cut off, two sprouted up, so that there were an hundred heads. But when Hyllus noticed this, he brought fire, and seared the head as it was cut off. In this way they were able to put an end to them all.[83]

50

or the Chimaera from Patara, because it had three, dissimilar ones ... (*Sermon* 4.94)

Fiftieth is the story about the Chimaera from Patara. It is this.[84]

Patara is a city of Lycia. It is said that there is a mountain there, in which mountain is a monster, which is a lion at the front, a serpent behind, and was a goat (*Chimaira*) in the middle; fire issued forth from the goat, and harmed those who passed by. Later, however, when Bellerophon came with the horse Pegasus, he killed the Chimaera.[85]

---

perished in such an invention. He sent the bull to Delphi as an offering to Pythian Apollo' (*Ep.* 222, *Epistolographi Graeci*, ed. R. Hercher, pp. 445–47. See n. 40 above for this collection of imaginary letters).

83 The Hydra was the offspring of Echidna and Typhon (Hes. *Theog.* 313–18), and lived in a lake near Lerna in Argos. It was killed by Heracles and his servant Iolaus, as described above (Hes. *Theog.* 313–18). Ps-N. supplies the wrong name, Hyllus (Heracles' son) for that of Iolaus, his servant, which is not given at this point in Gr.'s text. Hes. does not state if the Hydra has more than one head; D.S. mentions 100 (4.11.15) and Apollod., nine (*Libr.* 2.5.2). Gr. mentions the Hydra again in *Sermon* 4.115, *Ep.* 156.1, and *Poem* 2.1.11.1178–79 (Kurmann).

84 The recension *m* refers to *Comm.* 43.8 here and omits the whole story.

85 There is volcanic activity near Patara, hence its connection with a fire-breathing monster, which was first described by Homer (*Il.* 6.179–83) and Hesiod (*Theog.* 319) as having three heads, of a lion, a goat and a snake. The recension *n* adds after the word Pegasus: 'he thought up a plan, and, fixing a ball of lead to his spear, threw it into the jaws of the Chimaera. The lead was melted by the fire and fused its entrails, and thus', a passage not found in *Syr.* and *Arm.* but present in the *G.V.*, and in the mss. of Ps-N. used by Tzetzes in his commentary on *Alex.* 17. For the story of Bellerophon and for Pegasus, see *Comm.* 43.8 below. The Chimaera is mentioned again below, *Sermon* 4.115.

51

or Cerberus in Hades, because it had as many, but of a similar kind ...
(*Sermon* 4.94)

Fifty-first is the story about Cerberus. It is this.

There is a myth that there is a certain dog with three heads who is called
Tricranus. And he, they say, guards the gates of Hades. Though he wel-
comes and fawns on those who descend, he bites those trying to ascend
and does not allow them to do so. They say, then, that when Heracles went
down to abduct Persephone with Pirithous he killed Cerberus on his way
up.[86]

52

or the marine evil, Scylla, because she has six in a ring, and most repulsive
ones. And yet, they say, her upper part was good and kindly and not
unpleasant to see, for it was a girl, not unrelated to us: but the canine and
bestial heads from there downwards meant nothing good, as they devoured
whole expeditions and were as dangerous ... (*Sermon* 4.94)

Fifty-second is the story about Scylla. It is this.

There is a myth that there is a monster in the Tyrrhenian Sea which is a very
beautiful woman down to the navel, and then six dogs' heads grow on her
from either side; the rest of her body is in the form of a serpent. This

86 This appears to be the only version of the story in which Heracles kills Cerberus, again
mentioned below in *Sermon* 4.115. He was more usually commanded to bring him up to show
Eurystheus, as in Apollod. *Libr.* 2.5.12. The 'dog of Hades' (Hom. *Il.* 8.368; *Od.* 11.623) had
fifty heads in Hesiod (*Theog.* 310–12), but fewer in early art (Gantz, pp. 413–14) and in
Sophocles, *Women of Trachis* 1098, where the name, or rather adjective, *Tricranus*, 'three-
headed' appears. Ps-N. may be confusing this labour with that to do with Geryon (who also had
three heads, see story 2 above, and was killed by Heracles) and/or Geryon's dog (which had
two, and was also killed by him, Apollod. *Libr.* 2.5.10) – see Palaephatus 39 (40), where
Cerberus is explained as a dog of Geryon's, who came, like Geryon, from the city of Tricarenia,
and was a fine, large animal (but who was not killed by Heracles) and 'Nonnus', p. 297, n. 31.
Palaephatus was a 4th-century BC historian who attempted to rationalise and demystify the
myths about ancient heroes, heroines and monsters, although not those about the gods (see
Jacob Stern, 'Rationalizing Myth: Methods and Motives in Palaephatus', in *From Myth to
Reason?*, ed. R. Buxton, Oxford, 1999, pp. 215–22). For the fate of the would-be abductors of
Persephone, see story 39 above.

monster, they say, savagely and unsparingly devoured those that sailed by on these seas.[87]

53

as Charybdis opposite. (*Sermon* 4.94)

Fifty-third is the story about Charybdis. It is this.

There is a place in this Sicilian and Tyrrhenian Sea, in which there is an ebb and flood-tide in the sea.[88] The water divides itself so that the seabed, if that is possible, can be seen at this spot. An ebb is a drinking in, as it were, and swallowing up; the water recedes into certain cavities in the rocks and bursts out again. This latter is also called a flood-tide. This spot was dangerous and full of death for sailors. For a ship would be completely overwhelmed by the sea in this spot, if it happened to be sailing there when the ebb and flood-tide occurred. Homer (says) about these matters:

> On the one side is Scylla, on the other the divine Charybdis.

He called Charybdis 'opposite' when comparing her with Scylla.[89]

54

> But it is impossible for him (Julian) to conceal himself, not even if he were to make many a turn, and to become every shape he could devise, or even put on the helmet of Hades, as the saying is ... (*Sermon* 4.94)

87 Scylla is described by Homer, *Od.* 12.85–100, as having six long-necked heads with triple rows of teeth and twelve legs. When Odysseus sailed past her with his companions, her six heads snatched six of them from the deck of the ship. Ps-N.'s description of her is the same as that in Palaeph. 20.1–4 (before he rationalises it), and Hyg. *Fab.* 125.14, as of a part woman/ part snake (or fish, Hyg.) with dogs' heads around her waist. Apollodorus adds that she has twelve dog feet as well, *Epit.* 7.20.

88 The very slight tidal movements in the Mediterranean made any places where substantial currents and tides appeared, as here, and in the Euripus (see story 34 above), in the Red Sea and Maliac Gulf, worthy of remark. Hdt. uses these terms of the 'ebb and flow' of the tide in the Red Sea, 2.11, and of the Maliac Gulf in 7.198.

89 Charybdis was actually a whirlpool across from Scylla (*Od.* 12.101–07), which was supposed, as Ps-N. declares above, to be situated in the Straits of Messina, noted in Thuc. 4.24. The last-mentioned goes on to say, 'and the narrowness of the passage and the strength of the current that pours in from the vast Tyrrhenian and Sicilian mains have rightly given it a bad reputation'. The verse is quoted from *Od.* 12.235. Gr. mentions both Scylla and Charybdis in *Poem* 2.2.7.148–50, and Charybdis alone in *Poem* 1.2.28.140 (Kurmann).

Fifty-fourth is the story concerning the helmet of Hades. It is this.

Homer the poet introduces Zeus as creating a kind of invisibility and obscurity around the Greeks so that they could not be seen. He says, accordingly, in a rather mythical way, that he had put the helmet of Hades upon them so that they should not be seen. The helmet is the protective head-gear of Hades or Pluto.[90]

55

or the ring of Gyges, and turned the bezel ... (*Sermon* 4.94)

Fifty-fifth is the story about the ring of Gyges. It is this.[91]

Plato the philosopher introduces a certain myth in the *Republic* (this is a treatise of his with such a title). It says that Gyges was a shepherd in Lydia. He was once grazing his sheep on a mountain, when he came across a certain cave, which he entered and found within it a brazen horse, and he found within the brazen horse a corpse and a ring. The head of this ring was reversible, and it was turned round. The holy Gregory calls this head the bezel. So Gyges took the ring, they say, and went out. When the ring was in the correct position, he was seen by everyone, but when he reversed the bezel of the ring, he became invisible to them all. Plato, therefore, introduces this myth, because, he says, the just man, even if he were to possess the ring of Gyges so as not to be seen by anyone, ought none the less not to do wrong. For good should be practised for its own sake, and not for any other (reasons).[92]

90 The helmet of Hades concealed its wearer from sight (Apollod. *Libr.* 2.4.2–3, where it is worn by Perseus when he kills the Gorgon, Medusa – see also Hes. *Sh.* 226–27). Athene wears it in *Il.* 5.845 to hide herself from Ares. Ps-N. may also refer to *Il.* 17.268–70, where Zeus hides the Greeks in a mist. The recension *m* clarifies the matter by adding 'who was said to become invisible when he wore it' after the name Pluto.

91 The recension *m* refers to *Comm.* 43.5, and omits the rest of the passage.

92 Plato, *Rep.* 359d–60b. Ps-N. seems to be thinking of a ring with a reversible bezel, ornamented on both sides, such as were popular in Ancient Egypt and early Greece and among the Etruscans, M. Chatzidakis, 'Un anneau byzantin du Musée Benaki', *Byzantinisch-neugriechische Jahrbücher* 17 (1939–43), pp. 174–206. For examples made in the 4th-century BC in the north Pontic cities, see D. Williams and J. Ogden, *Greek Gold. Jewellery of the Classical World*, British Museum, 1994, items 108, 125 and 126. They became rarer in Late Antiquity, but a 5th- to 6th-century example is illustrated in Weitzmann, *Age of Spirituality*, item 470, and another from the 7th, item 305, discussed in Chatzidakis, 'Un anneau byzantin du Musée Benaki'. In Plato, Gyges' ancestor (or Gyges himself, *Rep.* 612b) turns the bezel of the ring around to the inside of his hand. Gr. uses the myth again in *Sermon* 43.21 (see *Comm.* 43.5) and in *Poems* 1.2.10.31–33 and 2.1.88.7–12.

56

Where, then, like the Lindians, is it pious to curse the Bull-eater, which is their way of honouring the god, that is by abuse of him, (*Sermon* 4.103)

Fifty-sixth is the story about the Lindians' cursing of the Bull-eater. It is this.

Lindos is an ancient city of Rhodes. Here those who are making sacrifice curse, slander and shower unholy abuse on the priest who is sacrificing and feasting upon the bull.[93]

57

or to sacrifice strangers, as among the Taurians, (*Sermon* 4.103)

Fifty-seventh is the story concerning the slaughter of strangers among the Taurians. It is this.[94]

We have already said that in Scythia there is a people, or a city, called Taurians. Artemis is honoured here. So when Iphigeneia, the daughter of Agamemnon, was brought here by Artemis, they sacrificed strangers who arrived there so that Iphigeneia's presence should not be disclosed by them on their return home.[95]

58

or the flogging at the altar, as among the Laconians ... (*Sermon* 4.103)

Fifty-eighth is the story 'the flogging of the Laconians beside the altars'. This has already been described before, and is mentioned now also.[96]

The Lacedaemonians, in teaching their children to be enduring, used severe whippings in teaching their children to be steadfast. They flogged them beside

---

93 Heracles landed in Rhodes, and, according to Apollod. *Libr.* 2.5.11 took a bullock from a cowherd's cart, sacrificed it and devoured it to the curses of the cowherd. Other sources, such as Conon, *Tales* 11 (Codex 186 in *Photius. Bibliothèque*, Henry, Paris, 1962, vol. 3, p. 13), make the cowherd a ploughman, as in Ps-N. See Frazer's note on Apollodorus' text for full references and the connection of the episode with other cursing rituals in Greek religion, as described in Burkert, 'Buzyge und Palladion. Gewalt und Gericht in altgriechischen Ritual', *Zeitschrift für Religions- und Geistesgeschichte* 22 (1970), pp. 364–67 (Kurmann, *ad loc.*). See the notes on story 41 above for the other appearances of the myth in Gr.

94 The recension *m* refers back to story 7, and omits the rest of the passage.

95 See story 7 above.

96 The recension *m* refers back to story 11 for this sentence, and omits the rest.

the altars, and to the one who was not faint-hearted but bore himself nobly they gave a prize.[97]

59

> or castration carried out while charmed by the sound of the double flutes and unmanned under the influence of dancing, as among the Phrygians ... (*Sermon* 4.103)

Fifty-ninth is the story of the 'Phrygians cutting themselves'.[98] This too has already been told by us, but we tell it now as well.[99]

Rhea, the mother of the gods, was honoured by the Phrygians. When they held festivals[100] to her, they used to cut their thighs and shoulders. Others played flutes so that the enjoyment of the flute (music) alleviated the pain of the cutting.

60

> and the rest (of obsolete items of vocabulary in the Greek language) be thrown away into Cynosarges, as bastards were long ago? (*Sermon* 4.105)

Sixtieth is the story 'the throwing away of bastards into Cynosarges'. It is this.

Cynosarges is a place in Athens in which bastards are adjudged as to whether they really are a person's son. Athenians call those of servile birth bastards. And these are bastards in relation to those of free birth. And these are judged and scrutinised as to whether they are wholly freeborn. The place is called Cynosarges for this reason: there was once a sacrifice in a nearby temple, and a dog went in and seized the meat of the sacrificial offering and brought it into this place. A temple was founded there and called Cynosarges,

---

97 See story 11 above.

98 See story 5 above. *Katatemnesthai*, 'castrate oneself' can also mean 'cut oneself'.

99 The recension *m* again refers back (to story 5) here and omits the rest of the text.

100 The recension *n* adds 'just as the Corybantes slashed her womb because of her many acts of fornication, restoring their goddess to health, they would say', here, and the words 'in honour of her lover, Atthis, and, at the same time' after 'played flutes'. The second hand of *L* adds a passage from the *Scholia Alexandrina* (A8) which explicitly refers to the rest of Gregory's text at the end of the passage as follows: 'And this is what the most holy Gregory means by "unmanned": for after the Phrygians cut off their genitals they probably degenerated into an effeminate nature'. This is written in a form of shorthand in the margin, and is transliterated by N.P. Chionides, *La brachigrafia italo-bizantina Studi e testi 290*, Vatican, 1981, p. 59.

as it were *Kunosarkes*, from the flesh (*sarkos*) and from the dog (*kunos*). But later the K dropped out and the G replaced it.[101]

61

for I laugh at your stately names, Moly, Xanthus and Chalcis, (*Sermon* 4.106)

Sixty-first is the story about Xanthus and Chalcis.

Homer (says):

Whom the gods call Xanthus, and men, Scamander.

and again:

The gods call her Chalcis, and men, Cymindis.

The holy teacher, then, is mocking at them.[102]

---

101 Cynosarges was the name of a gymnasium in Athens, where the sons of Athenian citizens by foreign wives gathered from the 6th century BC (Plut. *Themistocles* 1). Pausanias derives its name from the Greek for a 'white (or swift-footed) dog'– *kuōn argēs* (1.19.3, and *Schol.* on Demosth. 24.114). There was a temple to Heracles near it (Hdt. 5.63). From 451/0 BC onwards only those born of two Athenian citizens could be citizens themselves, and fathers with sons by foreign women had to depend on special legislation to enfranchise their sons. Ps-N. confuses the gymnasium with a law court near a different temple, that of Apollo Delphinius, the 'Delphinium', where those who asserted they had committed murder for a just cause were tried (*Constitution of the Athenians*, Ps-Xen. 57.3). This was also the spot where Aegeus, King of Athens, recognised Theseus, his son by a princess of Troezen, when the latter came to Athens in search of his father (Plut. *Thes.* 12.18).

102 As in story 36 above, *Syr.* provides a different and more informative text, although its identification of Xanthus is incorrect (see Brock, intro., p. 24): 'About Moly they say that when Circe made the companions of Odysseus into pigs in the house, Odysseus went to see if he could help them. And Hermes met him and said to him: "Not only will you not deliver them, but you will remain there." And he bent down and plucked a herb from the earth, which the gods called Moly, but men (another) such (name). And he said to him: "Take this, which will deliver you from the evil day" (*Od.* 10.275–306). Now Xanthos was the horse of Achilleus, immortal, he says; and when Achilleus was about to die it spoke, forsooth, like men, measured words, and it gave him an oracle about his death (*Il.* 19.405–24). And Chalcis is a certain bird that gods and men call by different names (lit. differently), as Homer says (*Il.* 14.291).' Ps-N. makes no reference to Moly (only the divine name of which is given in Homer, *loc. cit.* 305), but correctly notes the divine and human names of the river Scamander (*Il.* 20.74), with which Achilles fought, and of a bird (*Il.* 14.291). He possibly has little information about the background to these citations, and contents himself with a summary of Gr.'s expressed reaction to the terms. He may also be aware that Moly does not have a different name among men, but is difficult for them to uproot, though easy for the gods (*Od.* 10.305–06). Gr. speaks of the 'charm' given by Hermes to Odysseus in *Poem* 2.2.5.196–99.

62

> To play draughts and count and reckon on one's fingers ... who discovered
> these? Wasn't it an Euboean, if Palamedes was an Euboean, he who dis-
> covered many things, and was hated for that reason and brought to trial for
> all his wisdom and found guilty by those on the campaign against Ilium?
> (*Sermon* 4.107)

Sixty-second is the story about Palamedes. It is this.

Palamedes, a Euboean by race (Euboea is an island right opposite Attica), is
said to have discovered how to count and to play at dice and to use many
other systems of investigation. This Palamedes was one of those who joined
the campaign against Ilium. He was killed in Troy through the plotting of
Odysseus. For he had Odysseus as his enemy for the following reason: when
Agamemnon was pressing Odysseus to join the expedition to Troy, and
Odysseus was refusing to go, and pretended to be mad and took a donkey
and an ox, and was actually ploughing with them in a pretence of madness,
Palamedes showed that he was not mad at all. He showed him up by placing
his son Telemachus in front of the plough. Then, when Odysseus approached
the child he lifted the plough aside so as not to strike the child, and was seen
to be in his right mind. So as Odysseus cherished this grudge in Troy, he
composed a false letter from Priam as if to Palamedes about betraying the
Greeks, and planted it in Palamedes' tent. Later, when Palamedes was accused
of being a traitor, the letter was found, and he was put to death by Agamemnon and all the Greeks.[103]

63

> (Surely we must be deprived of all these) and suffer the fate of the jackdaw,
> to be humiliatingly stripped bare of our borrowed feathers? (*Sermon* 4.107)

Sixty-third is the story about the jackdaw and its feathers. This is the following tale.

---

103 Palamedes was famous for his discoveries, especially of the alphabet and of draughts
and dice (*Schol.* on Eur. *Or.* 432; Soph. *Fr.* 479.4), and for the fact that he was unjustly put to
death (Xen. *Mem.* 4.2.33; *Apol.* 26). The above description of how he exposed Odysseus and the
latter's revenge in Troy is found in Hyg. *Fab.* 95 and 105. Other writers give different details in
the story. He does not appear in Homer, but in one of the other epic cycles (the *Cypria*, see Paus.
10.31.1) and both Sophocles and Euripides wrote tragedies about him, which have not survived.
Gr. refers to his skill as surpassed by the flight of cranes, *Sermon* 28.25 (Demoen, p. 430).

There was a beauty contest, they say, among the birds, and Zeus was the judge of the contest. A day was appointed on which the birds had to gather before Zeus. On the day before the appointed day the birds flocked to the rivers to wash their feathers in the streams, so that the natural beauty of each should shine forth. The jackdaw, however, (this bird is both very small physically and of an ugly appearance) put the feathers that had dropped beside the waters upon himself, and himself came before Zeus, with the intention of carrying off the prize for beauty. But when a wind blew up so strongly that it scattered the feathers which were not his own, he found himself stripped of his beauty. In his own natural state of ugliness, then, he thus had joy of his humiliation.[104]

64

> Are poems yours? What, do they not rather belong to that old woman who was struck on the shoulder by someone running fast in the opposite direction, and, so the story goes, she abused him roundly in epic verse in the shock of the assault? Wasn't it this which pleased the young man so much and, when more carefully crafted, this which produced this wonderful poetry of yours? (*Sermon* 4.108)

Sixty-fourth is the story concerning the old woman who was shaken by the shoulder. It is this.

A certain woman called, as some say, Sibylla, as others, Phimonoë, and, as others again, Philyra, was shaken by a certain youth. The woman reacted quite abusively to the youth and abused him. The abuse she spoke was a line in metre. And, since the rhythm of the old woman's words pleased the bystanders, they picked up the metre of the line. Thus was the art of poetry invented.[105]

---

104 Ps-N. retells the well-known fable by Aesop (no. 103), mentioned again in *Poem* 2.2.29.55–58 (Kurmann).

105 Ps-N. correctly adds the name of the Sibyl Phemonoë (as two names), who (according to Paus. 10.5.7) was the first to use the hexameter, or epic metre, in her chanting of the prophecies of Apollo in his shrine at Delphi, to rework Gregory's account of the discovery of poetry (which was really that of iambic verse, Athen. 10.445b; see Bernardi *CJ* et al. *ad loc.*). The iambic metre was mainly used for abusive and comic verse and dialogue in Greek plays. Philyra was a sea-nymph and the mother of Chiron, the centaur, by Cronus (Pind. *Nem.* 3.78–83, and the *Schol. ad loc.*, with Ap. Rhod. 2.1241).

65

If you pride yourself on weapons, from whom do you get your weapons, most noble sir? Surely from the Cyclopes, who invented the forging of metal? (*Sermon* 4.108)

Sixty-fifth is the story about the Cyclopes. It is this.

The Cyclopes are said to have lived in the island of Sicily, in its mountains, following a shepherd's way of life, though living with more violence. These are said to eat human flesh and to have devoured the companions of Odysseus. Three of them are said to be the most outstanding, Brontes, Steropes, Arges. These same are said to be outstanding smiths by trade, who through their skill forged the thunder and lightning for Zeus. They are called the Cyclopes (Round-faced) according to Hesiod, because they had one round eye in their faces, but according to Telephatus, because they lived on a round island.[106]

66

And, if it is important to you, if not the most important thing of all, the purple, as a result of which you are such a wise man and the promulgator of such laws, should you not lay it aside for the Tyrians, where the shepherd's dog came from, who, when she had eaten the shell-fish and stained her lips, thereby discovered the dye for the shepherd, handing on to you emperors because of this an arrogant rag of mourning? (*Sermon* 4.108)

Sixty-sixth is the story concerning the purple robe. It is this.

In Tyre a shepherd's dog which was once walking along the shore found a shell-fish and ate it. Then the blood of the shell-fish dyed the dog's jaws. The shepherd, thinking that the dog had been hit, took some wool and wiped the

106 The land where the Cyclopes with whom Odysseus came into contact lived is not identified in Homer (*Od.* 9.105–542), though it was later thought to be Sicily (*Schol.* on Theocr. 1.7), where Theocritus locates his Cyclops, Polyphemus (11.7). In Hesiod, the Cyclopes, Brontes, Steropes and Arges, the sons of Uranus and Ge, are the first smiths, and each has one eye (Hes. *Theog.* 139–46). They were said to work at furnaces in the volcanic Lipari islands, which lie off the coast of Sicily (Call. *Hymn* 3.46). One of these is Strongyle, which is possibly the 'round island' referred to by Telephatus above. Some mss. (though not *Syr.*) give the name Palaephatus for Telephatus, who is otherwise unknown. For Palaephatus, see the notes on stories 51 and 52 above. As the first parts of the names are related in meaning, *palai* being the Greek for 'long ago' and *tēle* for 'far away', both may well stand for the same person, in Ps-N.'s rather insecure memory for names.

blood from her jaws. While the dog was found to be unharmed, the wool retained the purple dye. Then he realised that the shell-fish secreted that sort of natural dye, and publicised that very matter. So they harvested the shell-fish from the sea, and developed purple dyes.[107]

67

> What shall we say about agriculture and ship-building, if the Athenians were to exclude us from them, by telling of people like Demeter and Triptolemus and the serpents ... (*Sermon* 4.108)

Sixty-seventh is the story about agriculture and ship-building. It is this, just as the myth is told.[108]

Demeter had a daughter, Persephone. Pluto abducted her. As Demeter travelled around in her search for her daughter she came to Attica, and lodged with a certain Triptolemus in a village called Eleusis. So she learnt from Triptolemus that Pluto had abducted Persephone. In return for this good service she gave Triptolemus seeds, I mean wheat and barley, that is, commanding him not to begrudge them but to travel round and disperse the seed to all people, so that they might learn to sow and farm and eat cultivated crops. For long ago they used to eat acorns from oak trees; the verb to eat (*phagein*) comes from the oak (*phēgos*). It is said that Triptolemus, taking a chariot with winged serpents, and with Celeus as a companion, travelled round in this way distributing seeds.[109]

107 The purple robe has long been the mark of royalty, and the best purple dye came from the shell-fish (the murex) near Tyre on the coast of Palestine. Ps-N. retells Gregory's information, which is drawn from Achilles Tatius, *Leucippe and Clitophon*, trans. S. Gaselee, 1917, rev. 1969, 2.11.4–8, and others (Bernardi *CJ* et al. *ad loc.*), in a clearer and more intelligible manner.

108 The recension *m* alters the title to 'That about agriculture and ship-building. And (the story) about agriculture and Demeter and Core and Celeus and Triptolemus has been told in *On the Epiphany*, chapter 3' and omits all the story about Demeter.

109 Demeter was the goddess of corn and, according to the Homeric Hymn to her, she withheld the harvest in her grief when Pluto, the god of the Underworld, abducted her daughter. She only allowed the earth to bear produce again when Zeus had Persephone brought back. For the chariot drawn by winged serpents (a gift from Demeter), see Apollod. *Libr.* 1.5.2. Ps-N. sees, not the return of the harvest, but the change from a 'gathering' way of life to one of settled cultivation of fields. Acorns were noted as one of the earliest foods (Plut. *Coriolanus* 3.4) and the derivation of 'to eat' from 'oak-tree' above is also found in Servius (*on Ecl.* 1.1). Ps-N. also follows the Orphic version of the story (though Pausanias, who gives it, thinks it is spurious, 1.14.3) in which it is Triptolemus who tells Demeter where her daughter was. It was actually Celeus, the king of Eleusis, who gave Demeter lodging (*H.H.* 2.160–63), while Triptolemus

The holy Gregory also says that ship-building was discovered by the Athenians. I think he was speaking about the art of sea-fighting.[110] For the Athenians were principally sea-fighters. For the Phoenicians were said to have been the first to build ships, and Semiramis, triremes.[111]

68

and again of the people like Celeus and Icarius and all the mythology about these matters, which made these into a shameful mystery for you, one really deserving of the night? (*Sermon* 4.108)

Sixty-eighth is the story about Celeus and Icarius.

We spoke about Celeus in the previous story, that he wandered about with Triptolemus, giving out the seeds. This is the one about Icarius. It is said that wine was discovered by Dionysus, and for this reason they say that Dionysus is patron of the vine. When this Dionysus came to Athens, then, he met a certain Icarius, and gave him a vine-stock to plant. He planted it, and produced wine, and both drank it himself and gave it to shepherds to drink. The shepherds became drunk, and thinking that they had been poisoned by Icarius in their amazement at drinking (wine) for the first time, they put him to death. When his daughter, Erigone, however, discovered by means of his dog that Icarius was dead, she wailed and grieved. The gods took pity on her in her sufferings and transferred her into heaven. Erigone now is, they say,

---

distributed seeds. See M.-P. Masson-Vincourt, 'Interprétation d'un passage du Discours 39 de Grégoire de Nazianze', *Mélanges de Science Religieuse* XXXIII (1976), p. 4 (Bernardi *CJ*, *ad loc.*), for an examination of all Gr.'s references to Eleusis. In *Ep.* 196.1 he alludes to the scattering of seeds from above, without mentioning any names (Demoen, p. 427).

110 This difficulty is shared by modern commentators on Gregory's text (see Lefherz, 'Studien zu Gregor von Nazianz', p. 40; Bernardi *CJ*, Kurmann, and Lugaresi *4*, *ad loc.*). Kurmann considers that Gregory may be thinking here of Athene, the patron goddess of Athens, by whose advice the first ship was built (Apollod. *Libr.* 2.1.4; Hyg. *Fab.* 168.2), and Nonnus later writes of the 'skilled workmen of deft Hephaestus and Athena' (*Dion.* 36.409–11) who work on a fleet for Dionysus. The Athenians were famous for the sea battle of Salamis, in which they defeated the Persians in 480 BC.

111 For the Phoenicians as ship-builders, see Athen. 6.273e. Semiramis was the famous wife of Ninos, a king of Babylon, where she ruled in great splendour after his death (D.S. 2.4–20). She had transport vessels built in sections and took them with her in an unsuccessful attack on India to carry troops across the Indus (D.S. 16.6). Her story probably reflects the history of Sammuramat, the wife of Shamshi-Adad V of Assyria, who ruled as regent for her son Adad-Nirari III from 810–805 BC.

among the stars.[112]

As for the statement, '(which) made these into a shameful mystery for you', it does not refer to the story about Icarius, but to the myths told about Demeter. For she is said not only to have given them the seeds, but also a prescribed set of rites, which the Greeks perform. The said matters are viewed by them exactly as the god-taught Christians view baptism. Such a festival of the Greeks is called the *Mysteria* and the *Eleusinia* and the *Demetria*.[113]

69

> As for 'being initiated' (*mueisthai*) and 'initiating' (*muein*) and for 'worship' (*thrēskeuein*) where have these processes themselves come from to you? Surely it's from the Thracians, doesn't its name convince you? (*Sermon* 4.109)

Sixty-ninth is the story about 'worship' and 'being initiated'. It is this.

It is said that Orpheus, who was a Thracian and who discoursed about the Greek mysteries, taught both how and (...)[114] it was fitting to honour the gods. He then calls this honouring of the gods 'worship' as from a Thracian invention.[115] Others explain its origins by saying that (the word) worship has

112 Celeus and Icarius are grouped together by Gr., because Celeus welcomed Demeter and Icarius, Dionysus, when the two gods visited Attica (Apollod. *Libr.* 3.14.7), and Ps-N. follows this account of the gift of the vine to Icarius and the consequences of that gift. Erigone became the constellation of the Virgin, according to Hyg. *Astr.* 2.4, *Fab.* 130 and Serv. *on Georg.* 2.389. Ps-N. omits the fact that she hanged herself, a mode of death which links her in Hellenistic sources, if not before, with one aspect of the Ionian Greek festival of the Anthesteria (see the full discussion of both literary and artistic evidence in Burkert, *Homo Necans*, trans. P. Bing, ch. IV, especially pp. 240–43), and of the cult of Bacchus in Italy (see the discussion by the editor, A. Le Bœuffle, in the extra note (n. 12) on Hyg. *Astr.* 2.14).

113 Demeter is described as teaching Triptolemus, Celeus and others her rites, which confer benefits in the afterlife on those who are initiated in them (*H.H.* 2.473–82). These rites were held at Eleusis, and were called the Mysteries, etc. as noted above. Their religious significance is discussed in Burkert, *Ancient Mystery Cults*, passim. The Christians speculated much about their content, which was kept a deep secret by all the initiates (see *Comm.* 39.3 below), and Clement of Alexandria's disapproval of them (*Exhort.* 2.20.1–22.7) is echoed here by Gr., as in *Sermon* 39.4 and *Poem* 2.2.7.260 (Kurmann). Ps-N. appears more detached in his attitude.

114 There seems to be a lacuna in the Greek. *Syr.* reads 'taught in what way and how it was fitting', and *Arm.* (with some mss.), 'taught how it was fitting'.

115 The Greek for 'worship', had long been associated with Orpheus and his race (*Thrax/ Thrēx*, a Thracian), as noted in the *Schol.* on Eur. *Alcestis* 968. Orpheus was held to be the son of Calliope, one of the nine Muses, the daughters of Apollo, and Oeagrus, a mortal. He was renowned for singing and playing the lyre, for descending into the Underworld to reclaim his dead wife, Eurydice, from Pluto, and for 'inventing the mysteries of Dionysus' (Apollod. *Libr.* 1.3.2–3). See story 77 below for the works attributed to him and their influence.

rather come from *theoderkeuein*, as it were, that is, 'to see god'.[116] For *derkein* means 'to see'. As for 'being initiated' (*mueisthai*), it either comes from celebrating mysteries (*mustēria*) and secret rites, or from those who shut off (*muontas*) their sense-perception and pass beyond all physical illusion and thus receive the divine illuminations.[117]

70

As for making sacrifices, is it not from the Chaldeans, or from the Cypriots? The science of astronomy, from the Babylonians? Of geometry from the Egyptians? Of magian lore, from the Persians? (*Sermon* 4.109)

Seventieth is the story which concerns sacrifice, astronomy and geometry. It is not unclear.

It is said that the Chaldeans or the Cypriots discovered how to sacrifice to the gods. The story gives both names. The Chaldeans are a Persian people.[118]

The Babylonians are said to have been the first to have discovered astronomy through Zoroaster, and the Egyptians were the second to receive it.[119]

The Egyptians invented geometry, learning it from their vast land and by dividing up its parts, and then in this way making records and using them.[120]

116 *Syr.* omits the rest of this discussion about derivations.

117 The verb *mueō* 'I initiate' and the noun *mustērion* 'a mystery' have the same stem, which is similar to, but not identical with, that of the verb *muō* 'I close' or 'I shut off'.

118 Kurmann (*ad loc.*) considers that Gregory is referring to the practice of divination by consulting the entrails of sacrificial victims, which is what the Chaldeans (D.S. 2.29.2) and the Cypriots (Paus. 6.2.5, the first to use pigs in this way) are thought to have discovered. The Chaldeans were Babylonian, but Babylon became part of the Persian Empire in 450 BC, and Ps-N. uses the terms without distinction (see *Comm.* 39.16 below).

119 The founder of Zoroastrianism (Zarathrustra) was well known to the ancient Greeks. He is mentioned by D.L. (from a lost work by Hermodorus the Platonist, 1.2) as having existed 5000 years before the fall of Troy. Diogenes discusses the principal features of Zoroastrianism (as known to Aristotle, D.L. 1.8–9). He calls him a Persian, and derives his name (from another writer, D.L. 8) as meaning 'star-worshipper'. The Babylonians and the Egyptians were famous for their knowledge of astronomy (D.S. 2.29.2; D.L. 1.6 and 11). De Jong, *Traditions of the Magi*, pp. 346–402, makes a clear distinction between Iranian belief in Zoroastrianism, and the information in the Greek sources, which was once held to have influenced it, according to J. Bidez and F. Cumont, *Les Mages hellénisés, Zoroastre, Ostanès et Hytaspe*, I. *Introduction*, Paris, 1938, pp. 36–37.

120 For the Egyptians' claim to geometry, see D.L. 1.10–11. One ms. of *m* gives 'The Egyptians invented geometry, by dividing up their territory frequently, and then, in this way, making records and using them, because, whenever the Nile inundated their land, it overwhelmed each man's boundary marks' for this paragraph.

As for magic, he says, the Medes discovered it, and then the Persians, but first the Medes.[121] Magic (*mageia*) is different from witchcraft (*goēteia*) and witchcraft from sorcery (*pharmakeia*) in these respects, namely that magic is the summoning of beneficent divinities for some good communication, just as the utterances of Apollonius of Tyana had good intent. But witchcraft is the summoning of malefic divinities which haunt tombs for some evil communication. It is called witchcraft from the wails (*gooi*) and the mourning which take place near tombs. Sorcery is when someone gives someone else something by means of a deadly preparation, either as a love-charm or by mouth.[122]

71

From whom did you hear of divination by dreams, if not from the people of Telmesus? (*Sermon* 4.109)

Seventy-first is the story concerning divination by dreams. It is this.

Telmissus is a city of Lycia. This is an extremely ancient city. It existed,

---

121 The word for 'magic' in Gr.'s text is *mageuein* which means 'to be skilled in Magian lore' as well as 'to practise magical arts'. Ps-N. uses the word *mageia*, which has the same double meaning. The Magi were the wise men or priests among the Medes (Hdt. 1.101), and among the Persians, once they had conquered the empire of the Medes under Cyrus in 549 BC. They practised Zoroastrianism (but not witchcraft – Aristotle, D.L. 1.8). See de Jong on this passage among others, *Traditions of the Magi*, pp. 387–402. A clear summary of the history of Zoroastrianism is given in Mary Boyce, 'Zoroastrianism: a shadowy but powerful presence in the Judaeo-Christian world', 41st Lecture of the Friends of Dr Williams Library, 1987.

122 Ps-N., or his source, is conscious of the different meanings contained in the word 'magic', and breaks it down as shown. See G. Przychocki, 'De commentarii cuiusdam magici vestigiis', *BZ* 23 (1922), pp. 65–71, who developed a suggestion by P.A. Kremmer that stories 70–72 may have been derived from a handbook of magic spells, and my edition for the citations of this threefold division between *mageia*, *goēteia* and *pharmakeia* (the last meaning 'the use of drugs' or 'of spells') in later texts. Apollonius of Tyana (renamed 'Apollo' by the recension *m*) was a Neopythagorean sage and wonder-worker who lived in the 1st century AD. He was known for his 'white magic' in the 6th century AD, in the powers he was believed to exercise to drive away pests (see Malalas, *Chron*. 263–66), although earlier Christians, such as Eusebius, in the 4th century AD, dismissed him as a charlatan (see the *Life of Apollonius of Tyana*, composed by Philostratus in the 3rd century AD; E. Bowie, 'Apollonius of Tyana', *Aufstieg und Nieder-gang der römischen Welt*, II, 16.2 [1978]; and J.-J. Flinterman, *Power, Paideia and Pythagoreanism: Greek identity. Conceptions of the relationship between philosophers and monarchs, and political ideas in Philostratus' Life of Apollonius*, Amsterdam, 1995). It is cited in the *Souda*, as identified by Przychocki, 'De commentarii cuiusdam ...', pp. 66–67, though this has not been noted by Adler in her edition (see under *mageia*).

indeed, in the time of Croesus.[123] These are said to be the first to discover dreams, and to interpret portents. For they used to say, if anything happened, that it meant so and so, and whatever they said certainly turned out to happen.

72

> From whom, of augury? From whom else but the Phrygians, who were the first to study the flight and movements of birds? (*Sermon* 4.109)

Seventy-second is the story concerning augury.[124]

The Phrygians, accordingly, are said to have invented the whole science of augury. Augury consists of the divination of omens from birds, of omens from the home, of those from the wayside, from palmistry, and from involuntary movements.

Augury is when we say as this or that bird flies either before (us) or behind or to the right or left that it means such and such. Telegonus is said to have been the first to discover it.[125]

Divination from omens in the home is when one interprets domestic happenings, and says that they mean such and such. When a weasel appears on the roof, or a snake, or a mouse, or oil is spilled, or honey, or wine, or ashes, or anything else, (one says) that it means such and such. Xenocrates wrote a treatise on this subject.

Divination from wayside omens is when one interprets things that one meets on the way, by saying that if someone meets you with one kind of

123 The Greek mss. of Ps-N. agree in this spelling of the city's name. There were two cities of the same name in Asia Minor, one on the coast of Lycia and the other in Caria, near Halicarnassus, where there was also an oracle of Apollo. It is not clear from Hdt. 1.78 to which one Croesus (king of Lydia, 560–546 BC) sent for advice about a portent, but Christian writers attribute divination by dreams to the dwellers of the city in Caria (Tatian, *Sermon to the Greeks*, ed. E.J. Goodspeed, *Die ältesten Apologeten*, Göttingen, 1915, p. 1; Clem. Al. *Strom.* 1.74.5). Others, such as Cicero (*On Divination* 1.94) and Arrian (*Anabasis of Alexander* 2.18.1 and 2.3.3) make them knowledgeable about all kinds of portents.

124 Although Ps-N. takes up Gregory's word, *oiōnistikē*, 'augury', it is clear from his commentary that it has a more general meaning for him.

125 Telegonus, the son of Odysseus and Circe (Hes. *Theog.* 1014; Apollod. *Epit.* 7.16, 36) is the best-known bearer of that name; others are a son of Proteus (see 2 above), a king of Egypt who married Io after her wanderings (Apollod. *Libr.* 2.1.3 – for Io, see *Comm.* 5.28 and 39.20 below), or a descendant of hers (*Schol.* on *Eur. Or.* 932). None of the surviving literature about any of these figures, however, mentions this discovery.

burden, such a thing will happen to you, or if someone else does, then something else will. Polles wrote a treatise on this subject.

Palmistry is when we foretell someone's fortune from the opening of their hands and the lines (on them), either that they will marry, or have children, or some such thing. Helenus wrote a treatise on this subject.

Divination from involuntary movements is the interpretation of tremors of the body, (saying) that when the right eye trembles, for example, it means such and such, or the shoulder, or the thigh. Posidonius and many others wrote treatises about this.[126]

73

> For first of the Christians you have devised a revolt against the Lord, as they say the slaves did against the Scythians. (*Sermon* 4.109)

Seventy-third is the story concerning the revolt of the Scythians against their masters. It is this.

A band of the pastoral Scythians left Scythia to look for plunder. These left their slaves with their wives to make milk into cheese. The Scythians blinded their slaves and in this way had them make milk into cheese. Time went by, then, and since the Scythians who had left did not return, their wives grew familiar with the blinded slaves and had sexual intercourse with them, and conceived by them and gave birth. The children took the place of the Scythians who had left. They were slaves by breeding.

So, when the Scythians who had left so long ago returned, they found these, who had been begotten by the slaves, grown up and opposing them. And in the war which took place between the returning Scythians and those of servile breeding, those who had returned had very much the worse of it. So, one of them advised the ones who were defeated not to fight them with

---

126 Przychocki, 'De commentarii cuiusdam …', pp. 69–71 (cited in n. 122 above) finds some background to all these names, and supposes that Xenocrates (not the philosopher of 24 above, although the latter wrote a treatise entitled 'The Householder', D.L. 4.12) may be a doctor, Xenocrates of Aphrodisias, who is mentioned by the medical writer, Galen (AD 129–?199), as not being without a knowledge of witchcraft (12.793); Polles (from the second entry under that name in the *Souda*, which takes Ps-N.'s information as its first), to be a philosopher from Aegae who wrote a series of books on divination of various kinds; Helenus to be a mule doctor of that name (mentioned in the *Hippiatrica Berolinensia, Corpus Hippiatricorum Graecorum* I, ed. E. Oder and K. Hoppe, 77.14, Teubner, 1924); and Posidonius as the famous philosopher and historian (c.135–51/50 BC), who, like many of the Stoic school, also thought that divination was an actual science (D.L. 7.149).

weapons but with a whip. 'For', he says, 'to fight people with weapons, is war by equals against equals. To attack them with whips, is to go as masters against slaves.' So when the slaves' children saw the Scythians with whips they bowed their heads to them as to their rightful masters. This is how the war was brought to an end.[127]

74

> For, no more are the 'Thessalian mare' and the 'Lacedaemonian woman' and the 'men who drink from Arethusa' – I mean the Sicilians – distinguished from their fellows, as the oracle about them has it, than the Christians' own rites and customs are, which are most particularly appropriate to themselves and of such a nature that they cannot be rivalled by anyone else of those who wish to follow our ways ... (*Sermon* 4.112)

Seventy-fourth is the story about the Thessalian horse and the Lacedaemonian woman. It is this.

Every city has some unique feature which is special to it, as the region of Thessaly has horses, that of the Athenians, the silver mines, India, the gold-bearing sand, and likewise, Lacedaemon, hunting dogs (hence the Laconian hounds) and brave and undaunted women. Sicily, too, has a spring of water, called Arethusa, with whom the myth recounts the river Alpheus fell in love. The water of Arethusa was both unmixed and pure and sweet. The holy Gregory, then, says that just as some regions and cities and citizens had a certain special unique feature, thus the Christians' doctrine had all these, orphanages, hostels, hospitals, poorhouses, and all good things of that kind.[128]

---

127 Hdt. 4.1–5. See story 7 above for Scythia and the Scythians. The second hand of *L* adds a much longer note in brachygraphic script (transcribed by Chionides, *La brachygrafia italo-bizantina* [n. 100 above], p. 58), which follows the details in Hdt. more closely.

128 This story clarifies Gr.'s condemnation of Julian's attempt to establish lodging-houses, convents and so on (4.111) as a poor copy of the charitable centres established by the Christians. Ps-N. has no knowledge of the oracle to which Gr. refers (see the *Greek Anthology* 14.73, an anonymous oracle's response as to who were the best of the Greeks, of which there are many versions from different sources, discussed by Fontenrose, pp. 276–78). For Gr.'s own source, see Kurmann, *ad loc.* Ps-N. adds other, well-known, regional 'specialities' to the list, the silver mines of Laurium in Attica (Thuc. 2.55), the gold-bearing sand of India (Hdt. 3.102) and Lacedaemonian hunting dogs (Xen. *Hunting* 10.1.4). See *Comm.* 43.9 below for the myth of Alpheus and Arethusa.

75

> There is nothing like looking at this wonderful re-shaping or remodelling of
> theirs (of the Christian practices noted above), just as one watches a play,
> and finding out what their method of teaching was, and what the point of
> their congregations, so that as Plato said of his 'word-city', we can see their
> plan in action. (*Sermon* 4.113)

Seventy-fifth is the story about Plato's 'city in words'.[129]

Plato the philosopher composed a treatise which he called the *Republic*. In
this treatise he describes what a city ought to be like and of what number of
men it should be made up and by what customs and laws it should be
governed. This city only existed in theory; it never actually existed or was a
form of government. Thus, in this treatise he makes this remark, 'Let us
suppose that the citizens are making the following proposals, so that we can
see their minds at work.'[130]

76

> It would be a fine thing for them to declaim Hesiod's *Theogony* with its wars
> and routs, its Titans and Giants with their fearful names and deeds – Cottus,
> Briareus, Gyges, Enceladus, those serpent-footed monsters of yours, the
> gods armed with thunderbolts, the islands launched against them, that are
> both weapons and tombs to those who meet them, the bitter offspring and
> products of these, the monsters like the Hydra, the Chimaera, Cerberus, the
> Gorgons, a pride in everything bad. Let these fine passages of Hesiod be set
> before their hearers! (*Sermon* 4.115)

Seventy-sixth is the story about Hesiod's *Theogony*.

Hesiod is one of the poets who are now studied, three of whose poems, the
one called the *Theogony*, the one called the *Works and Days* and the one
called the *Shield*, are now studied.[131] In the *Theogony*, then, Hesiod is the
first to enumerate the origins of the gods, namely that so-and-so was born

129 The Greek, *en logōi*, means 'in word' or 'in theory'. Ps-N. misquotes it in the plural, *en
logois*, as *Syr.* and most of the Greek mss. show.

130 This is not a quote from Plato's *Republic*, but a reference to another dialogue, the
Timaeus, 19b–c, where Socrates speaks of his own wish to picture his imaginary city in action.

131 In the secondary schools with the works of Homer, as part of the literature syllabus,
though possibly only in excerpts. See the Introduction above, with n. 9. Gr. also speaks of
Hesiod in *Poems* 2.1.41.15–17 (as a sage, inspired by the Muses), and in 2.2.7.241–42 of
Orpheus, Hesiod and Homer breathing most sacrilegious songs.

from Chaos and Aether, Cronus from Uranus and Ge, and Zeus, Poseidon and Pluto from Cronus. Next he traces the lineage of families and the names of more recent gods, and how some gods warred against others, and how some were defeated, and others tore apart this one or those. For the Titans are said to have torn apart Dionysus.[132]

As for these names, such as Cottus and Briareus, which he (Gregory) mentions here, Hesiod states that certain men were born with a hundred hands, who fought on the side of the gods against the Giants. For the myth tells that the Giants rebelled against the gods until Zeus struck them with his thunderbolts. Hesiod speaks about the 'serpent-footed ones' in similar terms, namely that some men were born with serpents for feet. As for the 'gods who wield the thunderbolt', he here either refers to Zeus himself, because he struck the Giants with a thunderbolt, or to Steropes and Brontes, who forged the thunder and the lightning and the thunderbolts for Zeus. He also says that islands were hurled at the Giants by the gods as both weapons and tombs. These, then, are the myths he tells.[133]

As for the 'bitter offspring of these', he (Hesiod) says that the following death-bearing creatures were born from the blood of the Giants. These, which he (Gregory) himself enumerates, are the Hydra (this was the nine-headed serpent, which Heracles slaughtered), the Chimaera (which we mentioned previously, that its fore-part was a lion, its hinder part a serpent, and its middle a goat, and that Bellerophon had slaughtered it), and we have similarly already described how Cerberus was a dog with three heads at the gate of Hades, which fawned on those who went down to Hades, but devoured those who came up, and which was killed by Heracles.[134]

132 All of the above but the death of Dionysus Zagreus (the child of Zeus and Persephone, whose death played a part in Orphic writings, which are mentioned in story 77 below), added by Ps-N. to the passage, are described by Hes. *Theog.* 123, 137–8, and 453–8, respectively. Ps-N. gives a full account of Dionysus Zagreus in *Comm.* 5.30, below.

133 Gr. conflates the war of the gods against the Titans, the children of Uranus and Ge, in which they were helped by Cottus and Briareus (Hes. *Theog.* 149–51) with the war of the gods against the giants, some of whom had serpent scales on their feet, and who were crushed by the islands hurled against them (Apollod. *Libr.* 1.6.1–2), as noted by Bernardi *CJ* et al. *ad loc.*, and followed by Ps-N. The Titans were often confused with the Giants. See Gantz, pp. 445–54 for the early literary and artistic evidence for such battles. For Steropes and Brontes, see story 65 above. Briareus is mentioned again in *Sermon* 18.6 and in *Poem* 2.1.17.70 (Demoen, p. 426).

134 The Giants were born from the blood of Uranus when he was castrated by Cronus (Hes. *Theog.* 183–86), but the Hydra (see story 49 above), the Chimaera (see 50 above) and Cerberus (story 51) were the offspring of the monsters Typhon and Echidna (Hes. *Theog.* 306–20). The recension *m* omits the details about the Hydra, Chimaera and Cerberus as they have already been described.

The topic of the Gorgons is as follows, namely that they were three women whose faces were so terrifying that those who saw them died on the spot. Perseus is said to have killed one of them with his sickle-spear.[135]

77

Let Orpheus come forward with his lyre and all-embracing song. Let him roar out to Zeus the great and supernatural sayings and ideas of his theology:

Most glorious Zeus, the greatest of the gods, all rolled in dung
the dung of sheep
the dung of horses
the dung of mules.

So that I should suppose from this can be shown the generative and life-giving force of god which could not be done in any other way, nor should he spare the other boasts:

The goddess spoke and exposed both her thighs

in order to initiate her lovers with the postures which she still now uses for her initiations. (*Sermon* 4.115)

Seventy-seventh is the story which says, 'Let Orpheus come forward with his lyre'. It is this.

Orpheus was skilled in music, a Thracian by race, who is said to have sung so pleasantly that oaks and irrational creatures and rocks and rivers followed his song.[136]

Poems which the Greeks consider to be theological works are attributed to him. In these poems he describes by means of mythical allegories the ranks and lineage of the gods, what functions belong to which of them, the nature of rites due to each, and which created whom.[137] The holy Gregory then quotes certain lines by this Orpheus, which are about Zeus and Demeter. The

135 The Gorgons were the children of Phorcys and Ceto (themselves descended from Uranus and Ge), whose glance turned onlookers to stone. The one killed by Perseus, the son of Zeus and Danaë (see story 91 and *Comm.* 5.24 below) was Medusa (Hes. *Theog.* 270–74; *Sh.* 222–23); Perseus killed her with a sickle, given him by Hermes (Apollod. *Libr.* 2.4.2).

136 See story 69 and its notes. The recension *n* adds 'or rather his magic' to 'his song'. Gr. emphasises this aspect of Orpheus in *Poems* 1.2.29.169–70, 2.1.41.46, 2.2.3.212–14, 2.2.5.193–94 and 2.2.7.241. For the *Sermons*, see *Comm.* 5.13 and 39.17.

137 There are several types of poems attributed to Orpheus. Some are theogonies, as described by Ps-N. The fragments of these and literary references to their contents are collected in Otto Kern, *Fragmenta Orphicorum*, Berlin, 1922. The Derveni Papyrus, the remains of a 4th-century BC papyrus commentary on an Orphic theogony, discovered in Macedonia in 1963,

first is about Zeus, and the second about Demeter. The sense of the lines about Zeus is this, that 'Zeus, of high repute and greatest of all gods, contained in every kind of dung, both of sheep and of horses and mules'. *Mēleiē* is the dung of sheep, for *mēla* are sheep. By means of this saying Orpheus is supposed to show that Zeus extends his life-giving powers even to animal matter. The sense of the line about Demeter is this, namely, 'As the goddess approaches, she exposes her thighs' (he is speaking of her garments), so as, he says, to reward those who love her with sexual intercourse. Orpheus hints in these that the divine power is ready to give itself to those who long for it and to initiate them. The divine Gregory, then, disparages and ridicules them, by showing that the latter is shameful and that about Zeus unclean.[138]

78

> To all these may be added Phanes and Ericapaeus and he who swallows up all the other gods and gives them up again, so that he may become the 'father of gods and men'. (*Sermon* 4.115)

Seventy-eighth is the story which says, 'To all these may be added both Phanes and Ericapaeus'. It is this.

These two names are introduced with many others in the Orphic poems, where he describes Phanes as having a penis at the back, near his buttocks. They say, too, that he is the patron of the power of generating life. They also say that Ericapaeus is the patron of another power.[139]

---

adds much information (*Studies on the Derveni Papyrus*, ed. A. Laks and G. Most, Oxford, 1997). There are later hymns (late Hellenistic) associated with a Dionysiac cult in Asia Minor, the so-called 'Orphic Hymns', and an *Argonautica* (about the voyage of the *Argo*) and a *Lithica* (on the secret properties of stones), all of which, with the theogonies, are discussed by West. The Neoplatonists in Athens and Alexandria (3rd to 6th centuries AD) wrote clearly about the secret doctrines hinted at in the earlier literature on Dionysus Zagreus.

138 Ps-N follows Gr. in attributing these lines to Orpheus, although they are in fact by Pamphus, a 4th-century BC poet associated with the pre-homeric Orpheus by Pausanias and Philostratus (2nd to 3rd century AD), as noted by Bernardi *CJ* et al. *ad loc*. The passage about Zeus is said to derive from Stoic pantheistic beliefs (see Kurmann and Lugaresi *4, ad loc.*), while that about Demeter relates to an episode in her wanderings in search of her daughter (see story 67 above). When she came to Eleusis an old woman there made her laugh by exposing herself to her, an action transferred to Demeter by Gr. in his dismissive references to the mystery cults.

139 See the notes to story 77 above for the Orphic poems. Phanes is an early figure in the Orphic pantheon (West, p. 34) and Ericapaeus is a cult-name associated with Dionysus (West, p. 205, with n. 91 and 92). The above story is mentioned by West, p. 202, n. 85. Gr. associates Phanes with Oceanus and Tethys in *Sermon* 31.16.

As for the words 'He who swallowed all the gods', he is not talking about Ericapaeus but about Cronus.[140] For the latter is said to have swallowed his children up, and to have vomited out those he had already swallowed. For he is said to have swallowed a stone in place of Zeus, and when the stone went down he vomited them all up.

79

> Where do you put Homer, then, that great comedian about the gods of yours, or is he rather a tragedian? For you will find both aspects in his marvellous poems, some appropriate for disaster and others for laughter. (*Sermon* 4.116)

Seventy-ninth is the story which talks about Homer.

The story about this is well known. For throughout his poems he tells the myths of Cronus and Zeus, Hera and Aphrodite, and especially Athena, and, in a word, all those we know from his poetry.

He calls Homer a 'writer of comedy' because he describes some comic episodes to do with the gods, as when Hera, beautified and in glorious clothes, goes off to Zeus and deceives him, and sleeps with him, and other matter more amusing than this.[141]

He also calls him a 'writer of tragedy' because he tells some unhappy myths about the gods, as, for example, that he (Zeus) flung Hephaestus down into Lemnos, and that Aphrodite was wounded by Diomedes.[142] Such stories are indeed worthy of tears! For tears are caused by tragedy, and laughter by comedy.

---

140 Cronus, too, is included in the Orphic divinities. He swallowed all his children because he had been told that one of them would destroy him, until he was outwitted by his wife, Rhea. She gave him a stone wrapped up like a baby to swallow instead of her last-born child, Zeus, with the results noted above (Hes. *Theog.* 466–97). The recension *m* abbreviates all the text after 'Cronus' as follows: 'The story of the swallowing has already been told.' Gr. mentions gods 'who are cruel to their parents and to their children' in *Poem* 2.2.7.497.

141 *Il.* 14.159–360. The recension *m* omits all from 'as when ...' onwards. See story 81 below.

142 Zeus flung Hephaestus, Hera's son, down on to the island of Lemnos when he tried to protect his mother from Zeus' anger (*Il.* 1.590–94), and Aphrodite was wounded by the Greek hero, Diomedes, when she rescued her son, Aeneas, from him in battle (*Il.* 5.318–51). The recension *m* adds that Zeus flung Hephaestus down and adapts the passage about Aphrodite to 'some of them were wounded and others enchained'.

80

> It really is a matter of no little concern as to how Oceanus shall be reconciled to Tethys by Hera, dressed as a courtesan, since then there would be danger for the whole world if they were chaste, whether this means the dry principle should be exchanged for a watery one lest all should be cast into confusion because of the excess of one or the other, or for any other reason you could think of which is more absurd than the above. (*Sermon* 4.116)

Eightieth is the story about Oceanus and Tethys.

The poets bring this myth in as well, that Oceanus is the father of all the gods and Tethys the mother (Oceanus and Tethys are man and wife), and that, long ago, they separated from each other, and that through the mediation of Hera there was once more union and affection between them. The myth, he says, signifies that Oceanus is the wet medium and Tethys, that is the earth, the dry, and that long ago when the wet medium had no commerce with the earth, no living things were brought forth, and everything perished. Then Hera, as the patron of marriage, reconciled the two elements, and living things were again produced.[143]

81

> What does the wondrous union of Zeus the Cloud-gatherer and the revered Hera mean, when she seduces him to unseemly behaviour in the middle of the day, even if the poets flatter him with their verses, strewing dewy lotus beneath them and making crocus and hyacinth spring from the ground? ... At another time she drew to herself the whole girdle (*kestos*) of desires among her adornments put on for Zeus' benefit ... (*Sermon* 4.116)

Eighty-first is the story of Zeus the Cloud-gatherer with Hera.

Zeus felt more favourable to the Trojans and caused the Greeks to be defeated because of Thetis' intercession on behalf of Achilles, so that the Greeks might turn to Achilles in their hour of defeat. Hera supported the

---

143 The story of a rift between Oceanus and Tethys (*Il.* 14.200–05) is the excuse Hera makes to Aphrodite for asking her for the loan of her girdle (see story 81 below), by which she states she hopes to reconcile them, in her role as goddess of marriage. The allegorical interpretation of O. and T. as the wet element and the dry is found in both the Presocratic and Stoic philosophers, and in Clement of Alexandria as well, though he sees it as the separation of the water from the land in Gen. 1.9 (*Strom.* 5.100.5), as variously noted in Bernardi *CJ*, Kurmann and Lugaresi *4, ad loc.* Gr. refers to them again in *Sermon* 31.16.

Greeks.[144] And, as she did, she determined to beguile Zeus into sexual intercourse and sleep, after stirring him to a frenzy of lust, so that, while he slept, the Trojans would be unprotected, and be defeated by the Greeks. With this intention she took all the aids to beauty from the *kestos* of Aphrodite. The myth goes that the *kestos* is a little basket in which every aid to beauty, a good appearance and charm is stored up. Then, in all her glory, she went up to Zeus and moved him to lustful coition. The earth, too, they say, bloomed with plants, such as the crocus, the lotus and the hyacinth.[145]

82

> How can Hera be at one and the same time in your eyes the great sister and consort of Zeus, and now hanging in the upper air and the clouds, weighed down by iron anvils and honoured by golden handcuffs? (*Sermon* 4.116)

Eighty-second is the story of how Hera was suspended in the upper air and clouds, weighed down with iron anvils and chained with golden fetters. This is the story.

144 Thetis was a sea-goddess whom Zeus had once wanted to marry, but did not, either because she refused him, or because it was prophesied that her son by him would be more powerful than he. She was thus given in marriage to a mortal, Peleus (see *Comm.* 43.1 below), and the gods attended their wedding. For Thetis' intercession with Zeus for her son, see *Il.* 1.503–10. Achilles had quarrelled with Agamemnon because the latter took Briseis, one of Achilles' prizes, away from him to replace the loss of Chryseis, one of his own. Briseis was the daughter of a priest of Apollo, and had to be returned to her father to end the curse of disease he had laid upon the Greeks against her return. Achilles then refused to fight for the Greeks, despite all their inducements, until his friend, Patroclus, was killed fighting against the Trojans. His mother, Thetis, was anxious for him to fight to acquire the glory promised him at his birth. While the death of Achilles and the eventual fall of Troy were decreed by fate, Zeus, Hera and the other gods could support one side against the other from time to time to achieve the final issue. Hera hated the Trojans because the Trojan prince, Paris, had not given her the prize in the beauty contest between herself, Aphrodite and Athena (see the notes to story 2 above), and quarrelled bitterly with Zeus (*Il.* 1.511–21) over any help he gave them.

145 *Il.* 14.159–360. The *kestos* (originally an adjective, 'embroidered' with the noun, *himas*, a 'strap', of Aphrodite's charmed girdle which endowed the wearer with all attractions) stood for the girdle itself in post-homeric Greek. Ps-N. obviously thinks it is a container of some kind, a literal application of such metaphorical usage of the noun, *himas*, as is found in Gr. *Ep.* 32, of the collection of letters he is sending to Nicobulus: 'not of loves but of words' (suggestion of N.B. McLynn, Introduction, n. 105 above). The recension *n* gives a longer text for the last part of the story: 'in which every wanton aid to beauty, a good appearance, charm and a pretty face is stored up, forms of deceit as they are. Then in all her glory, she went up to Zeus and moved him, through this make-up, to lustful coition, surrounding herself with the scent of myrrh from the earth. The earth, too, they say, bloomed with plants, such as the crocus, roses, lotus, violets, lilies, with cassia, cinnamon, oil of myrrh and the other scents from perfumers and musk.'

Hera, as we know from many occasions, was jealous of Heracles. So, after his return from Troy when he had sacked it with Telamon, she harassed him by sea and raised a storm against him, after ordering the winds to distress Heracles' ship, and commanding Sleep to approach Zeus and to put him to sleep,[146] to prevent him from staying awake and helping the storm-tossed Heracles. When Zeus learnt about Hera's stratagem after his sleep, he punished her in this way; he bound an anvil to each foot, and her hands with unbreakable chains, and suspended her from the heaven in her punishment.[147]

83

What of the fear, then, when the gods bestirred themselves about the Laconian adulteress and the heaven sounded the trumpet, that the foundation of the earth would tear asunder, the sea change its order, the kingdom of Hades be revealed and things long hidden in time be brought to light? (*Sermon* 4.116)

Eighty-third is the story about the fear among the gods that, when the heaven sounded the trumpet, the foundation of the earth would tear asunder and Hades be revealed. This is also in Homer, in the twentieth rhapsody. It is this.

When Achilles was proving overwhelmingly successful, Zeus feared that Achilles would sack Troy, contrary to the decrees of Fate. Inspired by this fear, he urged any who wished to of the gods to go and help whichever side they wished to, so that some should help the Trojans and some the Greeks. When they had been so urged, Zeus thundered from the heaven, while Poseidon caused the sea to shake. At the shaking of heaven and earth, Hades was terrified that the underworld would be torn apart by the shaking of the earth, and his kingdom be revealed. The lines are the following:

In fear he leapt up from his throne and shouted, lest above him
Poseidon, the Earth-shaker, should rend the earth.[148]

---

146 The recension *n* rewrites the sentence from 'she harassed ...' as follows: 'Hera harassed the sea by enchantments and made it stormy, and roused the winds and storm-tossed Heracles' ship with violent waves, and by some magic she made Sleep approach Zeus and put him to sleep.'

147 See *Il.* 14.249–56 and 15.18–28. Hera hated Heracles because he was the son of Zeus and Alcmene (see story 3) above. The recension *m* omits 'in her punishment'.

148 See story 81 above for the powers the gods had to influence the course of the siege of Troy. This episode is described in *Il.* 20.1–63, from which these lines are taken. The recension *m* rewrites several passages in the story, omitting much of the repetition.

84

> What is 'the nod of the dark eyebrows and the movement of ambrosial hair, which shakes the whole of Olympus'? (*Sermon* 4.116)

Eighty-fourth is the story the 'nod of the eyebrows and the movement of the hair'. It is this.

Homer shows Zeus making a promise after the intercession of Thetis on behalf of Achilles, by moving his eyebrows in the promise and shaking his hair in the bowing of his head, and making the whole heaven stir as his own hair moved. He says the hairs are 'ambrosial', such as no mortal could possess.[149]

85

> What is 'Ares wounded' or 'shut up in a bronze jar'? (*Sermon* 4.116)

Eighty-fifth is the story of how Ares is wounded and shut up in a bronze jar. It is this.

As for the fact of his being wounded, the poet (Homer) says he was wounded by Diomedes. He says this in the fifth rhapsody. He was tied up by Otus and Ephialtes. These were the sons of Aloeus, who were tyrannical by nature. They lived in Thessaly. These plotted a rebellion against the gods. Ares, then, was the first to go out against them, was then defeated by them, and bound in a bronze jar. 'Bronze jar' (*Chalkos keramos*) is either a city of that name or a kind of stringent and almost escape-proof means of imprisonment. Otus and Ephialtes are said to have been nine fathoms high and nine cubits broad when they were nine years old.[150]

---

149 See story 81 above for this episode, from *Il.* 1.528–30. The adjective 'ambrosial' means divine or immortal. The name of the food of the gods, 'ambrosia' ('which confers immortality'), is taken from it.

150 Three episodes are conflated in this story. Diomedes wounds Ares (with the help of Athene) as told in *Il.* 5.855–61. Aphrodite's mother consoles her for her wounding by Diomedes (see story 79 above) by telling her that Ares himself was once imprisoned by Otus and Ephialtes (*Il.* 5.385–91). The scholiast on this passage explains *keramos*, 'a pottery jar' or 'jar', as a dungeon. Their size and their rebellion against the gods (see *Comm.* 43.12) are described in *Od.* 11.305–20.

86

> ... the gauche lover of golden Aphrodite, the careless adulterer, who was caught by the Limper, who gathered an audience of gods around himself as he misbehaved and was let off for a small ransom? (*Sermon* 4.116)

Eighty-sixth is the story about the lover of Aphrodite. It is this.

Aphrodite was the wife of Hephaestus. Ares was in love with her, and committed adultery with her. When Hephaestus learnt of this, as he was a smith by trade, he set snares for Ares when he came to commit adultery with Aphrodite. He fell into the snares and was held by them, and was caught in the act with Aphrodite. Hephaestus did not set them free until he had summoned the gods and put them on show. Ares was then set free, after paying a small ransom. He calls Hephaestus 'The Limper' because he was lame.[151]

87

> By what examples will they teach this? Will they speak of the wars of the gods ... (*Sermon* 4.120)

Eighty-seventh is the story about the wars. It is this.

Athena and Hera who supported the Greeks warred against Aphrodite and Ares who supported the Trojans. You could also mention the wars of the Giants against the gods and those of the Titans against Dionysus.[152]

88

> How will Cronus not inspire confidence as he castrates Uranus so that he may father no more gods and yet allow the waves to bring forth a god, the offspring of foam ...? (*Sermon* 4.121)

Eighty-eighth is the story about Cronus and the castration of Uranus. It is this.[153]

151 An accurate account of *Od.* 8.266–366. The recension *m* abbreviates the text from 'set snares for Ares ... lame' as follows: 'set snares for Ares in the bed. And when Ares came again to Aphrodite, they were caught by the snares when they fell into the bed.' The episode recurs in *Sermons* 5.32 (and is discussed by Ps-N.), 28.15 and in *Poems* 1.2.10.838–39 and 2.2.7.94 (Demoen, Inv. II, s.n.).

152 For the part played by different gods on different sides of the Trojan War, see story 81 above. See the notes on story 76 above for the wars of the gods with the Giants (all mention of which is omitted by *m*), and *Comm.* 5.30 for the death of Dionysus Zagreus.

153 The recension *m* notes 'It has already been told' for this sentence, and omits the rest. The myth appears in *Comm.* 39.4.

Uranus was the father of Cronus. Cronus, then, because he did not want him to have another child, took a sickle and cut his father's genitals off and threw the genitals into the sea. Foam gathered and Aphrodite was born from the foam. She was thus called Aphrodite as if from the foam (*aphros*).[154]

89

and Zeus in revolt against his Cronus in imitation of his father, (Zeus) the sweet stone and bitter tyrant-killer ... (*Sermon* 4.121)

Eighty-ninth is the story of the revolt of Zeus against Cronus. It is this.

When Zeus learnt that Cronus actually was a devourer of his children, he rose up against him and took his kingdom from him and made his own father, Cronus, fall from power.[155] He says, 'In imitation of his father', because Cronus, too, rose against Uranus and cut off his genitals, and took the kingdom.

He calls Zeus a 'sweet stone', and the same, a 'bitter tyrant-killer'. A 'stone', on the one hand, since, as they said, Rhea gave Cronus a stone to swallow in place of Zeus. He calls him 'Tyrant-killer' either because Zeus rose against Cronus, or because the stone which took his place made the other vomit up even those he had previously swallowed.[156]

90

How will the 'God of Profit' be set before them? (*Sermon* 4.121)

Ninetieth is the story about the God of Profit. It is this.

The Greeks call Hermes the God of Profit, because he is productive of profit. It is for this reason that Aristophanes the comic poet, too, when at a loss as to what to call Hermes says,

Let us set him up as God of Commerce,

that is as the patron of profit.[157]

154 Hes. *Theog.* 178–98.

155 The recension *m* rewrites 'and took ... from power' as 'and expelled him from his kingdom and put him down in Tartarus with the Titans'.

156 For Zeus' attack on Cronus, see Hes. *Theog.* 490–91, and for that of Cronus on Uranus, story 88 above. Story 78 above describes how Zeus escaped being swallowed by Cronus. According to Hes. *Theog.* 493–96, Rhea tricked Cronus into restoring his children to earth.

157 Aristoph. *Wealth* 1155. For Hermes' other titles, see *Comm.* 5.11 and 26 below. Gr. mentions Hermes in *Sermon* 4.101 and 102 (neither of which are commented upon by Ps-N.) and the 'God of Gain' in *Sermon* 14.29. He refers to 'thieving' gods in *Poem* 1.2.2.496 (Demoen, Inv. II, s.n.)

91

What next? Let them teach temperance and let them introduce self-control, the nearer, Zeus, who took on every shape for the sake of women and as an eagle was the dearest lover of Phrygian boys, so that the gods should feast as sweetly as possible with Zeus' favourites to pour their wine, and Heracles, the Three-Evening-One, who strove with the fifty daughters of Thestius on a single night, accomplishing this as his thirteenth labour, though I don't know why it wasn't numbered with the rest. (*Sermon* 4.122)

Ninety-first is the story about him who turns into every shape for the sake of women. He is referring to Zeus.

For Zeus became an eagle and abducted Ganymede, after falling in love with him homosexually. Ganymede was a Phrygian. The myth goes that Zeus abducted Ganymede to make him his cup-bearer when he entertained the gods to feasts. This Zeus turned into gold and had sexual intercourse with Danaë, abducted Europa as a bull, and became a swan to fornicate with Leda.[158]

As for the matter of the fifty daughters of Thestius, we have already said that Heracles had sexual intercourse on one night with the fifty daughters of Thestius. The same Heracles, too, was called the Three-Evening-One, as we have already said, because he was engendered in three days.[159]

158 The handsome Ganymede was carried off by the gods to be Zeus' cup-bearer, *Il.* 20.231–35, and later tradition states either that an eagle (or Zeus himself, in the form of an eagle – Ovid, *Met.* 10.155–56; Luc. *Dialogues with the Gods* 4.1) carried him away (Apollod. *Libr.* 3.12.2). The eagle was the bird sacred to Zeus. The recension *m* omits all from 'homosexually … feasts', while *n* adds 'by magic' after 'eagle'. Danaë was walled up in a chamber of brass underground (Apollod. *Libr.* 2.4.1) to prevent her from having a child who would kill her father, Acrisius, but Zeus had sexual intercourse with her as a shower of gold; he carried Europa off to Crete in the form of a bull (Apollod. *Libr.* 3.1.1), and became the father of Helen of Troy by Leda as a swan (Eur. *Helen* 16–21, 257–59). The recension *n* adds: 'As a bull again, he fornicated with Pasiphaë, he became a satyr, and carried out the other myriad evil deeds through lasciviousness and lust.' Gr. mentions Zeus' metamorphoses again in *Sermons* 5.32 and 39.4 (both duly commented upon by Ps-N.) and in 28.15.

159 See story 42 above for these myths about Heracles. The recension *m* omits this whole paragraph; *n* turns it into a separate story, number 92, and renumbers the following stories in accordance.

92

Let Ares restrain his wrath … (*Sermon* 4.122)

Ninety-second is about Ares' restraining of his wrath.

This is obvious, because Ares, who breathes anger, is said to be the patron of wars,[160] since we pray in wars for anger to be aroused within us.

93

Dionysus his drunkenness, (*Sermon* 4.122)

Ninety-third is the story about the drunkenness of Dionysus. It is this.

It is said that Dionysus is the patron of the vine and of wine and of drunkenness itself, and that they also depict him as drunken, as Hera had brought drunkenness upon him to drive him mad. For Hera was angry with him because he was a son of Zeus. For she used to envy those who were begotten of Zeus.[161]

94

Artemis her hatred of strangers, (*Sermon* 4.122)

Ninety-fourth is the story about Artemis, the hater of strangers. It is obvious.[162]

For we have already spoken about Iphigeneia and the Taurians. For Artemis is honoured by the Taurians in Scythia, and as she had Iphigeneia, the daughter of Agamemnon, as her priestess sacrificing strangers to her, she rejoiced in the killing of strangers.

---

160 *Il.* 5.891. The recension *m* changes 'since … us' to 'since those in wars pray for the arousal of wrath'. Ares is associated by Gr. with war in *Poems* 2.1.11.253, 2.1.51.9, 2.1.88.48 and *Ep.* 48.6, and anger is mentioned in connection with pagan gods in *Sermon* 28.15 (Demoen, Inv. II, s.n.).

161 For Dionysus and the vine, see story 68 above, and Apollod. *Libr.* 3.5.1 for Hera's influence on him (with Eur. *Cyclops* 3–4). See story 82 above for Hera's hatred of Heracles. The recension *m* ends the story at 'of wine'. Gr. refers to drunkenness of the gods in *Sermon* 28.15 (Demoen, Inv. II, s.n. Dionysus).

162 The recension *m* adds 'among the Taurians in Scythia' to 'strangers', and replaces 'It is obvious' by 'We have spoken about it above'. The rest of the text is omitted. See stories 7 and 57 above.

95

Loxias, their oracle-giver, his deceit (*Sermon* 4.122)

Ninety-fifth is the story about Loxias, the oracle-giver. It is this.

When Apollo was asked for an oracle, he gave oracles to those who consulted him neither clearly nor directly, but obscurely and ambiguously (*loxōs*); for this reason he was called Loxias, as giving as an oracle the opposite of what actually happened. Many, indeed, were deceived as a result of this, and none more so than Croesus the Lydian. For this was the oracle which was given to him:

> If Croesus crosses the Halys, he will destroy a great empire.

It was not clear which empire he would destroy. So Croesus, thinking that he meant the empire of his enemies, crossed the river Halys, and destroyed his own empire.[163]

96

> the lame god, the immoderate laughter, while the gods grieve and he stands firm on his slender thighs, (*Sermon* 4.122)

Ninety-sixth is the story about the measureless laughter. It is this.

The one about Hephaestus: when he bound Ares in snares because of his adultery with Aphrodite and summoned the gods, greatly, indeed, did they laugh at him.

He says that Hephaestus himself was a limping god; for this god was held to be lame by them. Hephaestus rejoiced in Ares' thighs because Ares fell by his thighs into the snares of Hephaestus.[164]

---

163 The story is told in Hdt. 1.53–54, 71 and 86, and the oracle itself cited in D.S. 9.31.1. Gr. mentions Apollo, or false or venal oracles, in *Poems* 1.2.10.375, 2.2.7.93 and 253–55 (Demoen, Inv. II, s.n. Apollo). In *Sermon* 5.32, Apollo is called a 'speechless statue' (*Comm.* 5.17).

164 The 'immoderate laughter' of the gods was aroused by the plight of Ares and Aphrodite (see story 86 above) but also by the sight of Hephaestus bustling around to serve the gods with nectar in *Il.* 1.599–600. His limp and 'slender thighs' are mentioned in *Il.* 18.411, as he started to work on the shield of Achilles, a reference not noted by Ps-N. The recension *m* alters the first phrase, 'The one about Hephaestus' to 'He says Hephaestus was a limping god. For he was lame to them, and when the gods saw him limping as he served them they laughed at him', and omits the second paragraph.

97

Zeus his gluttony as he runs with the rest of the demons to the rich feast with
the blameless Ethiopians, (*Sermon* 4.122)

Ninety-seventh is the story about 'Zeus running to the rich feast (*dais*)'.

This too is in Homer, that Zeus went away to Ethiopia to a feast, to which the
Ethiopians invited him and the other gods with him, once they had made it.
The feast of the Ethiopians and the *dais* are the same. It was a sacrifice to
Zeus. The lines are as follows:

> For yesterday Zeus went to the Ocean to join the blameless
> Ethiopians at their feast, and all the gods followed together.[165]

---

165 Cited from *Il.* 1.423–24. The Homeric Greeks believed that the Ocean encircled the
known world and that the Ethiopians, divided into two races, dwelt at the east and in the west
(*Od.* 1.22–24).

COMMENTARY ON SERMON 5

A SIMILAR COLLECTION AND EXPLANATION OF THE STORIES WHICH ST GREGORY ALSO MENTIONED IN THE *SECOND 'PILLAR-POSTED' ORATION AGAINST JULIAN*

1

> Again, tell me, you, about those stars of yours, Ariadne's Crown, Berenice's Lock, the lascivious Swan, the violent Bull, and if you like, your Snake-Holder, Capricorn and Lion … (*Sermon* 5.5)

First is the story about the Crown of Ariadne, the Lock of Beronice, and about the Swan and the Bull and the Lion and the Snake-Holder. They are these.

Ariadne was the daughter of Minos, the king of the Cretans. She fell in love with Theseus, the king of Athens, when he came to kill the Minotaur. Dionysus took her from Theseus, then, and carried her off to Naxos, and united with her. He also depicted a crown of stars in her honour in the sky.[1]

The (one) about the Lock of Beronice is this: A certain Beronice was the wife of the Ptolemy called 'The Benefactor' in Alexandria. So, when her husband, Ptolemy, was at war, she vowed that, if he returned unharmed, she would cut off a lock (of her hair) and dedicate it in the temple: Beronice then made the dedication. A certain Comon was an astronomer in her time and in flattery of her he said that the gods had placed this lock among the stars. And now there is, indeed, a cluster-shaped arrangement of stars in the sky which

---

1 See Gantz, pp. 114–16, 264–70, for a clear analysis of the three basic versions of the end of the Ariadne story (that she was killed by Artemis in childbirth, or was abandoned by Theseus and rescued by Dionysus, or was, as here, taken from Theseus by Dionysus). Ps-N. follows that most fully explained in D.S. 4.61.5–6. The Cretans extracted a tribute of seven youths and seven maidens every nine years from the Athenians to sacrifice to the Minotaur, a man with a bull's head, the child of Pasiphaë, queen of Crete, by a bull. Ariadne helped Theseus (the son of Aegeus, king of Athens) kill the Minotaur and escape when he came one year as one of the members of the tribute band. Dionysus saw her with Theseus, fell in love with her and took her from him. After her death, he placed the crown of stars in the sky in her memory (as in Aratus, c.315–240 BC, *Phaenomena*, 71–73).

they call the Lock of Beronice.[2]

The (one) about the Swan is this: Zeus, having fallen in love with Nemesis, as some say, or with Leda, as others, and wishing to have sexual intercourse with her without being seen by Hera, changed into a swan, and had intercourse with his beloved. So now this swan is fixed in the sky. The Swan, indeed, is depicted in the stars.[3]

The (one) about the Bull is this: A certain bull was produced in Greece by Poseidon. It ravaged the countryside and did much damage. Theseus attacked it and destroyed it. Since the gods both wished to magnify Theseus' act and to appease Poseidon, they fixed the bull in the sky. Now the Bull, too, is depicted in stars in the sky.[4]

The (one) about the Lion is this: There was a lion, a savage animal, in Nemea (this is a region of the Peloponnese). This lion, then, was attacking those in the region. So Theseus, who was king of Mycenae, and who was angry with Heracles, sent Heracles to kill the lion. Heracles went and killed it. Since the gods then wished to glorify Heracles' struggle they depicted the lion in stars in the sky. The Lion is also now among the stars.[5]

The (one) about the Snake-Holder is this: This Snake-Holder is said to be Asclepius, the patron of the art of healing. The snake is a symbol of

---

2 Ptolemy 'The Benefactor' reigned in Egypt from 246–221 BC. He married Berenice of Cyrenea in 246 BC. Her dedication of a lock of her hair when he went to war against Syria in that year, and its recognition as a constellation by Konon, a famous mathematician and astronomer of her time, are described in the lost *Lock of Berenice* by Callimachus of which only fragments remain and in Catullus 66, of the same name. Hyg. gives the full story, which is slightly abbreviated by Ps-N., in *Astr.* 2.24.1, and Ps-Erat. *Cat.* 1.12.18–20 mentions it briefly. Ps-N.'s version of the name, Comon, possibly refers to the verb *komaō*, 'I let my hair grow', or to the word comet, *komētēs*, which is also derived from the Greek for 'hair'.

3 See *Comm.* 4.91 above for Zeus and Leda. Nemesis (Retribution) is the daughter of Night. Isocr. *Helen* 59 makes both Leda and Nemesis the object of Zeus' love as a swan. In Hyg. *Astr.* 2.8 Zeus unites with Nemesis as a swan. She then bears an egg which is given to Leda; the child, Helen, emerges from the egg and is adopted by Leda as her daughter. He adds the other story, that Leda was the mother of Helen by Zeus in the form of a swan. Ps-Erat. refers to the Nemesis story alone, *Cat.* 1.25.1–7, while Apollod. also gives both versions (*Libr.* 3.10.7). See Gantz, pp. 318–20, for a full discussion of the evidence for the myths.

4 The constellation was more usually held to represent Zeus in his liaisons with either Europa or Io (Ps-Erat. 1.14.1–12; Hyg. *Astr.* 2.21.1; and the *Scholia Strozziana in Arati Phaenomena*, ed. Breyzig, on v. 174). This identification with the Marathonian Bull which was captured by Theseus (Plut. *Theseus* 14; Paus. 1.27.10) is only found in Ps-N.

5 Heracles had to expiate the crime of murdering his first wife and their children (see story 23 below) by performing the ten tasks to be imposed on him by Eurystheus (not Theseus, who was the king of Athens, as noted above), king of Tiryns and Mycenae, of which this was the first

agelessness: for the snake is said to cast its skin and to renew itself. So, because Asclepius renews mortal bodies through his healing art, they place him with a serpent. The gods, therefore, who wished to consecrate him instead of a statue (of him), consecrated him with stars in the sky.[6]

2

and to be like Salmoneus, thundering from a hide … (*Sermon* 5.8)

Second is the story about 'Salmoneus thundering from a hide'. It is this.

Salmoneus was the son of Aeolus and king of the Thessalians. He was impious to the gods, and by fastening stiff dry hides to chariots and by beating on cauldrons and hides alike, made an uproar; and, holding burning torches in his hands, he went on boasting that he was thundering and lightning just like Zeus until he was blasted by a thunderbolt and destroyed by Zeus.

He left a young daughter called Tyro. After she had been brought up by her paternal uncle Cepheus, she fell in love with Enipeus, a nearby river. Poseidon took on the form of this river and had sexual intercourse with Tyro instead of Enipeus. She conceived Pelias and Neleus and held them in her womb. She was married by Cretheus; Tyro later bore children, apparently by Cretheus, but, in fact, by Poseidon. Tyro also later had children by Cretheus himself as well.[7]

(Apollod. *Libr.* 2.5.1). These ten labours were subsequently increased to twelve by Eurystheus (see *Comm.* 4.2, 3, 41, 42, 49 et al. below). Gr. mentions Heracles and Eurystheus in *Ep.* 32. Hyg. *Astr.* 2.24.1 (who is closely followed by Ps-Erat. *Cat.* 12) states that Jupiter formed this constellation to honour the king of the beasts, or to mark Heracles' first labour.

6 Hyginus gives several explanations for this figure, *Astr.* 2.14.1–5, of which the last is Asclepius, the son of Apollo, and a detailed description of why he was associated with a serpent (he saw one serpent restore another to life with a certain herb, which he then used himself with similar results on a human). This is the only identification known to Ps-Erat., who does not mention the serpent (*Cat.* 6.1–9). Both say that Zeus had the constellation set in the sky (after blasting Asclepius' house with a thunderbolt because he was bringing too many dead to life) because of Apollo. See Gantz, pp. 91–92, for the earlier sources for Asclepius. Snakes had been long associated with healing powers in Greek thought, *Schol.* to Aristoph. *Wealth* 733: 'The snake is sacred to Asclepius, because it casts its skin (*gēras*, the Greek for 'old age' is also the term for the 'cast skin' or 'slough' of a snake, LSJ s.v.) and the art of healing preserves youth by thrusting back disease.' The cult of Asclepius was widespread in both Greece and Rome.

7 Ps-N. follows the account of Salmoneus' behaviour in Apollod. *Libr.* 2.9.7, although there the uncle who brings Tyro up is called Cretheus, not Cepheus. (Cepheus is the name of the king of Ethiopia, and father of Andromeda.) Homer also states that Cretheus married her and had children by her in addition to those begotten by Poseidon, disguised as Enipeus (*Od.* 11.235–59). Ps-N. may be confusing a Cepheus, the son of Aleus (Apollod. *Libr.* 2.9.16), with Cretheus here.

3

> For a certain nobleman among the Persians, in imitation of what Zopyrus
> (did) for Cyrus about Babylon … (*Sermon* 5.11)

Third is the story about 'Zopyrus in Babylon'. It is this.

As Cyrus, the king of the Persians, was spending a long time in the siege of
Babylon and fell into a long-lasting despair because it was hard to capture, a
certain Zopyrus, brave in spirit as the matter showed and not without honour
in Cyrus' opinion, devised the following scheme. After cutting off his nose
and ears and lacerating himself with scourges, he actually deserted to the
Babylonians, on the pretext that he had been terribly mistreated by Cyrus.
Once he had left he pretended to favour the Babylonians and suggested
certain attacks on Cyrus to them. In short, he inspired trust among the Babylonians by acting as a general on behalf of the Babylonians and destroying
many of Cyrus' men. After coming to an agreement with Cyrus on an
appointed day upon which he (Cyrus) should attack Babylon, he persuaded
the Babylonians to let him take the keys of the gates on that same day. He
then took them, opened up and led the Persians in. This is how Babylon was
taken. Herodotus mentions this in the Third Book of the *Histories*.[8]

4

> and a similar thing happened to him as had to Cyrus, son of Parysatis, who,
> when campaigning with the Ten Thousand against his brother Artaxerxes,
> and fighting boldly, lost his victory through rashness. (*Sermon* 5.13)

Fourth is the story about Cyrus the son of Parysatis.

Darius the Younger, the son of Xerxes, had two sons, Cyrus and Artaxerxes,
by Parysatis. When Darius died, the two quarrelled about the kingdom. Time
then brought Artaxerxes, as the elder, to become king; but the mother
preferred Cyrus, as the younger and beloved. Artaxerxes prevailed because
of time and himself became king. So Cyrus who was unwilling to give

---

8 Hdt. 3.153–60. This episode actually took place during the reign of Darius I (522–486
BC), although Gr. seems to confuse him with Cyrus I (557–530 BC) who also captured Babylon
(in 538), as noted in the *Scholia Oxoniensia*, *PG* 36 1133 D8–1136 A9 ('Nonnus', p. 294, n.
16). He did this by diverting the course of the river Euphrates, which flowed through the city,
and marching his troops in through its empty bed (Hdt. 1.191). *Syr.* and one early Greek witness
read Cyrus throughout the text of this story. The other mss. and *Arm.* give now Cyrus and now
Darius as the Persian king.

precedence to Artaxerxes asked his brother to give him the satrapy of Asia as a province. He took it and went down to Ionia. Settling there, however, he again fell to thinking about the kingship, and after gradually winning over about ten thousand Lacedaemonians and other Greeks, he persuaded them to accompany him. With these in company with him he went up as far as Persia. There was a battle then between Cyrus' and Artaxerxes' men, and Cyrus' men won, though they were much fewer (in number) than Artaxerxes' forces. For the Greeks knew how to carry out skilful manoeuvres in battle, and, though few in number, they were on the verge of defeating the many through their skill. Cyrus, then, carried away by his short-lived victory, rushed out from his phalanx against Artaxerxes' phalanx, with the intention, indeed, of cutting down Artaxerxes himself, but perished because he was on his own. And so he died without becoming king. Xenophon mentions these happenings in the *Hellenica*.[9]

5

And it is appropriate to quote the remark made by Herodotus about the tyranny of the Samians, that 'Histiaeus stitched the shoe but Aristagoras put it on', that is, the latter took up the matter which the former had initiated. (*Sermon* 5.15)

Fifth is the story about the 'tyranny of the Samians'.

Histiaeus, though a Samian by race, was a friend of Darius, the King of the Persians, and was taken by him to Persia. While living there he longed to see his native land. But, since he was not allowed to, he wrote to his nephew, Aristagoras, to arrange a revolt. And he persuaded some of the Ionians to revolt. This is how Histiaeus wrote: he took a trustworthy slave and, after shaving his head, he scratched what he wanted to disclose on the (other's) head. He then inked in the scratches and let him allow his hair to grow back. After it had grown back he sent him off, telling the slave to have it shaved once there so that Aristagoras could read the writing.

So when Aristagoras had read and had understood (the message), he caused the revolt of almost all the Ionians. The king then learnt (of this) in

---

9 Xen. *Anab.* 1.1.1–4. According to him, Cyrus was slandered to his brother, who then summoned him to kill him. Parysatis protected him and had him sent back to his command in Asia Minor where he won over the Greeks, with Xenophon, to support him in his attack on his brother. D.S. describes his defeat, 14.23.3–4 and 7. Xenophon then describes the long march of the Greeks ('The march of the Ten Thousand') back from the hinterland to the coast and safety.

Persia and consulted Histiaeus, as a Greek, as to what he should do. He was then advised by Histiaeus to send him to Asia as he was the right man to put an end to the revolt. So when Histiaeus went to Asia, and became the leader, as it were, of the whole affair, he heard this remark from Artaphernes the deputy governor of Sardis: 'Though Histiaeus stitched the shoe, Aristagoras put it on.' By 'shoe' he meant the whole affair. Herodotus tells this episode in Book Six (of the *Histories*).[10]

6

> So much did their robbery and greed surpass that of the Hundred-handed of old ... (*Sermon* 5.19)

Sixth is the story about the Hundred-handed.

We have told this in the stories of the *First Oration*, namely that there were two people, Cottus and Briareus, who had a hundred hands.[11] These fought on the side of the gods against the giants.

7

> What shall I say of the reversals and alterations of judicial verdicts, often being varied and changed in the middle of the night, as they say the tides ebb and flow? (*Sermon* 5.20)

Seventh is the story about the 'ebb and flow of the tides'.

The ebb, as we have already said, is the opposite of the flow of the tide. These movements are found in a narrow sea-strait closed in by either islands or lands.[12] An 'ebb' is, as it were, a swallowing and sucking down, when the water flows back to some crannies in its bed, and after a little while the water flows out again. So the sinking back of the water into the hollows of the earth is called the 'ebb', and the flowing out again of this is called the 'flow'. It is

---

10 Hdt. 5.24, 35, 36 and 106–7. The remark is made in 6.1. Histiaeus of Miletus was taken to Sardis by Darius in 511 BC and stayed there until 499, when the Ionian revolt began. See O. Murray, *The Cambridge Ancient History* IV.2, Cambridge, 1988, p. 486, for the probability of this account and the fate of Histiaeus.

11 *Comm.* 4.76 above.

12 See *Comm.* 4.53 above and the passage cited in the note there from Thuc. 4.24. Arist. *On Things Heard* 802b.34 notes that the narrowness of straits increases the force of the currents within it.

said that this happens often during the day, especially if a wind is blowing, and that the Euripus, the one near Greece, is subject to this movement; and that is why it is called the *Euripos* ('easily tossed') like something which is easily turned and changes easily. Aristotle is said to have thrown himself into it. We spoke about this in the *First Oration* as well.[13]

8

> Let them agree, nevertheless, that these (verdicts) were not worthy of the Elysian Plains nor of the reputation of Rhadamanthus there, the destiny which those cronies and companions of his think he deserves. (*Sermon* 5.20)

Eighth is the story about the Plain of Elysium and Rhadamanthus.

Just as the Christian doctrine states there is a paradise, so the pagans describe a certain place which they call 'The Islands of the Blest'. They also call it the Plain of Elysium, because those who have lived a good life will come (*eleusesthai*) there.[14]

Rhadamanthus is said to be the son of Zeus, who has judicial rank. It is therefore said that he judges those in Hades, and sends those worthy of punishment to Cocytus and Pyriphlegethon, but those who have lived a good life to the 'Islands of the Blest'.[15]

13 See *Comm.* 4.34 above with its notes for Aristotle and the currents of the Euripus. Procopius (as cited above) notes that the tides of the Euripus are not affected by wind. They were long a byword for change and instability of purpose (cf. Pollux 6.121), and much referred to by Gr., as in *Sermons* 6.19, 26.1 and 42.22; and *Poems* 2.1.1.470, 2.1.14.34 and 2.1.77.2.

14 The early scholia on Hes. *Works* 171 identify the 'Islands of the Blest' as paradise, as do those by the 5th-century AD Athenian philosopher Proclus (cited in the edition by Gaisford, *Poetae Minores Graeci*, II, on 169). Both passages speak from a Christian viewpoint, of the Isles being equivalent to Paradise for 'them' or 'the Greeks'. Gr. himself, in *Sermon* 43.23, speaks of the 'meadows of asphodel and the Elysian Plains, which are their representations of our paradise, derived from those books of Moses which are also ours'. This theory of a common (Mosaic) source for parallel pagan and Jewish and Christian ideas was well established in Jewish thought and in the early Fathers. Hesychius also cites Elysium as the equivalent to paradise (q.v.). Gr. mentions Elysium again in *Epitaph* 36 (Demoen, Inv. II, s.n.).

15 Rhadamanthus is described as the son of Zeus in *Il.* 14.322, and as the judge of the dead in Pl. *Gorg.* 523e. He sends the just to the Isles of the Blest and the wicked to Tartarus, *Gorg.* 526b, where the rivers Cocytus and Pyriphlegethon, respectively the 'River of Wailing' and the 'River of Fire' (*Od.* 10.513–14), await them (Pl. *Ph.* 114).

9

> There are those whom he favoured with invitations to dinner, with much
> drinking to their health amid throaty cries of 'Comrade', as the only induce-
> ment ... (*Sermon* 5.20) ... as for the toasts and loving cups which he
> publicly proposed to and received from courtesans ... (*Sermon* 5.20)

Ninth is the story in which he refers to the frequent throaty toastings 'Companion'. It is this.

Plato and all the (other) philosophers call the true lovers of letters 'companions', that is 'friends'. So Julian, as a philosopher, did not become
arrogant with kingship, but would imitate Plato and the rest by calling everyone 'companion'. This word, indeed, occurred often in his conversations.

'Toasts' is this. All the kings of old when holding a feast for all the
people, would, once the wine was mixed in gold and silver cups, take them
from the cup-bearer, drink a little from the cup, this being a sign of great
affection, and then hand it to whomsoever they wished, making them a gift
of the cup as well. This then was to 'toast' and the day (was called) 'of
friendship'.[16]

'To make throaty cries' is an imitation of the sound when, in delight with
what he is saying, (some) one in some way coughs over his words and seems
to hold them back in his throat.[17]

10

> As for his puffings and blowings, which ... he displayed while kindling the
> fire on the altar ... where shall we put them in our sermon? How fine it was
> to see the distended cheeks of the Roman emperor, providing much laughter
> ... Had he not heard that Athena, his own goddess, had even cursed the
> double flute, once she saw how it disfigured her by using a pool as a mirror?
> (*Sermon* 5.22)

Tenth is the story about Athena and the double flute. It is this.

Athena once took up a double flute and passed by a river as she played. But
when she saw her reflection with distended cheeks in the water, an unseemly

---

16 This practice is also described in the *Schol.* to Pind. *Ol.* 7.1, 4–5. It is usually the cup, not
the day, which was called 'of friendship' (Aristoph. *Lysistr.* 203), as explained in the scholia to
the same, *Acharn.* 984–85.

17 Dem. *About the Crown* 291 first uses the verb for showing approval. In Plutarch, it
describes the sound of crows cawing (*Moralia* 2.129a).

sight to her, she threw the flute away for causing ugliness. For in playing the flute the breath distends the cheeks and disfigures the flute player. Marsyas is said to have found the abandoned flute and to have competed with Apollo, and to have lost and been flayed by the river, which was then called the Marsyas.[18]

11

No longer do the greedy and deceitful demons hold power ... (*Sermon* 5.31)

Eleventh is the story about the greedy demons.

It is obvious that all demons are greedy for they enjoy savoury smells. Hermes is especially mocked (for this), which is why he is called *Deilakriōn*, as one who comes down to the meat when titbits of it are put out for him. They are deceitful above all, and especially on account of Apollo because he gave deceitful oracles.[19]

12

Throw down your Triptolemuses and Celeuses and the mystic serpents ... (*Sermon* 5.31)

Twelfth is the story about the Triptolemuses and Celeuses and the serpents.

We have already described these in the *First Oration* as well, as to how Triptolemus and Celeus took seeds such as corn and barley from Demeter and, with a winged chariot drawn by serpents, went all around the world providing corn for sowing and cultivation.[20]

---

18 This well-known myth is found in Melanippides (5th cent. BC) *Poetae Lyrici Graeci*, ed. Page, p. 393, Fr. 2; Arist. *Pol.* 8.6.14; and Apollod. *Libr.* 1.4.2, among others. Xen. also mentions the river in *Anab.* 1.2.8. Apollo won the contest by playing his lyre upside down, which Marsyas could not do with the flute (Apollod. *Libr.* 1.4.2).

19 This adjective, 'Wheedling' (Aristoph. *Peace* 193) is explained by the scholia as describing one 'who sees fragments of food, snatches them up and by breaking down turns the wrath of others against him to pity'. In the *Peace*, Hermes uses it of the farmer who offers him a bit of meat as a bribe. See *Comm.* 4.95 above for the deceitful oracles of Apollo.

20 See *Comm.* 4.67 above. The recension *m* adds 'has been told' to the title and omits the text. M.-P. Masson-Vincourt's explanation of the serpents as a reference to Zeus' metamorphosis into a serpent when he seduced his daughter Persephone (cited in Bernardi *CJ*, *ad loc.*) is further discussed in 'Nonnus', pp. 294–95, with n. 21. As stated there, it is not known to Ps-N.

13

Feel shame, for once, at the books of Orpheus, your theologian ... (*Sermon* 5.31)

Thirteenth is the story about the theologian Orpheus. We have already mentioned this, but will tell it now as well.

Orpheus, a Thracian by race, played the lyre, charming, as it is said, even inanimate things. Poems of his are circulated in which he actually writes a theology through mythical symbols, introducing series of gods and dimensions of beings and the actions and powers of gods. Orpheus composed these myths in a very unseemly, impious and violent way.[21]

14

No longer does the oak speak, no longer does the cauldron prophesy. (*Sermon* 5.32)

Fourteenth is the story about 'the oak no longer speaking nor the cauldron prophesying'. It is this.

Dodona is a city situated in Epirus in which an oak tree sacred to Zeus used to stand. In this was also an oracle, with women as prophetesses. Those in search of an oracle would go up to the oak and the oak would – allegedly – stir. Then the women would speak out, saying, 'This is what Zeus says'.[22]

The information about the cauldron is as follows. Matters to do with the cauldron also took place in Dodona; it is said to be something like this. It is said that in Dodona a statue holding a rod stood on a certain eminence. Those in search of an oracle would go to this spot and pray. When the god wished to give them an oracle, then, that statue would touch the cauldron with the rod. Then the cauldron would resound and an harmonious echo sounded from the cauldron. The prophetesses would be 'made full' and say what the demon inspired in them.[23]

21 See *Comm.* 4.77 above for Orpheus and his teaching. He was condemned in this way in Isocr. *Or.* 11.38–39 because he described the death of Dionysus Zagreus (see story 30 below), which was usually kept in secrecy by those who were initiates in Orphic beliefs. The recension *m* also omits this story, after a brief back reference in the title.

22 See *Comm.* 4.20 above for the 'speaking oak at Dodona' and its priests and priestesses, as discussed by Parke, ch. 1. Gr. refers to the 'oracles of the oak' in *Poem* 2.2.7.256 (Demoen, Inv. II, s.n. Dodona) and in *Sermon* 39.5 (*Comm.* 39.12).

23 While the oracle of the oak was of great antiquity (see Parke, as cited above), that of the 'cauldron' (*lebēs*) or 'bronze' (*chalkion*) seems to have been of later date. Parke, pp. 86–91,

15

> no longer is the Pythia filled with I know not what but myths and ravings …
> (*Sermon* 5.32)

Fifteenth is the story about the Pythia. It is this.

Phocis is a place in Greece. There is a city in it called Delphi. In this city is a temple to Apollo, which is called Pytho. The tripod and the oracular lots were in this temple. The oracular lots, indeed, were in the bowl of the tripod. So, whenever the person seeking an oracle asked about the prophecy, the lots would quiver and stir among themselves. So then the prophetess would become inspired and would say what Apollo wanted. The prophetess was called Pythia. At this point he (Gregory) says she was filled and made full and possessed by the god.[24]

16

> Castalia is silenced once more and is silent and the water is not oracular but ridiculed … (*Sermon* 5.32)

Sixteenth is the story about Castalia. It is this.

There is a spring in Antioch which Apollo is said to haunt, and to give

---

explains it as a reference to the resonance from the bronze votive objects at the shrine which included cauldrons, tripods and a statue of a boy with a whip, the lashes of which struck a cauldron when moved by the wind (described by the 3rd–2nd cent. BC traveller, Polemon; by Steph. Byz., in the account of Aristides, Book 2; and by Str. 7. *Fr.* 3). The loss of the lashes of the whip were noted in the 1st century AD, which possibly led to the speculation that the statue moved through the power of demons to strike a cauldron in answer to prayer, as well as a general association, both pagan and Christian, from that time onwards (if not before) of the 'Dodonaean bronze' with prophetic powers (Parke, pp. 90–91). The passage in the *Souda* discussed by Parke, p. 29, is derived from the above story, and its reference to the 'voices of demons being inarticulate' comes from story 17 below (see Adler, *ad loc.*). Parke rejects the theory that the priestesses at Dodona suffered a divine madness when they prophesied (Pl. *Phaedr.* 244b–c, a belief also promoted by the Christians: Origen, *Against Celsus* 7.3).

24 Pytho was the name of the region or of Delphi itself. It is derived from the verb, *puthein*, to rot or putrefy, of the body of the giant serpent killed there by Apollo. The information given here (and in *Comm.* 39.13 below) about the mantic lots is late and unique to Ps-N., though lots may have been drawn at Delphi to answer oracular enquiries. See Fontenrose, ch. 7, where all the evidence for the different types of oracles at Delphi is discussed. The authorities cited after the reference to Nonnus in n. 33 on p. 219 (Cosmas, the *Souda*, Adler, *ad loc.*) are later copies of Ps-N.'s material. According to the *Schol.* on Aristoph. *Wealth* 39, the Pythia was 'filled with madness' when she sat upon the tripod to prophesy.

prophecies and oracles to those who come to the water. It is also said that whenever one sought an oracle, the water sent up airs and breezes. And as the aforesaid exhalations went up, the priests around the spring would say what the demon wished.[25]

17

Apollo is once more a speechless statue, (*Sermon* 5.32)

Seventeenth is the story, 'Once more a speechless statue'.

We have found no information about this statue, then, as to where it used to stand or how it spoke. One must assume that it was the statue in Delphi, and that at that time it emitted an articulate voice. For one should know that the voices of demons are not articulate because they have no phonetic organs to form the voice into separate sounds as it is produced.[26]

18

Daphne is once more a plant bewailed in myth. (*Sermon* 5.32)

Eighteenth is the story about Daphne. It is a mythical tale.

Daphne, they say, was a girl with the good fortune to be the child of the river Ladon and Ge. She, they say, with her beautiful figure and lovely face,

25 See Bernardi *CJ*, pp. 358–59, n. 1, for a discussion at to whether Gr. is referring to the Castalian spring at either Delphi or to that in the shrine to Apollo and Aphrodite at Daphne near Antioch. (The latter was dedicated by Seleucus I at the beginning of the 3rd century BC and survived as a cult centre until the 4th century AD.) While the Delphic stream was not originally described as prophetic, there seems to have been a later tradition that it was in Clem. Al. *Protrept.* 2.11.1, with which Gr. (and others, including the last oracle cited above in the Introduction) appear to agree. Both recensions *m* and *n* add the name of the shrine, Daphne, to the text. Gr. refers to Castalia again in *Sermon* 39.5, and *Poems* 2.1.41.18 and 2.2.7.256 (Demoen, Inv. II, s.n.).

26 Despite his identification of Castalia with the stream in Antioch, Ps-N. shows no knowledge of the 'speaking statue' which was also at that shrine (as discussed by Bernardi *CJ*, *ad loc*.). I have noted elsewhere that Gr. may have no specific statue in mind ('Nonnus', p. 295). The recension *m* omits all the text after 'Delphi'. The sound emitted by the statue of Memnon in Egypt was but a single note, as described by Str. 17.1.46 and Paus. 1.42.1–3. For an interesting parallel to Ps-N.'s rationalisation of the inarticulate voices of demons (combined by the *Souda* with information from story 14, as noted above), see Gregory of Nyssa, *Life of Moses* 45 (*PG* 44 316 C), where 'the voice (of God) was articulate through divine power, without phonetic organs'.

stirred Apollo's love. Apollo then, stirred by love, pursued Daphne to see if he could have sexual intercourse with her. The girl, then, wishing to keep her virginity, prayed to her mother, Ge, for help. Ge opened her bosom and took the girl in, but, in a wish to console the god, she sent up a plant with the same name as her daughter, which Apollo took and used for a garland by his tripod, being consoled for Daphne, the object of his passion.[27]

19

Dionysus is androgynous once more, equipped with a band of drunkards and your great mystery (the Phallus), a god overwhelmed by passion for the fair Prosymnus. (*Sermon* 5.32)

Nineteenth is the story about 'that Dionysus was androgynous'.

They say that he (Dionysus) plays both the active part of a man and the passive part of women, and excites the Bacchae around him to frenzy as maenads and the Satyrs and Silens who dance around him. We have often said, indeed, that he was the discoverer and patron of wine and that he gave it to both women and men. They used to drink it and become drunk, and would dance with the women in drunkenness around him. Some say that the Satyrs are shepherds, but others that they are certain divine demons in attendance on Dionysus.[28]

---

27 There are different accounts of the parentage of Daphne, the child of the river Peneus according to Ovid, *Met.* 1.452–567, and Hyg. *Fab.* 203, or the river Ladon in Arcadia or its homonym near Antioch in Syria (Paus. 8.20.1 and 10.7.8; Philostr. *Apollonius* 1.16). The tale in Palaeph. 49 (50), which is similar to that of Ps-N., is an addition to the 4th-century BC text of unknown date. She is also described as the daughter of Amyclas in Parthenius, 1st century BC (*Love Stories* 15, with reference to Phylarchus, 3rd cent. BC). She is loved by Apollo and is either turned into a laurel tree to escape him (Parthenius, Ovid, Hyg.), or is replaced by one (Philostr., Ps-Palaeph. and Ps-N.). Laurel was associated with Apollo and his cult long before this aetiological myth arose.

28 The adjective *androgunos* can either mean an effeminate man, as here, or 'men and women together' (story 27 below) or 'a man and his wife', as in *Comm.* 4.80 above. Gr. speaks of 'androgynous gods' in *Poem* 2.2.7.94. Recension *m* rewrites the title as follows: 'The (story) about "that D. was androgynous and plays the active part of a man and passive part of women" has been told above.' The rest of the text is omitted. See *Comm.* 4.68 and 93 above for Dionysus and the 'invention' of wine. The Bacchae are his female worshippers, taking the title from one of his other names, Bacchus (see Gantz, p. 118). The Satyrs and Silens were minor deities, in the form of men with horses' ears and tails and sometimes with those of goats, and are associated with Dionysus. Silens are described by Paus. as 'older satyrs' (1.23.5). See Gantz, pp. 135–39, for a thorough review of the literary and early artistic evidence. Ps-N. never mentions their appearance.

We have already described the Phallus in the *First Oration*, that it was a leather phallus, which actors in the mimes now use and call *phalētarion*. They have this in the Dionysia, wearing it in their ceremonies and festivals, while they were at that time initiated.[29]

20

Semele is once more struck by a thunderbolt. (*Sermon* 5.32)

Twentieth is the story about Semele and the thunderbolt.

Semele was the daughter of Cadmus. Zeus was in love with her and had sexual intercourse with her. Hera, inspired by envy, made herself look like a nurse known to Semele and advised Semele: 'You should ask Zeus to have intercourse with you as he does with Hera.' (Zeus used to have intercourse with Hera with thunders and thunderbolts.) Hera gave Semele this advice so that, if Zeus came to her with thunderbolts, as a mortal she would be burnt up and she (Hera) would no longer have a rival: which is exactly what happened. For when Zeus visited Semele again, Semele asked him to have intercourse with her in the same way as he did with Hera. And, as he had intercourse with her, Semele was struck by a thunderbolt and died. Then Zeus took Dionysus, who was an embryo, and sewed him into his thigh. Later, in the seventh month, Hermes came and undid Zeus' thigh. Dionysus, then, as they say, was born. He (Hermes) took him to Nyssa in Thrace, and there he was suckled by the nymphs.[30]

29 *Comm.* 4.38. I discuss the continuance of the mimes and John Lydus' evidence for phalluses to do with Dionysus in 'Nonnus', p. 296, with notes 25, 26 and 27. Some festivities to do with Dionysus continued even in the late 7th century AD, as Canon 62 of the Council held at Trullo in AD 691–92 describes: 'there should be no wearing of masks, comic, satyric or tragic, nor should the name of the abominable Dionysus be cried out by those treading the grapes in the vats, nor should laughter be excited at the pouring of wine into wine-jars, by those acting like frenzied pagans through ignorance or light-mindedness. Any cleric acting like this with knowledge of these injunctions should be deposed from office, and any lay-person excommunicated' (*Die Kanones der wichstigsten altkirchlichen Concilien*, ed. F. Lauchert, Frankfurt, 1961, p. 126). The word, *phalētarion*, probably related to the Greek, *phalēs* (genitive, *phalētos*, a phallus), is not otherwise known (*Thesaurus*, Introd. §2.1.5, n. 32).

30 According to Apollod., Semele is tricked by Hera (*Libr.* 3.4.3); Hyg. adds the detail of the nurse, *Fab.* 167.2, 179.2–3, an account also found in Nonnus (*Dion.* 8.178–264). See Apollod. as cited for the rest of the story, and D.S. 4.2.3 for Dionysus and the nymphs. *Arm.* omits this story completely, while recension *m* retains the title alone. In Apollod., the nymphs dwell in Nysa in Asia, while Ps-N. follows *Il.* 6.130–35, in siting 'Nyssa' in Thrace, where Dionysus was attacked by the Thracian king, Lycurgus. A 'Mt Nysa' is associated with Dionysus in various areas, with no specific geographical identification (*Schol.* on Hom. *Il.* 6.133).

21

Hephaestus limps once more, though quick to discover adultery, a god covered in soot, but renowned for his skill, and an Olympian Thersites; Ares is in chains once more with terror, fear and uproar for his adultery, and a casualty for his rashness; Aphrodite once more a harlot, both shameful in origin and procuress of shameful unions. (*Sermon* 5.32)

Twenty-first is the story about limping Hephaestus. It is this.

Hephaestus was lame, and hence 'limping'. He was a bronze smith. Aphrodite was his wife and Ares committed adultery with her. Hephaestus then discovered the adultery in process by setting a trap. He (Gregory) calls the god himself 'covered in soot (*katēthalōmenon*) and smoke'; for soot (*aithalē*) is a kind of very thick smoke. He was covered in smoke because he was a smith. The poets say that he was 'renowned for his skill' (*klutotechnēs*) since he was notable in his practice of this skill of working in bronze.[31]

He (Gregory) calls him 'an Olympian Thersites' for the following reason: Homer introduced a certain man called Thersites, who was lame, squinting, hunchbacked, bald and foolhardy. He says that he accompanied the army not to make way but to excite ridicule. Since Hephaestus then was lame and covered in smoke, he (Gregory) says: 'Your Hephaestus is like Thersites'. He called him 'Olympian', meaning 'heavenly'. For Olympus is the heaven. So your god is an Olympian Thersites, lame and foolhardy.[32]

The phrase 'Ares in chains for adultery' is connected to the same story. For Ares was chained up by Hephaestus in snares while he was committing

---

31 See *Il.* 1.571, 18.142–44, where Hephaestus is so described. The recension *m* omits the first part of the passage about Ares and the snares, which is already recounted in *Comm.* 4.86 above. It adds the words 'and made the gods laugh' after 'Since H. was lame and covered in smoke', and omits the sentence 'For Olympus is "heaven"'. A part of the recension *n* then adds 'or, again, he (Gr.) calls him Olympian because he came from (Mt) Olympus where his workshop is, which is even until now said to be in Lycia in a part of Olympus, where fire spews up of its own accord, and it is called Hephaesteum; the Greeks of that time built him a temple there. Olympus is opposite Cyprus. Aphrodite fled here to dwell, and set up her adultery there, and took Adonis there.' (See *Comm.* 4.43 for Aphrodite and Adonis.) Mt Olympus, in northern Greece, is the highest mountain in Greece and was considered to be the throne of Zeus and home of the gods.

32 For the full account of Thersites, of which this is a brief but accurate summary, see *Il.* 2.1–278. When Agamemnon tested the resolve of the Greeks by advising them to abandon their siege of Troy, and they took him at his word, Odysseus, alerted by Athena, turned them back to hear what the other leaders had to say. Thersites abused Agamemnon loudly for this apparent change of mind, and was then beaten soundly by Odysseus to the approval of the rest of the soldiers.

adultery with Aphrodite. He (Gregory) says 'with Terror, Fear and Uproar' because these were the servants of Ares, the sons of War, and that they suffered the same fate as Ares, and that Hephaestus was not afraid of Terror, Fear and Uproar. He calls Ares 'a casualty' because he was wounded by Diomedes, when acting rashly in the war.[33]

The story about Aphrodite is connected as well, in that she was a 'harlot'; for she committed adultery with Ares. The pagans call her a 'procuress' because they say she is the patron of sexual intercourse.

22

once more Athena is a virgin and gives birth to a serpent, (*Sermon* 5.32)

Twenty-second is the story how Athena, though a virgin, gives birth to a serpent. It is this.

When Zeus wished to give birth to Athena from his brain, he needed a helper to take and strike his head so he could give birth. He discussed this matter with Hephaestus. Hephaestus would only split Zeus' head if he could deflower the offspring; Zeus agreed. So Hephaestus took his ox-goad and split Zeus' head. Athena emerged and Hephaestus pursued her to have sexual intercourse with her. As he pursued her he ejaculated on to Athena's thigh. Athena took some wool and wiped off the semen and threw it to the ground. A man with serpents for feet was born from the ground and the wool, who was called Erichthonius, taking the name from the wool (*erion*) and the earth (*chthōn*).[34]

33 Terror, Fear and Uproar are Ares' usual companions in battle (*Il.* 4.440 and 15.119 for Terror and Fear and *Il.* 5.593 for Uproar). Ares is the father of Terror and Fear (Hes. *Theog.* 933–35) and Uproar the servant of War (Aristoph. *Peace* 255). See *Comm.* 4.85, for Diomedes' attack on Ares. Ps-N. follows Gr.'s text in having Ares' battle companions attend him in adultery. Gr. mentions 'adulterous gods' in *Poems* 1.2.2.496 and 2.2.7.93 (Demoen, Inv. II, s.n. Ares).

34 Ps-N. does not explain, as the similar account in the *Schol.* to Plato's *Tim.* 23e does (see 'Nonnus' pp. 296–97, with n. 28), that when Zeus married Metis he was told that any child of hers would be more powerful than he. So he swallowed her and gave birth himself to Athene, with whom she was then pregnant (Hes. *Theog.* 886–900, 924–26; Apollod. *Libr.* 1.3.6). Hephaestus helped him to give birth for the above reward. Erichthonius, the child of Hephaestus and Athene by Hephaestus' attempting to gain a reward promised for other reasons as well (see Hyg. *Fab.* 166; Apollod. *Libr.* 3.14.6), was possibly confused with Erectheus, the first king of Attica, the child of earth, who was brought up by Athena (*Il.* 2.547–48), as discussed most recently by Gantz, pp. 77 and 233–34. The *Etymologicum Magnum* adds the passage from Ps-N. under the name Erectheus, as noted by Greene, *Schol. in Plat.*, *ad loc.* Gr. mentions 'half-serpent' divine children (among others) in *Poem* 2.2.7.104 (Demoen, Inv. II, s.n. Erichthonius).

23

> once more Heracles goes mad, or rather ceases from his madness, (*Sermon* 5.32)

Twenty-third is the story that 'Heracles is mad.'

Megara, for so she was called, the daughter of Creon, the king of Thebes, was married to Heracles. He had children by her. Hera, however, who hated Heracles for many reasons, inspired him with madness. And in his madness he killed his children by Megara.[35]

24

> once more Zeus takes on all kinds of forms through lust and depravity, the counsellor and highest of the gods, who alone draws the gods upwards, with all living things, (*Sermon* 5.32)

Twenty-fourth is the story how Zeus takes on all kinds of forms through lust. It is this.

Zeus is said, in his love for Danaë, to have become flowing gold, and to have had sexual intercourse with her in this way. In a similar way when in love with Ganymede, he became an eagle; when in love with Europa, he became a bull, and with Leda and Nemesis, a swan.[36] In this way, then, he would change his shape continuously, taking on every form through depravity, he the foremost god among them, and the one who draws all the other gods up to heaven.

25

> once more the tomb of Zeus in Crete is displayed. (*Sermon* 5.32)

Twenty-fifth is the story about the tomb of Zeus in Crete. It is this.

Zeus is said to have been brought up there in Crete and to have died, and that there is a tomb on which it is written that 'Zeus lies there', and that this a

---

35 This well-known episode in Heracles' life was the crime which he expiated by carrying out the twelve labours imposed on him by Eurystheus (see the notes on story 1 above). Hera hated him, of course, because he was a son of Zeus.

36 For these love affairs, see *Comm.* 4.91 and story 1 above. The recension *m* adds a cross-reference to the title and omits the text of the story.

refutation of those who say that Zeus is a god. They are refuted in that he was a man and died and lies in Crete.[37]

26

> If I catch sight of your God of Gain, God of Eloquence, your God in the Ring, I close my eyes and run past in shame at the sight, while you, for my part, may worship the vehemence of his words and his wallet. (*Sermon* 5.32)

Twenty-sixth is the story about the God of Gain.

It has already been said in the *First Oration* and it will now be repeated that the pagans say that Hermes is the patron of gain, which is why they make him hold a pouch, and the patron of eloquence and of theft. So they call him 'of gain', and 'eloquent' and 'messenger' and 'thief' and other such titles.[38]

27

> One thing alone is worthy of respect in your eyes, the honours paid by the Egyptians through a mixed crowd of men and women to the Nile ... (*Sermon* 5.32)

Twenty-seventh is the story about the honours paid to the Nile by the Egyptians.

Herodotus says nothing about this, but I read in the historian Aristaenetus, who relates that the Egyptians hold a pandemic feast to the Nile, and all, men and women alike, go round the theatres and there each man and woman feasts on what he or she has. After setting up choirs they sing the odes to the Nile which they sing to Zeus, namely that the Nile is doing the work of Zeus and watering the country. By 'honours of (a crowd of) men and women' he seems to mean the fact that all the people, men and women together, become frenzied and often even licentious, as if drunken.[39]

37 Rhea hid Zeus away in Crete (Hes. *Theog.* 468–80) to protect him from his father, Cronus (see *Comm.* 4.78 and 89 above). Call. *Hymn* 1.8–9 records that the Cretans built a tomb for Zeus (see Pfeiffer, *ad loc.*). This theme was also used by earlier Christian polemicists, such as Origen (*Against Celsus* 3.43). See Bernardi *CJ* and Lugaresi 5, *ad loc.*

38 See *Comm.* 4.90 and its notes. The recension *m* identifies the God of Gain as Hermes in the title, and rewrites the story as follows: 'They say that he is the patron of gain which is why they make him carry a pouch, and he is said to be the patron of eloquence and of theft.' Hermes was the messenger of the gods, and stole the cattle of his brother, Apollo, on the evening of the day upon which he was born (*H.H.* 4.18).

39 Such festivals in Egypt are described by Hdt. 2.60 and 62, and also by D.S. 1.36.10. Lugaresi 5 (p. 243) notes that Aristaenetus may be identified with A. of Byzantium, with reference to Jacoby, *Fragmenta Graecorum Historiorum* III, C.1, p. 158, no. 623. See story 19 above for the other interpretations Ps-N. gives to the word 'androgynous'.

28

The Isides and Mendesian Gods and Apides and all the other composite and bizarre monsters you mould or draw. (*Sermon* 5.32)

Twenty-eighth is the story about the Iseis and the Mendetes.

Isis is honoured by the Egyptians and greatly honoured. She is said to be Io, who was carried off by Zeus from Argos and changed into a cow. For they make horns on the head of the statue. And, as I said, she was one (of the gods) most honoured by the Egyptians.[40]

This is the one about the Mendesians. The Egyptians call Pan Mendes because they call a goat *mendēs*. Pan has the face of a goat. They so revere Mendes, or rather Pan, that they do not taste of goats' flesh because their god has the form of goats.[41]

The Apides are bulls venerated by the Egyptians. These used to be born long ago and were pure, and had a certain sign which showed them to be Apides. They were born at long intervals of time. When one was born, the Egyptians and certain priests, who were dedicated to this bull, would hold a great feast around the newborn bull.[42]

As for 'the drawing of bizarre and composite monsters', he (Gregory) means what I too saw in Alexandria, little statuettes with a dog's head, and sprouting next to it another of a cat, and another of a hawk. The Greeks would venerate these and draw likenesses of them. Not only did they depict that kind of thing but also other ugly creatures which the Egyptians used to venerate.[43]

---

40 Zeus fell in love with Io, the priestess of Hera in Argos, and turned her into a cow to evade the notice of Hera. She was pregnant with his child. Hera then had a gadfly drive her around the known Greek world until she came to Egypt, where she gave birth to her son and her wanderings ceased (Apollod. *Libr.* 2.1.3). Hdt. 2.40–41, notes the popularity of Isis in Egypt, and likeness between the statues of her and Io; D.S. identifies the myth of Io as the transference of Isis' cult to Greece, 1.24.8. Gr. refers to the worship of Isis with Apis, Mendes, Osiris and Sarapis in *Sermon* 34.5, and with the Nile and the others in *Poem* 2.2.7. 267–71 (Demoen, Inv. II, s.n.).

41 These customs of the Egyptians are described in Hdt. 2.42 and 46.

42 For the worship of Apis, see Hdt. 3.27–28.

43 Hdt. 2.65–76 lists the many creatures worshipped by the Egyptians. It was more usual for their animal-headed gods to have one head alone, although some composite deities are known from earlier times (G. Pinch, *Magic in Ancient Egypt*, British Museum Press, 1994, pp. 37–38, with pl. 17).

29

I laugh at your Pan and Priapus … (*Sermon* 5.32)

Twenty-ninth is the story about Pan and Priapus. The story about Pan is this.

It is said that when the suitors were visiting Penelope, the wife of Odysseus, they all had sexual intercourse with her and Pan was born. He was called Pan because he was conceived from all (*ek pantōn*) the suitors. The Egyptians say that Pan is the patron of sexual union itself, which is why they depict him with goat's legs, because the goat, which the Egyptians call *mendēs*, is promiscuous.[44]

This is the one about Priapus. It is said that after Aphrodite came up from Ethiopia she was endowed with measureless beauty, so that even Zeus himself fell in love with her. He had sexual intercourse with her and left Hera with boundless envy. So Hera, who at once foresaw the future and that her (Aphrodite's) child would be far more handsome than all the children of Zeus, took the initiative and touched Aphrodite's belly, and caused the child to be born with lewd desires. So when the child was born disfigured and the mother saw that the offspring would bring extreme reproach upon her because he was ill-formed, she took him and exposed him on a mountain. A certain shepherd came upon him, took him in and brought him up. And, because he thought his disability (that of his penis, I mean) was an indication of good harvests to come from the earth, he took him and established his worship, honouring him and naming him Priapus, which means, according to the Italians' language, 'the one who rescues from wandering those who are astray in the wilderness'. It is for that reason, then, that he is said to be honoured by the shepherds.[45]

---

44 See *Comm.* 4.40 above for the story of the birth of Pan, and Hdt. 2.46 for his cult in Egypt. The recension *m* adapts the title to 'The story about Pan and how he was begotten from Penelope and many suitors is told above', and omits this first part of the passage.

45 The statues of Priapus were ithyphallic and associated with fertility of all kinds. Syria, where the cult of Aphrodite is said by Herodotus to have originated (Hdt. 2.105), was once a part of Ethiopia (Pliny 6.182 and Tacitus, *Histories* 5.2). I discuss this passage in 'Nonnus', pp. 297–98 and n. 34, and agree with the hypothesis of Hans Herter in *De Priapo*, *Religionsgeschichtliche Versuche und Vorarbeiten* 23, Giessen, 1932, that Ps-N. introduced this version of the parentage of Priapus to explain Hera's emnity to him. He is elsewhere noted as the child of Aphrodite and Dionysus (D.S. 4.6.1; Paus. 9.31.2; *Schol.* on Ap. Rhod. 1.932) or of Aphrodite and Hermes (Hyg. *Fab.* 160). The reference to the derivation of Priapus from Italian is dismissed as 'rubbish' by the editors of the text of Ps-N. in *PG* 36 1053, n. 58. The recension *n* adds the explanation 'by magic' to Hera's action, and expands the description of the child to 'very lewd, shameful and fleshy'. The recension *m* describes the child's penis as hanging below

30

> and the gods who have mutilated themselves in madness or have been torn
> apart ... (*Sermon* 5.32)

Thirtieth is the story about the gods who are smitten and torn apart. This seems to me to be about the Titans and Dionysus. It is this.

Persephone bore Dionysus Zagreus, after conceiving him from Zeus. Once he was born, the Titans (these are an order of demons) who envied Dionysus his descent from Zeus, tore him apart. Others say that Dionysus was torn apart by the Titans at Hera's instigation.[46]

This, then, about Dionysus is about the gods who were torn apart; no story about those who were smitten occurs to us except that about the Giants. For when they wanted to fight against the gods, the gods drew up against them and went to war and smote them, and Zeus later sent a thunderbolt against them and burnt them up.[47]

---

his bottom, and then adds the following to the end of the story: 'Others say that Priapus was not the child of Zeus and Aphrodite, but of Aphrodite and Dionysus. For the statue of him is in the form of a small child, with a large and erect penis. The hierophants of their polluted mysteries say that Aphrodite is pleasure and Dionysus, drunkenness. They call that which is produced from both Priapus. For when pleasure takes part in drunkenness, it excites the body.' This last is derived from Theodoretus of Cyrrhus, *A Cure for the Afflictions of the Greeks*, ed. P. Canivet, with a French translation, *Théodoret de Cyr. Thérapeutique des maladies helléniques*, SC 57, Paris 1958, 1.112. Gr. speaks of the 'ithyphallic' children of pagan gods in *Poem* 2.2.7.104.

46 This first paragraph is completely rewritten by *m* as follows: 'This seems to me to be about the Titans and the ancient Dionysus, the child of Persephone and Zeus, whom the Titans tore apart at the instigation of Hera.' There were, in fact, two Dionysi: the first, the child of Zeus and his daughter Persephone, by his sister Demeter, the 'ancient' Dionysus or Dionysus Zagreus, was killed by the Titans (Call. *Aitia* 11, *Fr.* 43, 117, ed. Pfeiffer; Paus. 8.37.5; Clem. Al. *Exhort.* 2.17.2; Olymp. 1.3.1); the second Dionysus, the child of Zeus and Semele was the one which survived (see story 20 above). See 'Nonnus', p. 298, with notes 35–38. It is possible that Zagreus was originally not connected with Dionysus (see the most recent discussion in Gantz, p. 119). but so linked by the time of Callimachus. For the importance of the death of Dionysus in Orphic ritual and belief, see Burkert, *Greek Religion*, VI.2.3.

47 Gr. is probably referring to the castration of Cronus by Zeus, which is misunderstood by Ps-N. (as discussed in 'Nonnus', p. 293, n. 14). The recension *m* alters the second part as follows: 'About those who were smitten, he is surely talking about Cronus, whose genitals were cut off by Zeus, or about the Giants, who were smitten by the gods, and later blasted by a thunderbolt by Zeus who burnt them up.' See *Comm.* 4.78 and 89 for Zeus and Cronus and story 76 in that commentary for the wars of the gods and the Giants.

31

> but come on to your own arguments and fears, which suit not only poets but also philosophers, your Pyriphlegethons and Cocytuses and Acherons …
> (*Sermon* 5.38)

Thirty-first is the story about Cocytus and Pyriphlegethon. It is this.

When Plato was talking about the fates and final destinations of souls in the *Phaedo*, he said that those who had lived evil lives were punished in Cocytus and in Pyriphlegethon and in Tartarus. These are rivers, Cocytus being very cold, Pyriphlegethon very hot, and Tartarus a place in the middle of everything, in which there is a rising up of waters and sucking down of waters to the bottom of everything, a shadowy place without light. (He says) that the wicked are punished in that place. Acheron is a place in the middle as well, which is like a purgatory and not a place of punishment, cleansing and wiping away the sins of men.[48]

32

> … Tantalus, Tityus and Ixion. Your king … will be reckoned with these though he is not punished by thirst in marshes which come up to his chin, nor in fear, as tragedy has it, of a boulder overhanging his head, rolling back as often as it is thrust away, nor whirled around on a whistling wheel …
> (*Sermon* 5.38)

Thirty-second is the story about Tantalus, Tityus and Ixion. It is this.

Tantalus was the son of Zeus. He was granted the privilege of dining with the gods, but once privileged, he betrayed their mysteries and was punished with the following punishment for that reason. He stands in the prisons beneath the earth with a rock above him and below much water and trees covered in fruit; the rock hangs over him. So if, they say, he wants to drink of the water

---

48 This is a brief summary of Pl. *Ph.* 111c–14c, where the movement of the rivers in Tartarus (the underworld) and the nature of Tartarus are described. Within Tartarus is a fluid mass moving up and down, from which the rivers flow and into which they debouch. Pyriphlegethon is a river of fire, and Cocytus is presumed to be its opposite by Ps-N. The good dwell by the Acherusian lake into which the Acheron flows. The evil are sent to Tartarus. Some stay there for ever, but others have a chance of redemption. These are cast into Pyriphlegethon and Cocytus which circulate through the Acherusian lake, at which point they may beg for the forgiveness of those they have wronged. If this is not granted they are swept away, back into Tartarus, to circulate again and again until they are forgiven. Gr. refers to Pyriphlegethon in *Poems* 1.2.14.103, 2.1.43.29, 2.1.76.3 and *Epitaph* 40.4 (Demoen, Inv. II, s.n.).

around him, the rock falls on him in punishment. This is why he (Gregory) says that he (Tantalus) is racked by hunger and thirst, by seeing what one ought to eat and drink, but not being able to because of the rock hanging over him.

This one is about Tityus. Tityus fell in love with Leto, and in his love for her he seized her by her veil. Then Artemis and Apollo, who were Leto's children, shot arrows at him and killed him. And now, they say, he is in Hades, with the arrows fixed in him and he is punished for the above reason.

This one is about Ixion. Ixion fell in love with Hera. Hera told Zeus. As Zeus wished to know if he was in love with her, he made a cloud in Hera's likeness and stood it up. Ixion thought the cloud was Hera and had sexual intercourse with the cloud. Zeus was enraged and punished him in the following way: by stretching him out on a wheel, he made the wheel revolve continuously; and he rolls up and down continuously, in payment of this punishment.[49]

He (Gregory) says that Tantalus suffers from thirst, as we have said, 'in marshes up to his chin', because if his chin were to touch the marsh, it would dry up. Not only did the drying up act as his punishment, but also the fact that the rock hung over him and threatened to fall down upon him. As for the 'whirring on the wheel', it refers to Ixion. For he was stretched out on the wheel and revolved. 'Whirring' refers to the violent passage of the wheel.

33

nor is his liver torn by birds, never destroyed but ever regrowing, (*Sermon* 5.38)

Thirty-third is the story about the tearing of the liver by birds. It is this about Prometheus.

49 As noted by Bernardi *CJ* and Lugaresi *5* on this passage, Homer describes the punishment of Tityus and Tantalus in Hades, *Od.* 11.576–92, and Pindar, that of Ixion (*Pyth.* 2.21–41). Tityus lies supine on the ground as vultures feed on his liver, while Tantalus stands in a pool of water, which dries up whenever he seeks to quench his thirst from it. The third in this series is Sisyphus who endlessly pushes a huge stone up a hill, only to have it roll back downwards when it reaches the top. Gr. exchanges him with Ixion, possibly because Tantalus is also threatened by a huge stone in other sources, such as Pindar, *Ol.* 1.90, *Isthm.* 8.21 and others. Ps-N. alters the torments felt by Tityus to the continuing pain of the arrows which pierced his liver, and applies the following phrase about the liver 'ever-regrowing' (see story 33 below) to Prometheus. Ps-N. follows the simpler version of Apollod. *Epit.* 1.20 for the account of Ixion. Gr. refers to Ixion again in *Poem* 1.1.8.38 and Tantalus' thirst in *Epit.* 40.1 and *Ep.* 5.1 and 70.1 (Demoen, Inv. II, s.n.).

This Prometheus is said to have stolen fire from the gods and to have taken it to men, and that, in deceiving Zeus about the meat of sacrifice, he stirred him to a twofold anger. Wishing to punish him, he caused an eagle to devour his liver. By day the liver would be devoured and by night it would grow again. The eagle would come again and again until Heracles came and shot this bird with his bow.[50]

34

> we (Basil and Gregory) whom you honoured with the Cyclopean honour, saving us up for last in the persecution ... (*Sermon* 5.39)

Thirty-fourth is the story about the Cyclopean honour.

This Cyclops is said to be a robber hero and a shepherd who lived in Sicily and who had one eye. So, when Odysseus was on his wanderings after the Trojan War with his companions and came to Sicily, the Cyclops captured both Odysseus and his companions. He then ate the companions first, but in keeping Odysseus aside for last, he was unable to eat him because he ran away. He ran away by getting the Cyclops drunk, blinding him and getting out by hanging himself under the wool of a ram.[51]

35

> Let this be our pillar to you, higher and more prominent than the Pillars of Heracles. (*Sermon* 5.42)

Thirty-fifth is the story about the Pillars of Heracles. It is this.

---

50 As explained above, Ps-N. refers this to the punishment of Prometheus, whose liver was continuously devoured by an eagle by day and then grew back at night. Prometheus was first noted in Hes. *Works* 50–52 for his theft of fire, and in Hes. *Theog.* 535–55, for his deception of Zeus. Later authors, such as Hyg. *Fab.* 55 and Serv. *on Aen.* 6.595, note that Tityus' liver renews itself.

51 This is a fairly accurate account of Odysseus' escape from the Cyclops, as described in *Od.* 9, although there Odysseus escapes with most of his companions. The recension *m* provides the following text: 'After the Sicilian Cyclops in Homer had eaten Odysseus' companions, and after he had been pleased by Odysseus' gift to him of a wine wonderful to drink, he promised to give him a guest-gift and an honour in return for the wine he had drunk. This was, to eat him last of all the companions.' *Arm.* and a 14th-century addition to one manuscript also adds 'Thus the Theologian says that "Just as the Cyclops honoured Odysseus by (the promise of) eating him last, he made the same violent threat of punishment to Basil and me." And for this reason he says that "Persia avenged us."'

When Heracles got to Gadeira and could no longer go on further, for he could not cross the Ocean – for Gadeira is, as it were, an entrance from the Ocean to the Western Sea – once at Gadeira, he took pillars from the inhabitants of the place, as if both sea and land were both passable as far as them, and not beyond. The place was called the 'Pillars of Heracles'.[52]

52 According to Hdt. 4.8.2, Gadeira, or Cadiz, lay beyond the so-called 'Pillars of Heracles' (see the notes on *Comm.* 4. Intro. above, for the different meanings of *stēlē*), which were set up by Heracles to mark the boundaries of Europe and Libya (Apollod. *Libr.* 2.5.10), and were commonly held to represent the Straits of Gibraltar. Str. 3.5.5 (with Pliny 3.4), however, also speaks of pillars in the sanctuary of Heracles at Cadiz, to which Ps-N. here may refer. See Fraser's commentary on Apollod., *ad loc.*, for a full account of the two theories about the question. Both represent the ends of the known world to Ps-N., as to the scholiast on Pindar, *Ol.* 3.43. After the words 'inhabitants of the place' the second hand of *L* adds the comment: 'and set them up with the inscription: "Heracles and Dionysus came this far."'

COMMENTARY ON SERMON 39

COLLECTION AND EXPLANATION OF THE STORIES WHICH ST GREGORY MENTIONED IN THE *ORATION ON THE EPIPHANY*, WHICH BEGINS: 'AGAIN, MY JESUS'.

1

> These are not the births and thefts of Zeus, the tyrant of the Cretans, even if the Greeks are displeased; nor the shouts of the Curetes, and their rattling, and dancing in armour, hiding the sound of a wailing god, to help him escape the notice of a child-hating father; for it would be strange for the one swallowed like a stone to cry like a child. (*Sermon* 39.4 *PG* 36 337 A14–B5)

'These are not the births and thefts of Zeus, the tyrant of the Cretans.'

The theologians of the Greeks say that Zeus was born of Cronus, and, once born, was saved in the following way. Cronus, who was Rhea's husband, took and swallowed all the children she bore him. Since this happened many times in this way, Rhea remained childless. So, when she gave birth to Zeus, fearing that this baby too would be swallowed and perish, she swaddled a stone and gave it to Cronus to swallow as if it were a baby, and smuggled Zeus away to Crete. She put the Corybantes and the Curetes in charge of the baby to dance and rattle and clash their weapons, and for there to be enough noise to conceal and divert attention from the sound of the child's crying, to prevent Cronus from learning where he was hidden, seizing him and swallowing him.

So now he (Gregory) calls Cronus a 'child-hating father' and Zeus a 'crying child'. He calls the Curetes those appointed to dance with the Corybantes by Rhea. These Curetes and Corybantes are demons. He calls the Pyrrhic dance a 'dance in armour'. For they made a noise with their shields to drown the wailing of the child.[1] He said 'tyrant of the Cretans' because

---

1 Cronus had been told that he would be overcome by one of his children, and so swallowed them all as they were born. Rhea tricked him, as mentioned above, and in *Comm.* 4.78 and 88 (Hes. *Theog.* 453–91). The Curetes and Corybantes were long associated with the early days of Zeus in Crete (Eur. *Bacchae* 120–34), and the 'clashing dance' of the Curetes is described by Call. *Hymn* 2.51–53, and elsewhere. The Pyrrhic dance was a war-dance in full armour, either

while the theologians of the Greeks say that both Cronus and Zeus were gods, the common story, with which the holy Gregory also agrees, says that this Zeus was the tyrant of Crete. His subjects, then, wishing to flatter him, as he was a mortal, invented the tale that he was descended from the god Cronus and from Rhea; that is why he adds, 'even if the Greeks are displeased'. For the Greeks do not wish him to be a mortal and the tyrant of Crete, but a god.[2]

2

nor the mutilations of the Phrygians and flutes and Corybantes, and all the ravings of men about Rhea, consecrating to the mother of the gods and being initiated into such ceremonies as befit the mother of such gods as these. (*Sermon* 39.4 *PG* 36 337 B5–9)

'Nor the mutilations of the Phrygians and flutes and Corybantes.' This story is also placed among the stories of the '*Pillar-posteds*'.[3] It is this.

In Phrygia was worshipped Rhea, the mother of the gods, Zeus, Poseidon, Pluto and Hera, the mother, then, of these gods, and the wife of Cronus. Certain rites, accordingly, were held in her honour in Phrygia. And in their ecstasy and derangement those who were carrying out the initiations and those who were being initiated cut themselves with swords, without noticing that they were cutting themselves. Some others would play the double flutes, beguiling them and inciting them to mutilation. Up to the present day, too, in the mountains of Caria, some most foolish Greeks still slash themselves, in obedience to this custom.[4]

---

named after its inventor, Pyrrichus (Aristoxenus *Fr.* 46, *Fragmenta Historiorum Graecorum*, ed. C. Müller, II, p. 269; Str. 10.3.8), or because it was first danced at the funeral pyre (*pura*) of Patroclus, the friend of Achilles (Aristot. *Fr.* 519).

2 See the discussion of this point in *Comm.* 5.25 above.

3 See *Comm.* 4.5 and 59 above.

4 Many pagan practices continued in the mountain fastnesses of Asia Minor until the 5th and 6th centuries AD, as noted by F. Trombley, 'Paganism in the Greek World at the End of Antiquity: The Case of Rural Anatolia and Greece', *Harvard Theological Review* 78 (1985), pp. 334f., 344 and 349–51, and *Hellenic Religion and Christianization*, I, p. 170 and n. 318. The passage he cites on p. 171 of the latter work from Cosmas of Jerusalem (n. 319, from *PG* 38 502), however, is a quotation of the above story, and may not, therefore, reflect practices contemporary with Cosmas, who dates from the 8th century AD. S. Mitchell, *Anatolia, Land, Men and Gods in Asia Minor*, vol. II, Oxford, 1993, pp. 118–19, discusses the survival of paganism in Caria, most notably in the city of Aphrodisias. The two Asclepiodoti taught there

3

Nor have we any abduction of a maiden (Core), nor wandering of Demeter, nor her introduction of certain Celeuses and Triptolemuses and serpents, nor what she did and what she suffered. For I am ashamed to bring into daylight that ceremony of the night, and to make a sacred mystery of obscenity. Eleusis knows these things, and so do those who are eyewitnesses of what is there guarded by silence and well worthy of it. (*Sermon* 39.4 *PG* 36 337 B9–C1)

'Nor have we an abduction of Core.' This story is also placed in the '*Pillar-posteds*'.[5] It is this.

Demeter, who is said to be a goddess, bore a daughter to Zeus, whom they called both Core and Persephone. Pluto fell in love with her, and in his love carried her off and went down to Hades. Demeter then travelled around looking for Core, and, after many wanderings, she came to Attica. When she came there after she called the place to which she came Eleusis, because she had come (*elēluthenai*) there, she learnt from Keleus and Triptolemus that Core had been carried away by Pluto and was in Hades. So, once the goddess had learnt this, she ceased from her wandering. In return to the men for this favour, she gave them seeds, corn and barley and pulses. For Demeter is said to be the patron of seed-bearing crops. When she gave the seeds, she also gave them serpents and winged chariots so they could go around and give corn and barley to everyone. For humans had not yet learnt to eat bread or to make use of corn, but lived a nomadic life. Not only did she give them corn and all the seed-bearing crops, but she also initiated them in the mysteries, and taught them how they should initiate and be initiated. The rite in Eleusis takes place by night. For a temple was built there to this Demeter.

---

as pagan philosophers in the late 5th century AD (Athanassiadi, *Damascius*, pp. 348–49, where the evidence for both remaining there is summarised). C. Roueché, *Aphrodisias in Late Antiquity*, London, 1989, pp. 91–92, argues that A. the Younger left Aphrodisias and did not return. These details apart, there seem to have been influential groups of both pagans and Christians at Aphrodisias in the late 5th century AD. The many conversions effected by John of Ephesus from AD 535–565 in Asia Minor, Caria, Phrygia and Lycia and the destruction of an important pagan shrine at Daeira, near Tralles, in Caria, referred to by both Trombley and Mitchell, also indicate the survival of pagan activity (as described in John's *Historiae Ecclesiaticae*, ed. and Latin trans. E.W. Brooks, Paris, 1936, repr. Louvain, 1952, 3.36 [for the mission against the pagans and destruction of Daeira] and his *Account of the Refugees in Constantinople*, *Lives of the Eastern Saints* II, ed. and English trans. E.W. Brooks, in *PO* 18, 1924, p. 681, for the mission again, and the conversion of 80,000 pagans in Asia, Caria, Phrygia and Lydia).

5 In *Comm.* 4.67 above.

He (Gregory) said, 'On the one hand she gave benefits, and on the other, she received benefits', because of the fact that Demeter both received benefits when she heard about her daughter and ceased from her wandering, and that she granted benefits to Celeus by giving the seeds and performing the mysteries. As for the (phrase) 'Eleusis knows these things', he is speaking about the village to which Demeter came and in which she set up the mysteries. And he said, 'of those things which are guarded by silence and well worthy of it', because of the fact that there is a law which commands that none of those who were initiated and fully instructed in the mysteries should disclose the rite, but should keep it in silence and not mention it to those who were not initiates.[6]

4

Nor are these Dionysus, and a thigh in travail with a premature foetus, just as a head was previously with another; nor an androgynous god, nor a band of drunkards and an enfeebled army; nor of the folly of the Thebans in honouring him; nor of the thunderbolt of Semele which they worship. (*Sermon* 39.4 *PG* 36 337 C1–5)

'Nor are these Dionysus and a thigh in travail.'

Semele was the daughter of Cadmus, the king of Thebes. Zeus fell in love with her and had sexual intercourse with her, and stirred Hera, his wife, to jealousy and envy. Hera, then, in her jealousy, went away to Semele and said to her, 'You are completely taken in, for it is not Zeus who is sleeping with you. For when Zeus has sexual intercourse with me', she said, 'he has intercourse with me with lightnings and thunderbolts. So, if Zeus comes to you, say to him, "Have sexual intercourse with me in the same way as you do with Hera." And if he has intercourse with you with thunders and thunderbolts, it really is Zeus who is having intercourse with you. If he does it in any other way, it is not Zeus.' After Hera had made these suggestions, and Zeus came to Semele, he was asked by her to have intercourse with her in the same way as he did with Hera. Then, while he had intercourse with her amid thunderbolts, she could not endure the thunderbolts and died. So Zeus swiftly took the embryo which was in Semele, and put it into his thigh and sewed it up until it was nine months old. This was Dionysus. 'A premature

6 See *Comm.* 4.68 for the Mysteries of Demeter at Eleusis. The initiates celebrated them at night (Aristoph. *Frogs* 445–48) and all preserved a vow of silence about their content – see Hdt. 2.171, Paus. 1.38.7 et al.

foetus', then he calls this embryo which was put into the thigh. He says, 'a thigh in travail', because the thigh of Zeus was pregnant with him.[7]

He calls Dionysus himself 'an androgynous god' because he sometimes behaves like a woman, and sometimes like a man. He says the Satyrs and the Bacchae and the Silens are a 'band of drunkards'. These are demons, companions and followers of Dionysus. He also calls these very deities a 'dissolute army'; he calls them dissolute because of drunkenness. For since Dionysus is the patron of wine, it is reasonable for them to introduce the demons with him as drunkards.[8] As for 'the folly of the Thebans in honouring him', (it is) because Dionysus was a Theban by race, as he was born of Semele; for we have said that Semele was the daughter of Cadmus the Theban. He is right to say 'folly of the Thebans', since the Thebans are ridiculed for their stupidity, and there is a proverb which says, 'Boeotia is a pig'.[9] And why is the thunderbolt worshipped? Because it burnt Semele up.

As for 'Just as a head (was) previously with another (premature foetus)', it is a different story, but since it is connected to this one it itself too must be explained.

The head of Zeus became a head in travail, just as his thigh became 'a thigh in travail' when he sewed Dionysus within it. For his head once became a head in travail when he had Athena in it. For Athena is said to have been born from the head of Zeus. For Zeus felt birth-pains for her there, and, taking a blow to his head from Hephaestus with an axe, he gave birth to Athena from it.[10]

5

Nor are they the harlot mysteries of Aphrodite, who was shamefully, as they themselves say, both born and honoured. (*Sermon* 39.4 *PG* 36 337 C6–7)

Fifth is the story about Aphrodite and her shameful mysteries.

For it is said that Aphrodite had her origin from the genitals of Uranus. For Cronus, they say, the son of Uranus, took the sickle and cut off his own father's genitals and threw them into the sea. Once these genitals had fallen

---

7 In *Comm.* 5.20 above, q.v., Hera deceives Semele in the guise of her nurse, a version found elsewhere in Hyg. *Fab.* 167.2, 179.2–3.

8 See *Comm.* 5.19 above for Dionysus and his companions.

9 The Boeotians were proverbial for their rustic ways (Pindar *Ol.* 6.152, with the scholia), and this proverb is applied by Olymp. 64.b3–4, to Simmias' comment on his countrymen, as one who came from Thebes.

10 See *Comm.* 5.22 for Athena. *m* makes this story 5, and renumbers the rest in sequence.

and had attracted foam, they gave birth to Aphrodite, which is why she is called Aphrodite, since she was born from the foam (*aphros*) and the descent (*katadusis*) (sc. into the sea). This is why he says, 'shamefully ... both born and honoured'. For, in the same way, her rites and feasts are celebrated through shameful activity, luxurious indulgence and prostitution, as Aphrodite is also the patron of prostitution itself.[11]

6

Nor certain Phalli and Ithyphalli, shameful both in form and in actions; (*Sermon* 39.4 *PG* 36 337 C8–9)

Sixth is the story, 'Nor certain Phalli and Ithyphalli'. This is obvious.

At the feast of Dionysus the Greeks used to put leather phalli formed into the shape of a man's penis upon themselves in honour of the god. While they hung some of the phalli from their necks, they tied others, which they also call ithyphalli, upright to their loins, imitating an erect penis; so that of the phalli, some were 'erect phalli' and others, 'oblique phalli'. They did this in honour of the lover of Dionysus. For it is said that a young lad fell in love with Dionysus, but then, before he could gain his licentious aim, he was drowned in Lerna and died. So Dionysus, wishing to satisfy the love of the dead youth, hewed a phallus out of fig-wood and hung it around his neck, and went about like that. And in honour of Dionysus because of this, the Greeks put phalli upon themselves.[12]

7

Nor the Taurians' slaughter of strangers ... (*Sermon* 39.4 *PG* 36 337 C9–10)

Seventh is the story about the slaughter of strangers of the Taurians.

The Taurians are a Scythian people, where there was a temple to Artemis, in which Iphigeneia, the daughter of Agamemnon, was priestess. In this temple they sacrificed every visiting stranger to Artemis. We have clearly spoken about this story in the stories of the '*Pillar-posteds*'.[13]

---

11 Aphrodite's birth is also described in *Comm.* 4.88 above. In *Comm.* 5.21, *ad fin.*, she is called the patron of prostitution.

12 This passage summarises information already given in *Comm.* 4.38.

13 See *Comm.* 4.7, 57 and 94 above.

8

nor blood of Laconian ephebes shed on the altars, shed as they scourged themselves with the whips; and in this case alone use their courage badly, who honour a goddess and her a virgin. For those same people both honoured effeminacy, and worshipped boldness. (*Sermon* 39.4 *PG* 36 337 C10–340 A4)

Eighth is the story, 'the blood of the[14] Laconian ephebes on the altars'. It is this.

The Lacedaemonians, in their training in endurance, used to hold a festival in which they flogged each other. They were trained in a kind of courage as a result of this in order to be enduring in wars. The Laconians used to honour Artemis in the festival of the whips. For he says she is a virgin goddess. For she is resolute and above all cowardice and emotion.[15]

He (Gregory) says that the Lacedaemonians honoured effeminacy, either because they used to hold a certain festival – I mean the *sussitia*, that is – in which they all ate together and fared sumptuously and became effeminate, or because there they honoured the passion of paederasty, as we know about Pausanias and the Argilian, that the Argilian was once the catamite of Pausanias. As for 'They worshipped boldness', the account was about endurance and bravery.[16]

9

And where will you place the butchery of Pelops, which feasted hungry gods, that bitter and inhuman hospitality? (*Sermon* 39.5 *PG* 36 340 A7–9)

Ninth is the story about the butchery of Pelops. It is this.

14 Ps-N. adds the article here, after previously citing exactly from Gr. in his titles.

15 See *Comm.* 4.11 for these contests.

16 Ps-N. misrepresents the frugal arrangements of the adult male citizens of Sparta, who ate together regularly, each providing a set amount of rations for his mess (of 15 members) from the land tilled for him by helots until the 2nd century BC. The scholia on Plato's *Critias* 112b notes that they ate in common, and the meetings were also called *philitia*, 'because they were gatherings of friendship'. Citizens' sons were also trained in separate age groups and messed together. Paederastic relationships were institutionalised. Thuc. 1.132 states that the Spartan general Pausanias (who captured Byzantium in 478 BC, but was suspected of encouraging the helots to revolt against their masters and starved to death in the shrine in which he took refuge to evade arrest, c.470) had a trusted servant, 'the man from Argilos (a city near Amphipolis)', who was once his favourite.

Pelops was the son of Tantalus. The gods, then, once visited this Tantalus. Tantalus, then, wishing to entertain them, sacrificed his son, and cooked him and set him before them. The gods, both amazed at and filled with pity for Tantalus, collected the pieces of flesh and put Pelops together. And he came to life and was found to be alive. But, as one of the gods had eaten a part of his shoulder from the meat of Pelops, he put a segment of ivory in the shoulder when the body was put together. Pelops was restored to life like this, with an ivory shoulder. All the Pelopidae were recognised by their shoulders. For the descendants had an ivory segment in their shoulders.[17]

10

Where the horrible and dark spectres of Hecate? (*Sermon* 39.5 *PG* 36 340 A9–10)

Tenth is the story about Hecate.

The Greeks consider Hecate to be a goddess; some say she is Artemis, others, the Moon, and others that she is a certain independent goddess who appears in certain extraordinary apparitions to those who summon her; she especially appears to the accursed. Her apparitions appear as serpent-headed men, of surpassing height and size, so that their sight alone astounds and terrifies those who see them.[18]

11

and the underground puerilities and oracles of Trophonius, (*Sermon* 39.5 *PG* 36 340 A10–11)

---

17 In *Comm.* 4.4, q.v., the deity who ate of Pelops' shoulder was said to be Demeter.

18 Hecate was first known as a kindly, nurturing goddess (Hes. *Theog.* 411–52) who was later associated with the Underworld and magic (Aristoph. *Tagenistae* 500–01; Ap. Rhod. 3.861f., under the name Brimo; Theocr. 2.12, et al.). Curses appealing to her (with other chthonian deities) are known to have been composed as late as the 3rd century AD – Gager, *Curse Tablets and Binding Spells from the Ancient World*, pp. 207–08. The scholia on Ap. Rhod. 3.861 identifies Brimo as Hecate and speaks of the apparitions she sends forth. That on 3.1214–15 mentions that she is crowned with snakes. The terrifying apparition Empusa is sent by her (*Schol.* on Arist. *Frogs* 293). The scholia on the same, *Wealth* 594, also speak of offerings of food set out to her at the new moon, and associate her with the Moon goddess and with Artemis. There are several cults of Artemis Hecate in different parts of the Greek world, among other titles. See the excellent overview of the many aspects of her cult in the *OCD*, 3rd ed., by Albert Henrichs, s.n. Ps-N. elaborates on Gr.'s statement with his own adaptations of literary reminiscence. Gr. mentions her again, with her apparitions in *Poem* 2.2.7.265 (Demoen, Inv. II, s.n.).

Eleventh is the story about Trophonius. It is also placed in the (*Orations*) *against Julian.*[19] It is this.

Trophonius and Agamedes were two brothers, seers by profession. Of these, Trophonius, through vainglory, hid himself under the earth, so that in appearing to have disappeared, he might be thought to have been carried up to the gods. But having been hidden away in a certain cave, he breathed his last. Then the gods in pity on him, they say, made the spot in which he breathed his last give oracles. And they went down into the cave and, carrying out certain rites, they came up in the belief that they had received an oracle. For it is said that everyone who went down into that cave was gloomy from that time onwards.

12

or the ravings of the Dodonaean Oak, (*Sermon* 39.5 *PG* 36 340 A11–12)

Twelfth is the story about the Dodonaean Oak.

Dodona is a city in Old Epirus. In this (city) was an oak tree, in which Zeus was said to dwell and to give prophecy to those who asked for prophecies. Certain prophetic stirrings proceeded from the oak itself.[20]

13

or the sophistries of the Delphic tripod (*Sermon* 39.5 *PG* 36 340 A12)

Thirteenth is the story about the Delphic tripod.

Delphi was a city in Phocis, and Phocis a province of Greece. In this Delphi was a temple of Apollo, in which was the Pytho, (and) in which stood the bronze tripod, from which bronze tripod the oracle issued. For above the tripod was a bowl in which the oracular lots leapt and sprang whenever Apollo prophesied. It was 'three-footed' (a tripod) for this reason, because it gave prophecies about the three aspects of time. For true prophecy speaks about both those things which are past and those which are present and those

19 This summarises the information in the second part of *Comm.* 4.1.

20 Again a summary of previous information, in *Comm.* 4.20 and 5.14. The recension *m* adds 'and these were clear to the prophets at the place; for Zeus gave oracles there by means of women' to the end of the story.

which are to come.[21]

14

or the prophetic draught of Castalia? (Sermon 39.5 PG 36 340 A12–13)

Fourteenth is the story about Castalia.

This is a spring near Antioch over which Apollo used to preside. A certain oracle used to be produced in this spring, from a such flow of water, not from words. For no voice sounded forth, but simply a certain echo of both rising air and flowing water, by which certain people who stood by and understood these signs predicted the future.[22]

15

Nor is it the sacrificial art of the Magi, and their prognostication by incisions … (Sermon 39.5 PG 36 340 A14–15)

Fifteenth is the story about the sacrificial prognostication of the Magi. It is this.

The Magi made their forecasts from sacrifices, through examining the livers of victims. For as they sacrificed and cut victims up, they looked for certain signs in the cuts and in the livers and in the other parts by which they foretold the future. The Magi are a Median race, from which those who foretell the future by examining livers come.[23]

16

nor the Chaldaean astronomy and horoscopes, comparing our lives with the movement of the heavenly bodies … (Sermon 39.5 PG 36 340 A15–B2)

---

21 See *Comm.* 5.15, where the Pytho is explained as the temple of Apollo. *Syr.* translates the word as 'Pythia', and *Arm.* as 'the enquiries'. It is possibly intended to represent the inner chamber of the shrine. The last sentence refers to the description of Calchas in *Il.* 1.69–70, the 'best of seers, who knew what is, what will be and what was'.

22 Ps-N. again refers to the shrine of Apollo at Daphne near Antioch (see *Comm.* 5.16 above) rather than to that in Delphi, which was the older foundation.

23 The Magi are confused here (by Gr. as well) with the Chaldaeans who were the first to examine the livers of sacrificed victims for foretelling the future. Both the Magi and the Chaldaeans were also astronomers (see story 16 below and *Comm.* 4.70 above).

Sixteenth is the story about the astronomy of the Chaldaeans.

The Chaldaeans, of whom the first was Zoroaster and his successor Ostanes, understood the movement of the heaven and said that the fortunes of the newly born responded to such movements of the heavenly bodies. The Greeks learnt astrology from these Chaldaeans, and were the first to connect those newly born with the movement of the stars.[24]

17

> Nor are these Thracian orgies, from which the word 'worship' (*thrēskein*) is said to be derived; nor the rites and the mysteries of Orpheus, whom the Greeks admired so much for his wisdom that they devised for him a lyre which draws all things by its music. (*Sermon* 39.5 *PG* 36 340 B3–7)

Seventeenth is the story about the Thracian orgies.

It is said that the Thracians began to worship and serve god and perform rites and organise mysteries first of all mankind. *Thrēskein* (worship), that is reverence of the holy, is derived from these Thracians. And Orpheus is said, first of all the Thracians, to have introduced the rites and how they should be performed, and (to have taught) which was appropriate to which god. This Orpheus was the one who was said to have bewitched even inanimate things and to have soothed wild beasts through the sounds of his lyre.[25]

18

> Nor the torment of Mithras which is deservedly suffered by those who can endure to be initiated into such things; (*Sermon* 39.5 *PG* 36 340 B7–9)

Eighteenth is the story about the torments of Mithras.

Different people have different opinions about Mithras; for some say he is the Sun, others the patron of fire, and others a certain independent power. Certain rites are performed to this Mithras, and especially among the

24 See *Comm.* 4.70 above for Zoroaster. Both he and Ostanes were also described as Magi by D.L. 1.2. Tamsyn Barton, *Ancient Astrology*, London and New York, 1994, gives a thorough account of the Christian attitudes to astrology (attacked by Gr. in *Sermon* 5.5) and the casting of horoscopes in ch. 3.

25 The Thracian origins of divine worship and the importance of Orpheus are discussed in the notes to *Comm.* 4. 69 and 77 above. The recension *m* omits the last part of story 17, from 'and which was appropriate ... lyre.'

Chaldaeans. Those who were initiated into the rites of Mithras were initiated through a range of torments. For first they accepted the slighter ones, and then, in this way, the more severe; as, for example, first they made those to be initiated fast for fifty days, then, if it happened that they bore up well, they had them flogged for two days, then, again, they made them spend twenty days in the snow, and thus by gradually increasing the severity of the torments, if the candidate showed himself to be resolute, they finally initiated him into the full rites.[26]

19

nor the tearing apart of Osiris, another misfortune revered by the Egyptians. (*Sermon* 39.5 *PG* 36 340 B9–10)

Nineteenth is the story about the tearing apart of Osiris.

Osiris is considered to be a god by the Egyptians. Some say he is the same as Dionysus, but others that he is different from him. They say then that this Osiris was torn apart by Typhon, and that there was great grief among the Egyptians, so that they commemorated the tearing of Osiris in perpetuity. And, just as they say Dionysus was torn apart by the Titans, so was Osiris by Typhon. This Typhon is a demon.[27]

20

Nor the ill-fortunes of Isis … (*Sermon* 39.5 *PG* 36 340 B10–11)

Twentieth is the story about Isis.

Isis is considered to be the same as Io, who was carried away by Zeus. For Zeus, they say, carried Io away, and, fearing Hera, his wife, he changed Io into a heifer, sometimes into a white one, at another to a black, and at

26 See *Comm.* 4.6 above for the worship of Mithras and the value of Ps-N.'s comments.

27 The connection between Osiris and Dionysus was of long standing, due, among other reasons, to the similarity of their deaths. It was only hinted at by writers such as Herodotus because of religious scruples (Hdt. 2.61; see also Plut. 360e6–f4), but openly stated by D.S. 1.11.3. Typhon, who is also called Typhoeus in Hes. (see Gantz, pp. 48–51, for a clear description of his/their origins and history and links with Egypt), was identified with Seth, Osiris' brother and murderer, in Plutarch (as cited above) and D.S. 1.21.2f. Seth actually cut Osiris' body up, rather than having it torn apart (see 'Nonnus', p. 298 and note 35, with its reference to West, p. 160, with notes 71 and 72). The death of Dionysus is discussed in the notes to *Comm.* 5.30.

another to a violet (*iazousan*) one. And in this way he roamed around with her. Zeus then came to Egypt in his travels with Io. And the Egyptians honour Io or Isis. For this reason they carve a cow's horns on the head of her statue, signifying the girl's metamorphosis into a heifer.[28]

21

and the goats more venerable than the Mendesians, (*Sermon* 39.5 *PG* 36 340 B11–12)

Twenty-first is the story about the Mendesian goats.

In Egyptian the he-goat is called *mendēs*. Some of the Egyptians worship the he-goat, as being sacred to the power of generation. For the goat is said to be a lascivious animal. Those who dwell around the Mendesian mouth of the Nile, then, do not eat goats, through reverence of the god of fertility. They also greatly honour goatherds. There was a temple to Mendes among the Egyptians, in which temple the statue was goat-legged and had an erect member.[29]

22

and the manger of Apis, the calf that luxuriated in the folly of the people of Memphis, (*Sermon* 39.5 *PG* 36 340 B12–13)

Twenty-second is the story about the manger of Apis.

A long time ago over periods of time a bull, conceived from a moonbeam, would be born to the Egyptians. The bull would be called Apis by them. It had certain signs round its tail and tongue, and was identified as Apis by these signs. Whenever this bull was born, then, the Egyptians would hold a festival as if a god were visiting them. They would set a large amount of all kinds of food before the bull in a manger, feasting their god, Apis.[30]

---

28 See *Comm.* 5.28 for Isis and Io. Apollod. notes that she was turned into a white cow (*Libr.* 2.1.3). Io wandered around the Greek world pursued by a gadfly, sent by Hera, until she came to Egypt and bore Epaphus, her son by Zeus, and then regained her human form. Her name, Io, has a similar form to the Greek for a violet, *ion*, which may be why Ps-N. introduces the colour violet at this point.

29 Again, most of this material already occurs in a shorter form in *Comm.* 5.28 (q.v.). See Hdt. 2.48 for the statue of Pan.

30 See *Comm.* 5.28 for the worship of Apis.

23

nor all the honours with which they outrage the Nile, while themselves proclaiming it in song to be the Giver of fruits and corn (*Sermon* 39.5 *PG* 36 340 B13–C1)

Twenty-third is the story about the Nile.

They honour it as a god when it rises, and bless it as the cause of prosperity, thinking that the rising water itself is a god.[31]

24

I pass over their honours to reptiles and animals and their worship of vile things. (*Sermon* 39.6 *PG* 36 340 C4–5)

Twenty-fourth is the story that the Egyptians worshipped animals and reptiles.

They used to worship the ibis, crocodiles, snakes, cats and some species of fish, from their foolish reverence drawing disrespect upon themselves.[32]

---

31 Also described in *Comm.* 5.27 above.
32 Hdt. lists the different creatures worshipped by the Egyptians in 2.65–76.

COMMENTARY ON SERMON 43

COLLECTION AND EXPLANATION OF THE STORIES WHICH ST GREGORY MENTIONED IN THE *FUNERAL ORATION ON BASIL THE GREAT*, WHICH BEGINS: 'HE WAS THEN ABOUT TO ...'

1

the Pelopidae and Cecropidae and the Alcmaeones, the Aeacidae and the Heraclidae, and the highest of them all are of no account to me. (*Sermon* 43.3)

First is the story concerning the Pelopidae and the Cecropidae and the other names with them.

When the rhetors and sophists 'from outside' want to show that the subject of their praise is extremely well-born, they say that he traces his descent, perhaps from Pelops or Cecrops or Heracles or from one of the rest of those who are considered to be heroes or of men who have achieved fame in some other way.[1] The holy Gregory then says that the forefathers of the most holy Basil were greater and more noble than those who were considered to be noble by those 'from outside'. This then is what St Gregory means, and it must now be explained who these people such as Pelops and Cecrops and Alcmaeon and Heracles are. For it is the descendants of these who are in future called after them, the Pelopidae from Pelops, the Cecropidae from Cecrops, the Alcmaeonidae from Alcmaeon, the Heraclidae from Heracles and the Aeacidae from Aeacus.

Let us first then say who Pelops is. Pelops was the son of Tantalus, the king of Phrygia. As this Tantalus was at war with Ilus, the founder of Ilium on the Troad, and feared defeat, he enjoined his son, Pelops, to take money and depart for Epirus, with the following words: 'If I am victorious, return to

---

1 This *Sermon* in praise of Basil the Great, like *Sermon*s 4 and 5, follows the rules of rhetoric for its arrangement (see the notes to *Comm.* 4, Intro. above, and Bernardi *43*, pp. 28–32). This passage is also discussed by Bernardi *43*, *ad loc.*, n. 5. See the Intro., n. 27 above for the phrase, 'from outside', used twice in this story, for 'pagan'.

Phrygia, but, if I am defeated, stay in Europe.' So Pelops took the money and went to Greece, to the region called Apia. This region Apia had Oenomaus as king, he who had a daughter called Hippodameia. Then Pelops had a chariot race here with Oenomaus and, being victorious, he took Oenomaus' daughter Hippodameia to wife, and took possession of the region. And, instead of Apia he called it the Peloponnese, that is, the 'island (*nēsos*) of Pelops'. All the descendants of Pelops then are called the Pelopidae, such as Atreus, Thyestes, Agamemnon and Menelaus and finally Orestes.[2]

So much then concerning Pelops; that about Cecrops will now be told. Cecrops was the king of Athens, whose rule brought great benefits to Attica. He is the one who was called 'of two natures'. He was called 'of two natures' because he knew two languages, the one of Greece and the other of Egypt. For it is said that the Athenians were colonists of the Egyptians, from the city of Saïs. Cecrops then was the leader of the colony. When he came to Greece he learnt the language of Greece, being already in possession of Egyptian. The tale which tells that the Athenians were autochthonous is a myth, taking its fiction from the fact that those who dwelt in Attica had never moved, or rather been driven out. For since the country is thinly covered with soil, it was not so much coveted that the original inhabitants were driven out and replaced by others.[3]

2 See *Comm.* 4.4 and *Comm.* 39.9 for the earlier history of Pelops, and *Comm.* 5.32 for the fate of Tantalus, the wealthy king of Phrygia (Str. 15.5.28). Ps-N. explains Pelops' travels to Greece as the result of the latter's war with Ilus (D.S. 4.74.4), and gives a summary account of Pelops' successful contest with Oenomaus, king of Elis (Apollod. *Epit.* 2.2–7). The Peloponnese was also called Apia after Apis, a legendary king of Argos (Aesch. *Suppliant Women* 260; Paus. 2.5.7). Atreus and Thyestes were Pelops' sons and Agamemnon and Menelaus, his grandsons (or great-grandsons), and Orestes was the son of Agamemnon. Thyestes seduced his brother's wife, for which Atreus murdered Thyestes' sons and set them before him as a meal; then Agamemnon and Menelaus led the Greeks against Troy to regain Menelaus' wife Helen, who had fled there with Paris (see *Comm.* 4.2). While Agamemnon was away, Thyestes' son, Aegistheus, committed adultery with Agamemnon's wife, Clytemnestra, who then murdered Agamemnon on his return for sacrificing their daughter, Iphigeneia, to Artemis (*Comm.* 4.7, 57, *Comm.* 39.7 and story 3, below). Orestes then executed his mother and was pursued by the Furies for this deed (*Comm.* 4.7 above). Gr. refers to the Pelopids again in *Poem* 2.2.4.128 (Demoen, Inv. II, s.n.).

3 Cecrops, the legendary first king of Athens, was more usually described as being part-man and part-snake. He gave the Athenians their first laws and established the institution of marriage. His association with Egypt is later, found in D.S. 1.28.7 and in the scholia on Aristoph. *Wealth* 773. The latter scholion also gives other reasons for his 'double-nature', though not that found above. Malalas, too, notes he came from Egypt (*Chron.* 70–72). The scholia on Aelius Aristides (on *Panath.* 95.7) mention that the historian Charax (?1st cent. AD) describes Erechtheus as the leader of a colony from Saïs in Egypt to found Athens, who knew both Greek and Egyptian, and was thus called 'double-natured'. For the myth of Erichthonius/Erechtheus,

Enough then concerning Cecrops; the story of Alcmaeon must now be told. This Alcmaeon was an Athenian by race, and very famous, who wished to preserve the liberty of the Athenians for ever. When the city then was under the tyranny of Pisistratus, he left as he could not endure to see Athens in slavery. Once he had left, however, he schemed and kept watch as to how to restore freedom to the Athenians. He went to Delphi, then, to the temple of Apollo, and hired the temple from the Delphians. As he had hired it, and then had all the male and female servants of the god in his pay, he persuaded the priestess, the Pythia, that, if ever a Lacedaemonian came to consult the oracle, she should say no other thing to him but that 'The god bids you set the Athenians free.' As this happened constantly and most frequently, the Lacedaemonians were stirred into action and came and expelled the tyrants from Athens. So Alcmaeon achieved great glory then, for freeing Athens by his wisdom. But so much concerning Alcmaeon.[4]

Let Aeacus be the fourth to be treated by us. This Aeacus is said to be the son of Zeus, and especially just. For that reason, once, when there was no rain in Greece, the leaders of the cities came to him, asking him to pray to his father for rain. He stood and prayed, and through his prayer he ended the drought. The rains flowed, watering Greece. The piety of Aeacus was especially proved as a result of this. He then begot two sons, Peleus and Telamon, of whom, Peleus fathered Achilles and Telamon, Ajax. These were called the Aeacidae, who are, as a result of this, offered the honour won by their grandfather.[5]

---

the child of Hephaestus and Earth, and another early king of the Athenians, who had serpents for feet, see *Comm.* 5.22 above; Thucydides rationalised the myth of autochthony by explaining that Attica had never changed its inhabitants because of its poor soil (1.2.5). Gr. speaks of the Cecropids again in *Poem* 2.2.4.120–31 (Demoen, Inv. II, s.n.).

4 The Alcmaeonid, Cleisthenes, bribed the oracle at Delphi (Hdt. 5.62–66), not the founder of the family. See Fontenrose, pp. 309–10, where this passage is discussed with reference to the indirect (but earlier) sources of Q124. The event is dated to 510 BC. The first Alcmaeon was said to be a descendant of Nestor, the Homeric king of Pylos. He fled to Athens when expelled from Messenia, and gave his name to a noble family there (Paus. 2.18.7–9). It was his descendant, another Alcmaeon, who was allowed to visit his treasury by Croesus and to keep all he could carry away (see *Comm.* 4.19, for Solon's visit to the same). He so loaded himself down with treasures and gold dust that he could scarcely walk (Hdt. 6.125).

5 This description follows Isocrates 9.14 most closely, in combination with Clem. Al. *Strom.* 6.3.28. The mention of an oracle in the latter, however, with Apollod. *Libr.* 3.12.6, and others, is dismissed by Fontenrose, p. 373, on L46, as a later interpolation. Achilles, son of Peleus and Thetis (see *Comm.* 4.81 and 84 above) and Ajax, son of Telamon, were famous Greek heroes in the Trojan war. Ajax carried Achilles' body to safety after he was killed in Troy (see *Comm.* 4.9 above), but then killed himself, in shame for his madness after he was not awarded Achilles' arms.

Finally, then, Heracles is left for us. This Heracles is said to have been the son of Zeus. For Zeus put on the form of Amphitryon and had intercourse with Alcmene. And Heracles, who performed those great labours, was born. Many, then, were descended from Heracles, of whom the first was the famous Hyllus, from whom even the kings of the Lacedaemonians descended. So, all the kings of the Lacedaemonians were said to be Heraclidae.[6]

2

> You, tell me about your Elapheboluses, and Orions and Actaeons, the ill-fated hunters … (*Sermon* 43.8)

Second is the story concerning the Elapheboluses and Orion and Actaeon.

They say that Artemis is the patron of archery. This goddess then is said to shoot (*ballein*) unerringly at deer (*elaphoi*), so that Artemis is known as the goddess, shooter of deer (*elaphēbolos*).

As for Orion and Actaeon, these were also hunters. Actaeon hunted with hounds, and saw Artemis naked. This, seeing the gods naked, and especially the virgin ones, was unlawful. So Artemis in her anger made Actaeon's dogs go mad, and they found him and killed him in such a way that it was said that Actaeon was dragged down by dogs.[7]

This Orion is the constellation. He came into being as a result of the gods' urinating on the hide of the ox which was slaughtered by Hyrieus, the king of Thebes, being born at a time when he entertained the gods. Orion, then, was born in this way and, being a hunter, fell in love with Artemis. Then the goddess was angered and sent a scorpion against him. He was stung and died, and for that reason he is in the heaven with the Scorpion.[8]

6 See *Comm.* 4.3 for the birth and parentage of Heracles, and of his eldest son, Hyllus. The Dorian rulers of Sparta traced their descent from him.

7 The recension *n* rewrites this last sentence as 'So Artemis in her anger made Actaeon's dogs go mad, and they saw him as if he had the horns of a deer and seizing him, they killed him in such a way that it was said that A. was killed, dragged down by dogs.' In some versions of the story, Actaeon's dogs just go mad, as in Call. *Pallad.* 110–18 and Paus. 9.2.3 (who rejects the metamorphosis). In Apollod. *Libr.* 3.4.4, he is changed into a deer. According to this passage, the dogs were then inconsolable when they could not find their master, until Chiron (see story 4 below) made them an image of him 'which soothed their grief'. Gr. mentions Actaeon again in *Poem* 2.2.3.60–61 (Demoen, Inv. II, s.n.).

8 See Palaeph. 51 and Hyg. *Fab.* 195 for this aetiological version of Orion's birth (*ouron* is the Greek for urine). He had long been described as a constellation (*Il.* 18.486; Aratus *Phaen.* 634–46) and as a hunter (*Od.* 11.572–75). Although Ps-Erat. *Catast.* 32 states that he was the

3

> you, who wonder at myths and the substitution of a deer for a virgin ...
> (*Sermon* 43.8)

Third is the story about the substitution of the deer for the maiden, which is placed in the seventh story in the *First 'Pillar-posted' Oration against Julian*. It is this.

On the naval expedition of the Greeks from Greece against Troy, when a sacrifice to Artemis took place in Aulis in Boeotia, and Iphigeneia, the daughter of Agamemnon, was offered up for sacrifice, Artemis took pity on the maiden, snatched her away and carried her off to the Taurians in Scythia, and made a deer appear in place of the maiden, which the Greeks took and sacrificed. Iphigeneia, however, was a priestess of Artemis in Scythia.[9]

4

> not boasting of a Thessalian mountain cave, as the workshop of his virtue, nor of some braggart Centaur, the tutor of the heroes of his day; nor was he taught under such tuition to shoot hares, and run down fawns, or hunt stags, or excel in war, or in breaking colts, using the same person as teacher and horse at once; nor nourished on the fabulous marrows of stags and lions,
> (*Sermon* 43.12)

Fourth is the story concerning the Thessalian Cave. It is this.

Once Achilles was born he was given by Thetis to Chiron to have for a nurse and at the same time a teacher of archery. This Chiron was a Hippocentaur, who lived in a certain cave and grotto in Thessaly. Chiron, then, took Achilles and set him on his back, on his equine part, and trained him and taught him archery in this way, rearing him not on bread and milk, but on the marrows of deer and other wild beasts, for which reason he was called Achilles, as one who took no share (*a-*) of provender (*chilos*); for provender is sustenance.[10]

---

son of Poseidon by a daughter of Minos, king of Crete, he also adds that Orion's death was caused by Artemis' wrath (as in Palaeph., as cited above; Ps-Erat. *Catast.* 7; Call. *Hymn* 3.264–65; and Aratus *Phaen.* 634–46) with other reasons.

9 This story gives a slightly different emphasis to the material from the accounts in *Comm.* 4.7, 57 and 94 above.

10 Chiron was the 'wisest of the Centaurs' (*Il.* 11.831), and the half-brother of Zeus (Xen. *Hunting* 4). He acted as tutor to many heroes (Xen. *Hunting* 2), including Peleus, the husband of Thetis (see story 1 and *Comm.* 4.81 and 84 above for these, and Bernardi *43, ad loc.*, n. 5).

5

> of which we thought more than Gyges of the turning of his ring, if this is not
> a legend, on which depended his Lydian sovereignty; (*Sermon* 43.21)

Fifth is the story concerning the turning of the ring of Gyges. This story is
also mentioned in the '*Pillar-posteds*', in the fifty-fifth story. It is this.

In the *Republic*, Plato says that this Gyges was a shepherd, and, as he looked
after his sheep, he found a hollow bronze horse. Within this horse he found
a dead man lying, wearing a ring. He took the ring and kept it. When he
turned the bezel of the ring one way he became invisible, and when he turned
it back, people saw him again. The bezel is the eye of the ring. This one
rotated. So, with this ring, he went to the palace of the Lydians, and twisting
the bezel, became invisible, and entered and killed the king and took the
kingdom. Herodotus gives a different account about Gyges, saying that
Gyges killed Candaules and became king at the command of the queen.[11]

6

> or than Midas did of the gold through which he perished, in answer to his
> prayer that all he had might turn to gold. (*Sermon* 43.21)

Sixth is the story about Midas.

This Midas was king of Phrygia. He was a lover of money and mad after
gold, as what happened shows. He prayed, then, that whatever he touched
should turn to gold. This request, then, was granted, and whatever he
touched, by hand or mouth, became gold. Thus everything was gold for him.
But since he could not eat, he died. For the food which passed into him

---

Ps-N. follows Gr. exactly, taking up his specific reference to Achilles' upbringing (as found in
Apollod. *Libr.* 3.13.6), but giving his own derivation for the name Achilles. Apollod., q.v.,
derives it from *a cheilē*, that is, the privative *a* (= without) lips [*cheilē*] (sc. to the breast). Gr.
speaks of Chiron's wife elsewhere, in *Poems* 2.2.3.168 and 2.2.6.99 (Demoen, Inv. II, s.n.).

11 As noted in *Comm.* 4.55 above, Pl. associates this story first with an ancestor of Gyges,
rather than with Gyges himself. Both he and Hdt. (who makes no mention of the ring) link
Gyges' succession to the throne of Lydia with the queen. Pl. attributes it to the adultery with her
that Gyges was able to effect by means of the ring; Hdt. explains it by the queen's anger at the
king for allowing Gyges, the captain of his bodyguard, to see her naked. The king made him
stand behind their bedroom door so as not to be seen, but she caught sight of him as he left, and
forced him to avenge the insult by murdering the king and becoming her husband (Hdt. 1.8–12).
See *Comm.* 4.50 above for Gr.'s other references to the myth.

through his mouth turned into gold. So he died of starvation.[12]

Others recount that he received an oracle and survived. The oracle said that he should drive a chariot and stop and found a city wherever the chariot halted. He did so, and founded Ancyra in Galatia. For an anchor (*agkura*) is the iron stay of a barge, which held back the chariot and brought Midas to a stand. This is why the city was founded and called Ancyra.[13]

7

> For why should I speak of the arrow of the Hyperborean Abaris (... to whom flight through the air was not of such consequence ...) (*Sermon* 43.21)

Seventh is the story about the arrow of Abaris. Herodotus mentions this story in the Fourth Book. It is this.

Abaris was a man from the Hyperboreans. The Hyperboreans are more northerly and further inland than the Scythians. This Abaris, then, after being inspired by a god, is said to have travelled round Greece in a circle with an arrow and to have uttered certain oracles and prophecies, as one who was inspired by a god. The rhetor Lycurgus mentions Abaris in his *Oration against Menesaechmus*, saying that when a famine arose among the Hyperboreans, Abaris came to Greece, and hired himself to Apollo, and was taught how to utter oracles by him. Thus, holding the arrow as a symbol of Apollo (for this god is an archer) he travelled all round Greece, giving oracles.[14]

---

12 Ps-N. follows some of the brief information about Midas given by the scholia on Aristoph. *Wealth* 287, with no reference to the notorious ass's ears he was said to have, as described there and elsewhere. He introduces the mention of his death. Ovid, *Met.* 11.85 onwards and Hyg. *Fab.* 191 explain that Dionysus, who had granted this prayer because he had rescued his attendant, Silenus, allowed him to free himself from it by bathing in the river Pactolus. His immersion turned the waters gold in colour. Gr. refers to him again in *Poems* 1.2.10.392 and 497, in 1.2.28.148–50, 2.1.12.435, 2.1.88.13–17, and *Epigr.* 34.1 (Demoen, Inv. II, s.n.).

13 Paus. 1.4.5 notes, without giving any explanation, that the anchor discovered by Midas still existed in his time and that he had founded the city. Steph. Byz. describes how Mithradates I and his son Ariobarzanes drove some Egyptian invaders back to the coast and took the ships' anchors back as trophies to the city which they founded after the victory, and named Ancyra (s.v.).

14 Hdt. 4.36 refuses to comment ('I have nothing to say') about Abaris 'who is said to have been an Hyperborean and to have gone with his arrow all around the world without eating'. His story is known to Pind. *Fr.* 270, who is cited by Harpocration (2nd cent. AD) as dating his travels to the time of Croesus. The scholia on Aristoph. *Knights* 729 mention Abaris and his oracles, and the above reference to the *Menesaechmus* of the 4th-century BC orator Lycurgus (see Photius, *Library* cod. 268) is cited as a fragment of this work (*Lycourgi oratio in Leocratem*, ed. N.C. Comonis, Teubner, 1970, 14.5a). Ps-N. describes the arrow as a symbol

8

> or the Argive Pegasus, to whom flight through the air was not of such consequence. (*Sermon* 43.21)

Eighth is the story about Pegasus. It is clearly the one about Bellerophon.

When the Chimaera from Patara (which this holy Gregory mentioned in the '*Pillar-posteds*', in the fiftieth story) emerged and damaged the country of the Lycians, and when Proetus was king of Lycia, Bellerophon was ordered to kill the Chimaera. The beast was just as we described it there. For at the front it was a lion, at the back a serpent, and in the middle a goat (*chimaira*). Fire proceeded from this goat, and the beast was difficult to capture. Bellerophon, then, with the help of a god, found Pegasus (which was said to have wings and to drip water from its hooves), and came and killed the Chimaera, helped by the horse's power of flight, for, as I said, it had wings.[15]

9

> And if there is, or is believed to be, a river flowing with fresh water through the sea, or an animal which can dance in fire, the consumer of all things, such were we among all our comrades. (*Sermon* 43.21)

Ninth is the story about the Alpheus. It is this.

Alpheus is a river of Arcadia. Arcadia is a city of the Peloponnese. There is also a spring in the island of Sicily called Arethusa. This river, then, fell in

---

rather than the means of conveyance it is seen as by Gr. (and Iambl. *V.P.* 91). He refers to both Pegasus (see below) and Abaris' arrow in *Poem* 1.2.10.50–51 (Demoen, *Inv.* II, s.n.).

15 Proetus was the king of Argos. His wife, Stheneboea, fell in love with Bellerophon, and when he refused her advances she told her husband that he had tried to rape her. Proetus then sent him to his father-in-law, the king of Lycia, with a letter, asking him to see that Bellerophon came to grief. He was thus sent against the Chimaera in the hope that the Chimaera would kill him (*Il.* 6.155–83). Athena helped Bellerophon capture the winged horse Pegasus (Paus. 2.4.1 and the *Schol.* on Pind. *Ol.* 13.116), or Poseidon gave it to him (Eustathius, *Schol.* on Hom. *Il.* 6.155), and with the horse's help he killed the Chimaera (Pind. *Ol.* 120–29). Pegasus was so named because it was born 'beside the springs (*pēgai*) of Ocean' according to Hes. *Theog.* 280–83. Ps-N. derives the name from *pēgazein*, to gush forth. At least two fountains are said to have been created by a kick from its hoof (Paus. 2.31.9, 9.31.3). It was the child of Medusa and Poseidon, springing from a drop of her blood, when she, after intercourse with Poseidon in the form of a horse or a bird, was decapitated by Perseus (see *Comm.* 4.76 above). The recension *n* again adds that Bellerophon put a ball of lead at the end of his spear, which was melted when he flung it into the mouth of the Chimaera and caused her death, as in *Comm.* 4.50 above, *ad fin.*, q.v.

love with the spring Arethusa. In his love he passed through the sea and came up in Sicily next to the spring, without mixing in the brine of the sea, but keeping his waters pure for his beloved.[16]

After this is the story about the salamander. It is this. The salamander is an animal about the size of a lizard or a small land crocodile. The animal is so extremely cold that if it enters a fire, it quenches the flames, but is not burnt itself.[17]

10

as we ran on foot against that Lydian chariot, (*Sermon* 43.22)

Tenth is the story concerning the Lydian chariot.

This is a proverb about those who wish to compete and are not able to catch up. The proverb is 'He is running against a Lydian chariot.' The proverb is derived from Lydian chariots because they are very fast and cannot be overtaken.[18]

Others say that the proverb comes from the chariot of Pelops. For some say that Pelops was a Lydian and not a Phrygian. He then defeated Oenomaus in his own chariot, and the proverb then arose 'He is running against a Lydian chariot.'[19]

16 Arcadia is a part of the Peloponnese, not a city. The myth of Alpheus and his love for Arethusa is old, referred to by Pind. *Nem.* 1.1–2 (see the scholia *ad loc.*) and Ibycus, *Poetae Melici Graeci*, ed. Page, *Fr.* 42, and told in full in Paus. 5.7.13. It recurs in Gr. *Poems* 1.2.2.596–99, 1.2.9.22–24, 1.2.10.826, and 2.1.11.217–18 (Demoen, Inv. II, s.n.).

17 The salamander is described in much these terms in the scholia on the 3rd–2nd-century BC Nicander of Colophon's *Alexipharmaka* 537, on antidotes (see Declerck, 'Les *Commentaires Mythologiques* du Ps.Nonnus sur l'homélie XLIII de Grégoire de Nazianze', *Byz.* 47 (1977), *ad loc.*). The 1st-century AD medical writer Dioscorides notes that the belief that the salamander is impervious to fire is wrong (2.62.1). Bernardi *43* states that several mss. have drawings of the salamander and the river Alpheus on the margins of this text (*ad loc.*). The recension *n* separates this part of the story into story 10, giving 19 stories altogether.

18 This phrase is derived from Pindar, *Fr.* 243 (ed. Turyn), and is noted as a proverb in Diogenianus' collection, 6.28 (2nd cent. AD), *Corpus Paroemiographorum Graecorum*, I.

19 Pelops is said to be a Lydian in Pindar, *Ol.* 1.24. This explanation is added to the discussion of the proverb by Apostolius (15th cent. AD), *Collectio paroemiarum*, I.11.1–4, *Corpus Paroemiographorum Graecorum*, II.1. See story 1 above for the chariot race between him and Oenomaus.

11

Orestes and Pylades were nothing in their eyes; (*Sermon* 43.22)

Eleventh is the story concerning Orestes and Pylades. It is this.

This Orestes is the son of Agamemnon. He had so deep a friendship with Pylades and Pylades with him, that when Pylades died, Orestes went down to Hades with him.[20]

12

or the sons of Molione, the wonders of the Homeric scroll, celebrated for their union in misfortune, and their splendid driving, as they shared in reins and whip alike. (*Sermon* 43.22)

Twelfth is the story about the Molionidae.

Molione was a certain woman who lived in Thrace. She had two sons, the one Otus, the other, Ephialtes. Every year these grew a cubit taller and a span wider. They were violent and arrogant and reached such a pitch of insolence that they decided to rebel against the heavenly gods. They decided, accordingly, to pile Ossa on Athos, and to climb up them to heaven. Ossa and Athos are two mountains in Thrace. Zeus, then, in anger, hurled a thunderbolt and blasted them. They perished. An oracle about their destruction by a thunderbolt had been previously given to their mother, that they would be blasted by thunderbolts because of their arrogance.[21]

---

20 Pylades was the constant friend of Orestes. He accompanied him in his travels to the Taurians (see *Comm.* 4.7 above), and married his other sister, Electra. There is no known source for Ps-N.'s statement, which has long been recognised as reflecting a pun on Pylades' name (*pulē* being the Greek for a gate and *hadēs*, Hades).

21 Ps-N. does not recognise this reference to Homer, *Il.* 23.638ff., about the two sons of Molione, who may have been, from a fragment of Hes. (R. Merkelbach and M. West, *Fragmentea Hesiodea*, Oxford, 1967, *Fr.* 17) to have been 'Siamese twins' (see Gantz, pp. 424–26, for a recent discussion of this). In Homer *Il.* 23.638ff. they drive a single chariot together, one holding the reins and the other the whip. Ps-N. misidentifies them as the Aloadae (briefly mentioned in *Comm.* 4.85 above). In *Od.* 11.305–20, the latter attempted to pile the mountains Ossa on Olympus and Pelion on Ossa in their attack on the gods and were killed by Apollo. Ps-N. gives them the same fate as the Giants (Apollod. *Libr.* 1.6.2).

13

> it would be easier to emerge from the labyrinths than to escape the nets of his
> words. (*Sermon* 43.23)

Thirteenth is the story about the Labyrinth. It is this.

In the island of Crete there is a mountain in which there is a cavernous grotto
which is troublesome to descend into and difficult to come out of, into which
the Minotaur is said to have been cast. So, since it is difficult to get out of the
Labyrinth, the holy Gregory has now applied this to compelling arguments
which no one could evade, but by which they would be ensnared. For he is
referring to hunting nets. A hunting net is a kind of net made out of thick
rope which they set up in the hunting of bears, deer or other, more powerful,
animals.[22]

14

> To those who have had experience of him, Minos and Rhadamanthus were
> mere trifles, whom the Greeks thought worthy of the meadows of asphodel
> and the Elysian plains, which are their representations of our Paradise ...
> (*Sermon* 43.23)

Fourteenth is the story concerning Minos and Rhadamanthus. It is this.

Minos and Rhadamanthus are said to be the sons of Zeus, of whom Minos
was a law-giver, having received that ability from his father, and Rhadamanthus an upright judge, as having learnt justice from his father.[23] The poets,
then, and Plato himself say about these, that when they died darkness did not
receive them but the Isles of the Blest and the Plain of Elysium. The name
Elysium is as it were 'an escape' (*alusion* from *aluō*) and 'a deliverance'
(*apolusion* from *apoluō*), not of punishment. So they say that the just among

22 The first Labyrinth was a building designed by Daedalus for the imprisonment and
concealment of the Minotaur, as noted above. He was a man with the head of a bull, the son of
Pasiphaë, queen of Crete, by her adultery with a bull, sent by Poseidon to Crete. Poseidon
intended it to be sacrificed to himself, but Minos, King of Crete, kept it alive instead. Ps-N. may
also be thinking of the cavern, identified in various mountains in Crete, in which Rhea hid Zeus
away from Cronus (see *Comm.* 39.1 above, and Hes. *Theog.* 482–84). Hdt. mentions a similar
building in Egypt (2.148). Standing nets were regularly placed to block animals' escape-routes
when hunting them, as noted by Xen. *Hunting* 6.5.

23 See *Comm.* 4.44 above for Minos and *Comm.* 5.8 for Rhadamanthus. They were the
children of Zeus by Europa (*Comm.* 4.90, et al.), and judged the dead in Hades, Pl. *Gorg.* 524a.
Alusion and *apolusion* are first cited by Ps-N. – *Thesaurus*, Intro. §3.15.2.

them will take up residence there after death. As for the name asphodel, it is the name of a plant with a not unpleasing scent and a delightful flower.[24]

15

> Such was the case and his galleon was laden with all the learning attainable by the nature of man; for beyond Gadeira there is no passage. (*Sermon* 43.24)

Fifteenth is the story about Gadeira.

Gadeira is a place in the West. This place is the ending of the sea and, as it were, an outflow from our sea out to the Atlantic sea. It is said that sea is no longer navigable after Gadeira because it is full of reefs and dark. It is called Gadeira from land (*gē*) and *deira*. For the neck is called *deira*. From the fact that there is a kind of neck of land there it is called Gadeira.[25]

16

> so, after a brief stay at Athens, my longing desire made me, like the horse in Homer, to burst the bonds of those who restrained me, and prancing o'er the plains, rush to my mate. (*Sermon* 43.24)

Sixteenth is the story about the horse which broke its bonds. It is this.

The poet Homer, in wishing to express the keenness and enthusiasm for war of Diomedes, describes him by means of a comparison in the following words:

> Just as when a stabled horse, well-fed at the manger ...[26]

---

24 For Elysium and the Isles of the Blest, see *Comm.* 5.8 above. Homer speaks of the 'meadow filled with asphodel' in Hades (*Od.* 11.539). The asphodel is a member of the lily family and grows wild and profusely in Greece. The recension *n* adds 'and it has a useful root' to the end of the story. It was used in medicine, Diosc. 2.291, and *Schol.* to Hes. *Works*, 41.

25 See *Comm.* 5.35 for the literary significance of Gadeira, or Cadiz, the port of which lay on the long narrow island of Erytheia off the coast of Spain. Steph. Byz. also speaks of its situation in this way (s.v.).

26 The full citation has more relevance to Gr.'s words. It continues, 'breaks his halter and gallops over the plain in triumph to his usual bathing place in the fairflowing river'. The simile occurs twice, in *Il.* 6.506–08, and 15.263–65, but describes Hector and Paris, respectively. Cosmas of Jerusalem notes this error, when he makes use of the story in *PG* 38 614.

17

> but a prelate is easily found, without laborious training, with a reputation of recent date, being sown and springing up in a moment, as in the legend of the giants. We manufacture those who are holy in a day, and bid those to be wise who have had no instruction ... (*Sermon* 43.26)

Seventeenth is the story about the giants[27] who were sown and sprang up on the same day. It is this.

It is said in Thebes of Boeotia that Cadmus, or someone else, sowed the teeth of the Delphinian dragon in the earth. And armed men were produced. They were produced from the thighs upwards, and they stood like that and fought with each other and the others.[28]

18

> Why should I compare with this work (the refuge for the poor and sick built by St Basil at the gates of Caesarea) Thebes of the seven portals, and the Egyptian Thebes, and the Walls of Babylon, and the Carian tomb of Mausolus, and the Pyramids, and the immeasurable bronze of the Colossus, or the size and beauty of shrines that no longer exist, and all the other objects of men's wonder and historic record. (*Sermon* 43.63)

Eighteenth is the story concerning seven-gated Thebes and that of the Egyptians. It is this.

The holy Gregory intends to tell us about the wonders[29] here. Seven-gated Thebes is that of Greece, the one which was founded by Amphion and

---

27 Ps-N. repeats Gr.'s text, but does not explain the reference to giants. Earth bore the giants when sprinkled with the drops of blood from Cronus' severed genitals (see *Comm.* 4.88 above). A later scholion to Euripides' *Phoenician Women* 5, however, speaks of 'giants' sprouting from the dragon's teeth once they had been sowed by Cadmus (Creuzer, *Meletemata, ad loc.*).

28 Both Cadmus and Jason (whom a part of the recension *n* mentions after Cadmus) sowed teeth from the same serpent, either the one who guarded a spring in Boeotia or that of Castalia at Delphi (for its Boeotian origins, see Euripides, *Phoenician Women* 931–32; Ap. Rhod. 3.1176–80; for the other, Hyg. *Fab.* 178.5), Cadmus in Thebes and Jason in Colchis, on his quest for the golden fleece. Five of the earth-born survived in Boeotia, from whom the kings of Thebes were to descend; all the earth-born died in Colchis, either at each others' or at Jason's hands. The same group of manuscripts adds 'The story about Jason is told by Apollonius.'

29 Lists of the 'Wonders' or 'Sights' of the world were established by the 2nd century BC, though they did not all concur in detail. They were usually seven in number. Gr. adds the two cities of Thebes here (as good comparisons with Basil's city of hostels) and omits the Hanging Gardens of Babylon. His other items, the walls of Babylon, the tomb of Mausolus, the pyramids, the Colossus and at least one temple are found elsewhere. The city of Thebes in Greece was only

Zethes with a lyre. The Egyptian Thebes is that of a hundred gates. It was very large a long time ago, so large indeed that it had a hundred gates.

The Walls of Babylon are said to be extremely strong. For they were built of baked brick and dissolved limestone, with a great width and length and a great circumference.

The tomb of Mausolus the Carian is itself also very big. For Mausolus was the tyrant of Caria who established a tomb at great expense on a mound lying within a marshy lake. It is called a 'Carian tomb' as a possessive. It is also called 'Carian' because it was the race of Mausolus the Carian.[30]

The Pyramids are themselves worthy of viewing, and were built in Egypt at great expense. The Christians say they are the granaries of Joseph, but the Greeks, among whom is Herodotus,[31] that they are the tombs of certain kings.

As for the Colossus in Rhodes, he says that it is a very large statue and worthy of admiration.[32]

---

previously listed as a wonder by Pliny, *N.H.* 10.36. Ps-N. does not commit himself to a number, nor does he recognise the references to the temple of Diana at Ephesus or of Zeus at Olympia.

30 For Amphion and Zethes see *Od.* 11.260–65, and Ap. Rhod. 1.735–41, with Apollod. *Libr.* 3.5.5 and others. Zethes toiled at carrying the stones to build the walls: Amphion played his lyre, and the stones piled themselves up to the sound. Hundred-gated Thebes is mentioned in the *Iliad*, 9.381–83, and the walls of Babylon are described by Hdt. 1.178–79. They were so wide that a four-horse chariot could turn within their width. The tomb of Mausolus was built from 367–351 BC (and finished after his death by his wife Artemisia). Pausanias notes its size and beauty and that the Romans adopted the term 'mausoleum' for their own great tombs (8.16.4). The pyramids – *puramides* – (of Memphis) are first mentioned by Hdt. 2.8, and the building of some of them is described in 2.124–27. They were thought to be granaries by the Christians because of Joseph's well-known action to prevent famine and because the Greek for 'wheat' is *puros*. Ps-N. uses a Latin loan-word 'horreum' for 'granary' here. Another etymology in Pl. *Tim.* 56b relates the name to the pointed shape of a flame (*stoicheion puros*, an element 'of fire', LSJ s.v.). The Colossus of Rhodes was a bronze statue of Apollo and stood 105 feet high. It was felled in an earthquake (Str. 14.2.5). It was made at the end of the 4th century BC by the sculptor Chares, and collapsed in the next. All the Greek and Latin texts listing the wonders are collected, printed and edited by K. Broderson, *Reiseführer zu den Sieben Weltwundern*, Insel Taschenbuch 1392, 1992. For text of Ps-N. above (item 12) he uses manuscripts from different and later parts of the Greek tradition. Another list of the 'Wonders' by Gr. is quite allusive, see *Epigr.* 50.1–3: 'a wall, a statue, gardens, pyramids, a temple, a statue, a tomb'.

31 The recension *n* then adds: 'It is probable that after the time of Joseph and the exodus of Israel that the Greeks made them the tombs of kings'.

32 One part of the recension *n*, *y* then continues: 'So, quickly summing up what they (the pagans) call the seven Wonders, he says that they are as nothing in comparison with the hostels which St Basil built. And even now outside Caesarea, near the Argennon, appear the so-called Basileiae, about which the holy Gregory says in his Funeral Oration on him, "Go forth a little way from the city and behold the new city, etc."'

APPENDIX 1

ADDITIONAL STORIES FOUND IN SOME WITNESSES AT THE END OF *COMMENTARY* 5[1]

36[2]

Thirty-sixth is the story about Actaeon; it is this.

Actaeon was a hunter; he saw Artemis naked. It was not lawful to see the virgin goddesses naked. So Artemis, in anger, made Actaeon's dogs go mad and they killed him. Actaeon was then killed by his own dogs.

37

Thirty-seventh is the story about Orion; it is this.

A certain Hyrieus was a king of Boeotia. The gods, who wanted to see if men were hospitable to strangers, came to him in order to be entertained by him. He received them and sacrificed an ox and feasted them. So after the feast the gods went out and saw the hide of the slaughtered ox lying on the ground. They urinated upon it and created Orion from the urine and the ox-hide. When he grew up he fell in love with Artemis. She sent a scorpion against him, and he died, stung in the ankle. So the gods took pity on him and established him in stars in the sky with the Scorpion.[3]

---

1 These additional stories are from different parts of the Greek, Syriac and Armenian traditions. They appear, in various combinations, at the end of *Comm.* 5, but have no links at all with the text of *Sermon* 5.

2 These two stories are found in *Syr.* and the recension *n*.

3 The recension *m* combines the titles of 36 and 37 into one (36) and adds a reference to *Comm.* 43.2, completely omitting their texts. It then adds the following story: 'About the phallus of Osiris or Dionysus who was torn apart by Typhon.

'They say that his sister Isis gathered his limbs together with much hard work, but could not find his phallus. She made a copy of the phallus because of this and ordered it to be worshipped by everyone. There used to be a festival among the Greeks, then, which they called the Phalla-gogia.' (See *Comm.* 5.30 and *Comm.* 39.19 for the death of Osiris/Dionysus. Isis was Osiris' sister and wife. She brought his body back to life to be impregnated by it with their son, Horus.)

38[4]

Thirty-eighth (is) the (one) about Adonis and Aphrodite.

Myrrha was the daughter of Cinyras. She slept with her own father and conceived a child from him. In deep shame and not enduring her guilt, she exposed the child, once it was born, on a mountain. The so-called nymphs, whom they call the 'Mountain Nymphs', brought him up. He was handsome in appearance; and he became a hunter. Aphrodite, a wanton little woman, fell in love with him. Her lover, Ares, in jealousy of him, turned himself into a boar and killed him. Aphrodite grieved and was possessed by complete mourning. As she could not bear her love she went down to Hades in search of her beloved. She asked Pluto to give him to her. Persephone, his wife, hindered the request, because she was greatly taken with Adonis. As Aphrodite did not yield in her request, they decided to divide his company between themselves, and that the one should have it for half the year on earth and the other for half the year in Hades.[5] Aphrodite then assented to this and told her worshippers that Adonis had come back to life, so that they should celebrate festivals, giving up their mourning and their groans. It is a race beyond the Ethiopians who worship this little woman with some care. So they wrote letters and sent them out to sea in a pot after certain rites. This pot turned up of its own accord in Byblos in Palestine, and when Aphrodite's fellow-worshippers there received it, they held a feast, rejoicing together with their so-called goddess, who had found her lover. And (from) the letters: They recognised them and said it was what Isaiah the prophet says: he who sends out papyrus letters into the sea as pledges (that is as securities for their love).[6] For by means of the letters it told those who were mourning for Adonis that he had come to life. Those from Israel took over this drama and grieved for Tammuz; for that is what Adonis was called by them.[7]

4 Stories 38, 39 and 40 are found in *Syr.*, *Arm.* and in a 14th-century addition to one Greek ms., *F.* Their Greek text, like that of 36 and 37 above, is edited by J. Declerck, 'Five unedited Greek scholia of Pseudo-Nonnos', *L'Antiquité Classique* 45 (1976), pp. 183–86, and reproduced in the edition of the *Commentaries*, pp. 268–72, by the author's kind permission.

5 Several versions of the parentage of Adonis are given in Apollod. *Libr.* 3.14.4. This, as noted by the editor, is found in Hyg. *Fab.* 58. Apollod. makes Zeus the arbiter of the dispute, but, although he mentions that Adonis was killed by a boar while out hunting, he makes no reference to Ares (see *Comm.* 4.43 above).

6 Isa. 18.1–2 (Revised Version) reads as follows: 'Ah, the land … beyond the rivers of Ethiopia: that sendeth ambassadors by the sea, even in vessels of papyrus upon the waters, saying …'

7 Ezek. 8.14–15, of Ezekiel's vision: 'Then he brought me to the door of the gate of the Lord's house which was towards the north; and, behold, there sat the women weeping for

39

Thirty-ninth (is) the (one) concerning Pandion.

Pandion was the king of (the) Athenians. As he was at war against the Lacedaemonians he persuaded Tereus to be his ally; he was a tyrant of the Thracians. But he said he would not be an ally unless he first promised his elder daughter to him in marriage. For Pandion had two daughters, Procne and Philomela, who loved each other so much that they both decided that whatever catastrophe the one suffered, the other would voluntarily inflict the same upon herself. So he promised Procne to Tereus … He took her home and had children by her. After much time had gone by, she (Procne) longed to see her own sister and asked her husband to go to Athens and bring her sister. So he went and with Pandion's permission he took Philomela, the other sister, as well. But on the way, he, like the barbarian he was, became drunk and raped the girl. In shame at his deed, he cut out Philomela's tongue so she could not speak about the lawless deed and abandoned her beside the road. But, as she was a Greek woman and practised in the finest weaving, she wove a robe and depicted the event within it, and sent it to her sister. Once she realised what had happened, she took her sister in; but, taking the child she had had by Tereus, she cut him up and cooked him and set him before her husband on his return from hunting. He realised what had been done, and, mad with rage, he pursued her and her sister. So Zeus, in pity for them, changed the former into a swallow and the other into a nightingale, and in this way they ended the chase.[8]

40

Fortieth (is) the (one) concerning Priapus.

This idol is in the form of a little child, with a larger penis fitted on him than

---

Tammuz.' Brock (q.v. *ad loc.*) has identified material very similar to 38 in the commentaries of Cyril of Alexandria, *PG* 70 440–44 and Procopius of Gaza, *PG* 86 2137, on this passage on Isaiah. Some phrases in 38 are similar to those used by Cyril in his descriptions of Aphrodite and the Nymphs, which may indicate a common source.

   8 This account of the story of Pandion, Procne and Philomela follows Apollod. *Libr.* 3.148 in outline, which was probably derived from Sophocles' lost play *Tereus*. In Apollodorus, however, Procne becomes a nightingale and Philomela a swallow. Hyg. *Fab.* 45 makes the swallow Itys' mother, as above. See Gantz, pp. 239–41, for a full discussion of the sources. Tereus is usually turned into a hoopoe, or a hawk.

is appropriate to his age, which they call a phallus. The pagans tell the myth that he is the son of Dionysus and Aphrodite; and those who know the mysteries of these say that this is born through pleasure and drunkenness, which is why they name him Priapus. For when someone is overcome by drink and pleasure, he has an erect penis.[9]

9 See *Comm.* 5.29 above for the alternative parentage of Priapus. Material similar to the above is found in the recension *m*, as described in the notes to that story, and derived from Theodoretus of Cyrrhus, *A Cure for the Afflictions of the Greeks*, 1.112–13. *Syr.* translates the final phrase as 'a man becomes a pagan'.

APPENDIX 2

STORIES LISTED IN ORDER OF APPEARANCE IN THE *COMMENTARIES*

Numbers in parentheses denote *Sermon* and chapter for each story.

4.   Intro. Nature of a 'Pillar-posted' oration (*Sermon* 4, Title)
4.1   Empedocles, Aristaeus, Empedotimus, Trophonius (4.59)
4.2   Proteus, Paris and Helen (4.62)
4.3   Pyre of Heracles (4.70)
4.4   Butchery of Pelops (4.70)
4.5   Cult of Rhea in Phrygia (4.70)
4.6   Torments of Mithras (4.70)
4.7   Slaughter of strangers among the Taurians (4.70)
4.8   Sacrifice of the royal maiden (Polyxena) (4.70)
4.9   Self-sacrifice of Menoeceus (4.70)
4.10   Deaths of daughters of Scedasus (4.70)
4.11   Cult of Artemis in Sparta (4.70)
4.12   Slaughter of strangers among Taurians (4.70)
4.13   Hemlock of Socrates (4.70)
4.14   Leg of Epictetus (4.70)
4.15   Anaxarchus in the mortar (4.70)
4.16   Leap of Cleombrotus (4.70)
4.17   Pythagorean precept against beans (4.70)
4.18   Theano's contempt for death (4.70)
4.19   Endurance of Epaminondas and Scipio (4.71)
4.20   Selli (4.71)
4.21   Insatiability of Solon (4.72)
4.22   Socrates' love of beauty (4.72)
4.23   Plato's greed (4.72)
4.24   Epicurism of Xenocrates (4.72)
4.25   Banter of Diogenes (4.72)
4.26   Dweller in the tub (4.72)
4.27   Epicurus (4.72)
4.28   Crates (4.72)

4.29   Threadbare cloak (4.72)
4.30   Antisthenes (4.72)
4.31   Philosopher in the sun (4.72)
4.32   Potidaea (4.72)
4.33   Arcadian riddle (4.72)
4.34   Aristotle and the Euripus (4.72)
4.35   Well of Cleanthes (4.72)
4.36   Strap of Anaxagoras (4.72)
4.37   Heraclitus and Democritus (4.72)
4.38   Phallic cult of Dionysus (4.77)
4.39   Buttockless and Black-buttocked (4.77)
4.40   Begetting of Pan (4.77)
4.41   Heracles the Bull-eater (4.77)
4.42   Heracles the Three-Evening-One and the daughters of Thestius (4.77)
4.43   Julian the Idolian, Pisaean and Bull-burner (4.77)
4.44   Fox in a lion's skin (4.79)
4.45   Melampus and Proteus (4.82)
4.46   Mt Etna (4.85)
4.47   Torments of Mithras (4.89)
4.48   Cruelty of Echetus and Phalaris (4.91)
4.49   Hydra (4.94)
4.50   Chimaera (4.94)
4.51   Cerberus (4.94)
4.52   Scylla (4.94)
4.53   Charybdis (4.94)
4.54   Helmet of Hades (4.94)
4.55   Ring of Gyges (4.94)
4.56   Bull-eater in Lindos (4.103)
4.57   Cult of Artemis among the Taurians (4.103)
4.58   Cult of Artemis in Sparta (4.103)
4.59   Cult of Rhea in Phrygia (4.103)
4.60   Cynosarges (4.105)
4.61   Xanthus and Chalcis (4.106)
4.62   Palamedes (4.107)
4.63   Jackdaw and its feathers (4.107)
4.64   Discovery of poetry (4.108)
4.65   Discovery of metal-working (4.108)
4.66   Discovery of purple dye (4.108)

5.7   Ebb and flow of the tides (5.20)
5.8   Elysium and Rhadamanthus (5.20)
5.9   Julian's feasts (5.20)
5.10   Athena and the flutes (5.22)
5.11   Greedy and deceitful demons (5.31)
5.12   Triptolemus, Celeus and the serpents (5.31)
5.13   Orpheus the theologian (5.31)
5.14   Dodonaean oak and cauldron (5.32)
5.15   Pythian oracle (5.32)
5.16   Castalian spring (at Antioch) (5.32)
5.17   Speechless statue (5.32)
5.18   Daphne (5.32)
5.19   Dionysus and his rout; the phallus (5.32)
5.20   Semele and the thunderbolt (5.32)
5.21   Hephaestus, Ares and Aphrodite (5.32)
5.22   Athena, though virgin, bears a serpent (5.32)
5.23   Madness of Heracles (5.32)
5.24   Amours of Zeus (5.32)
5.25   Tomb of Zeus (5.32)
5.26   Titles of God of Gain (5.32)
5.27   Nile worship (5.32)
5.28   Cult of Isis, Mendes, Apis and other animals in Egypt (5.32)
5.29   Pan and Priapus (5.32)
5.30   Gods who were smitten or torn apart (5.32)
5.31   Rivers in Hades (5.38)
5.32   Punishments of Tantalus, Tityus and Ixion (5.38)
5.33   Punishment of Prometheus (5.38 – refers to Tityus)
5.34   Odysseus and the Cyclops (5.39)
5.35   Pillars of Heracles (5.42)

39.1   Birth of Zeus (*Sermon* 39.4)
39.2   Cult of Rhea in Phrygia (39.4)
39.3   Demeter, Core/Persephone and Eleusinian Mysteries (39.4)
39.4   Births of Dionysus and Athena (39.4)
39.5   Birth of Aphrodite (39.4)
39.6   Phallic cult of Dionysus (39.4)
39.7   Slaughter of strangers among the Taurians (39.4)
39.8   Cult of Artemis in Sparta (39.4)
39.9   Butchery of Pelops (39.5)

SELECT BIBLIOGRAPHY

PRIMARY TEXTS

Unless otherwise stated, the texts and translations are to be found in the Loeb Classical Library.

Aelian, *On the Characteristics of Animals*, Eng. trans. A.F. Schofield, 3 vols, 1958–59

——, *Historical Miscellany*, ed. N. Wilson, 1997

Agathias, *Historiae*, ed. R. Keydell, *Agathiae Myrinaei historiarum libri quinque (Corpus fontium historiae byzantinae 2. Series Berolinensis)*, Berlin, 1967; Eng. trans. J.D.C. Frendo, Berlin and New York, 1975

Anonymous Prolegomena to Platonic Philosophy, ed. and Eng. trans. L.G. Westerink, Amsterdam, 1962

Apollodorus, *The Library, Epitome*, Eng. trans. J.G. Frazer, 2 vols, 1921

Apollonius Rhodius, *Argonautica*, Eng. trans. R.C. Seaton, 1912

——, *Scholia in Apollonii Rhodii Argonautica* (scholia vetera), ed. K. Wendel, Berlin, 1935 (repr. 1970)

Aratus, *Phaenomena*, Eng. trans. G.R. Mair, in *Callimachus and Lycophron*, 1921

Aristophanes, Fragments: *Poetae Comici graeci* 3.2, ed. R. Kassel and C. Austin, Berlin, 1984

——, Plays: Eng. trans. J. Henderson, 3 vols, 1998, 2000

——, *Scholia graeca in Aristophanem*, ed. Fr. Dübner, Paris, 1883

Aristotle, *Nicomachaean Ethics*, Eng. trans. H. Rackham, 1926

——, *Politics*, Eng. trans. H. Rackham, 1932

Arrian, *Anabasis of Alexander*, Eng. trans. P.A. Brunt, 2 vols, 1976, 1983

Athenaeus, *The Deipnosophists*, Eng. trans. C. Burton Gulick, 7 vols, 1927–41

Augustine, *City of God*, Eng. trans. Henry Bettenson, Harmondsworth, 1972

Basil of Caesarea, *On the Value of Greek Literature*, ed. N.G. Wilson, London, 1975; Eng. trans. Roy J. Deferrari and M.R.P. McGuire, in *St. Basil, Letters*, vol. 4, 1934

Callimachus, Fragments: *Callimachus*, ed. R. Pfeiffer, vol. 1, Oxford, 1949

——, Hymns and Epigrams 1–60: *Callimachus*, ed. R. Pfeiffer, vol. 2,

Oxford, 1953; Eng. trans. of Hymns, A.W. Mair, *Callimachus and Lycophron*, 1921

Cicero, *On Divination*, Eng. trans. W.A. Falconer, 29 vols, vol. 20, 1923

——, *Tusculan Disputations*, trans. J.E. King, vol. 18, 1927

Clement of Alexandria, *The Exhortation to the Greeks*, Eng. trans. G.W. Butterworth, 1919

Cosmas of Jerusalem, *Commentarii in Gregorii Nazianzeni Carmina*, PG 38, ed. J.-P. Migne, Paris, 1862

Damascius, *The Philosophical History*, Eng. trans. P. Athanassiadi, Apameia Cultural Association, 1999

Demosthenes, *Orations*, Eng. trans. J.H. Vince (vols 1–3), A.T. Murray (vols 4–6) and N.W. De Witt and N.J. De Witt (vol. 7), 7 vols, 1926–49

——, *Scholia Demosthenica*, ed. M.R. Dilts, 2 vols, Leipzig, 1983, 1986

Diodorus Siculus, *Library of History*, Eng. trans. C.H. Oldfather (vols 1–6), C.L. Sherman (vol. 7), C. Bradford Wells (vol. 8), Russell M. Geer (vols 9–12), 12 vols, 1933–67

Diogenes Laertius, *Lives of the Philosophers*, Eng. trans. R.D. Hicks, 2 vols, 1925

Dioscorides, *De materia medica*, ed. M. Wellmann, *Pedanii Dioscuridis Anazarbei de materia medica libri quinque*, 3 vols, Berlin, 1907, 1906, 1914, repr. 1958; Eng. trans., *The Greek Herbal of Dioscorides, illustrated by a Byzantine AD 512, Englished by John Goodyer AD 1655: edited and first printed, AD 1933, by R.T. Gunther*, Oxford, 1934

Elias of Crete, *Commentarii in Gregorii Nazianzeni Orationes III et IV* (sc. IV and V) in *Sancti Patris nostri Gregorii Nazianzeni opera*, vol. II, ed. J. de Billy, Paris, 1583, repr. 1630 (in a Latin translation)

Epictetus, *Discourses*, Eng. trans. W.A. Oldfather, 1925

Pseudo-Eratosthenes, *Catasterismi: Pseudo-Eratostheni catasterismi* (*Mythographi Graeci* 3.1), Leipzig, 1897; Eng. trans. Theony Condos, *Star Myths of the Greeks and Romans: A Sourcebook*, Michigan, 1997

Etymologicum Magnum seu verius Lexicon, ed. T. Gaisford, Oxford, 1848

Euripides, *Plays*, Eng. trans. D. Kovacs, 4 vols, 1994–99 (2 vols in preparation)

——, *Scholia in Euripidem*, ed. W. Dindorf, 4 vols, Oxford, 1863; ed. E. Schwarz, 2 vols, Berlin 1887, 1891

Gregory of Nazianzus, *Sermons* 4 and 5: *Grégoire de Nazianze. Contre Julien. Discours 4–5*, ed. and Fr. trans. J. Bernardi, SC 309, Paris, 1983; Eng. trans. C.W. King, *Julian the Emperor, containing Gregory Nazianzen's two invectives and Libanios' monody, with Julian's extant theosophical works*, Bohn's Classical Library, London, 1888

——, *Sermon* 39: *Oratio* XXXIX, *In Sancta Lumina PG* 36 335–60; Eng. trans. C.G. Browne and J.E. Swallow, *Select Orations of Saint Gregory Nazianzen*, in *A Select Library of the Nicene and Post-Nicene Fathers of the Christian Church*, ed. Henry Wace and Philip Schaff, Oxford and New York, 1894, repr. 1996, vol. 7, pp. 352–59

——, *Sermon* 43: *Grégoire de Nazianze, Discours 42–43*, ed. and Fr. trans. J. Bernardi, SC 384, Paris, 1992; Eng. trans. C.G. Browne and J.E. Swallow, *Select Orations of Saint Gregory Nazianzen* (cited above), pp. 395–422; *Sermons* 39 and 43 are also translated into English in *Funeral Orations by Gregory of Nazianzus and Ambrose*, ed. L.P. McCauley et al., Washington, 1968

——, *Sermons* 1, 2, 3, 7, 8, 12, 16, 18, 21, 27–31, 33, 34, 37–43 and 45, Eng. trans. in *A Select Library of the Nicene and Post-Nicene Fathers*, vol. 7, cited above; *Sermons* 27–31 are translated into English by L. Wickham and F. Williams in F.W. Norris, *Faith gives Fullness to Reasoning*, Leiden, 1991

——, *Poems*, Latin trans., *PG* 37 397–1600; *Poems* 1.1.1–5, 7–9, Eng. trans. D.A. Dykes, *St Gregory of Nazianzus Poemata Arcana*, ed. C. Moreschini, Oxford, 1997; *Poems* 1.2.9 and 10, Ger. trans. M. Kertsch, *Gregor von Nazianz: Carmina de Virtute 1a/1b*, ed. R. Palla, Graz, 1985; *Poems* 2.1.39, 2.1.11, 2.1.19, 2.1.34 and 2.1.92, Eng. trans. C. White, *Gregory of Nazianzus, Autobiographical Poems*, Cambridge, 1996; *Poem* 1.2.10, It. trans. C. Crimi, *Gregorio Nazianzeno, Sulla virtù, Introduzione, testo critico e traduzione di C. Crimi, commentario di M. Kertsch*, Pisa, 1995

——, *Epigrams*, Eng. trans. W.R. Paton, *Greek Anthology*, Book 8, *The Epigrams of St Gregory the Theologian*, 1917

——, *Epitaphs*, Latin trans., *PG* 38 col. 11–82

——, *Epistles*, *Gregor von Nazianz. Briefe*, ed. Paul Gallay, Berlin, 1969

Herodotus, *Histories*, Eng. trans. A.D. Godley, 4 vols, 1920–24

Hesiod, *Theogony, Works and Days, Shield of Herakles*, Eng. trans. Hugh G. Evelyn-White, *Hesiod, Homeric Hymns, Epic Cycle. Homerica*, 1914

——, *Scholia in opera et dies* (scholia vetera), ed. A. Pertusi, *Scholia vetera in Hesiodi opera et dies*, Milan, 1955

Hesychius, *Lexicon*: *Hesychii Alexandrini lexicon*, ed. K. Latte, vols 1–2, Copenhagen, 1966; ed. M. Schmidt, vols 3–4, Halle, 1861, 1862, repr. Amsterdam, 1965

Homer, *Iliad*, Eng. trans. A.T. Murray, 2 vols, 1924, 1925; rev. edn William F. Wyatt, 1999

——, *Scholia in Iliadem* (scholia vetera), ed. H. Erbse, *Scholia Graeca in Homeri Iliadem* (*scholia vetera*), vols 1–5 and 7, Berlin, 1969, 1971, 1974, 1975, 1977, 1988

——, *Odyssey*, Eng. trans. A.T. Murray, 2 vols, 1919; rev. edn George E. Dimock, 1995

——, *Hymns*, Eng. trans. Hugh G. Evelyn-White, *Hesiod, Homeric Hymns, Epic Cycle. Homerica*, 1914

Hyginus, *De Astronomia*: *Hygin: L'Astronomie*, ed. and Fr. trans. A. Le Boeuffle, Paris, 1983; Eng. trans. Theony Condos, *Star Myths of the Greeks and Romans: A Sourcebook*, Michigan, 1997

——, *Fabulae*: *Hygin: Fables*, ed. and Fr. trans. Jean-Yves Boriaud, Paris, 1997

Iamblichus, *De Vita Pythagorica*: *Iamblichi de vita Pythagorica*, ed. U. Klein (post L. Deubner), Leipzig, 1937, repr. Stuttgart, 1975; Eng. trans. Gillian Clark, *Iamblichus: On the Pythagorean Life*, Liverpool, 1989

Jerome, *Select Letters*, Eng. trans. F.A. Wright, 1933

Lucian, *Works*, Eng. trans. A.M. Harmon (vols 1–5), K. Kilburn (vol. 6), M.D. Macleod (vols 7–8), 8 vols, 1913–25, 1959, 1961, 1967

——, *Scholia in Lucianum*, ed. H. Rabe, Leipzig, 1906, repr. Stuttgart, 1971

Lycophron, *Alexandra*, Eng. trans. A.W. Mair, *Callimachus and Lycophron*, 1921

——, *Scholia in Lycophronem*: *Lycophronis Alexandra* (scholia vetera et recentiora partim Isaac et Joannis Tzetzae), ed. E. Sheer, *Lycophronis Alexandra*, vol. 2, Berlin, 1958

Malalas, *Chronicle*, ed. L. Dindorf, Bonn, 1831; Eng. trans. E. Jeffreys, M. Jeffreys, R. Scott et al., *The Chronicle of John Malalas*, Australian Association for Byzantine Studies 4, Melbourne, 1986

Nonnus, *Dionysiaca*, Eng. trans. W.H.D. Rouse, 3 vols, 1940

Nonnus: Pseudo-Nonnus, *Commentaries* 4, 5, 39 and 43: *Pseudo-Nonniani in IV Orationes Gregorii Nazianzeni Commentarii editi a Jennifer Nimmo Smith, collationibus Versionum Syriacarum a Sebastian Brock Versioneque Armeniaca a Bernard Coulie additis*, Corpus Christianorum Series Graeca 27 Corpus Nazianzenum 2, Brepols, 1992; K. Weitzmann translates passages from *Commentaries* 4, 5, 39 and 43 as part of his discussion of miniatures in mss. of Gregory's sermons and the *Commentaries*, *Greek Mythology in Byzantine Art*, Princeton, 1951, pp. 6–92

——, 'Nonni narrationes viginti' (*Commentary* 43), ed. F. Creuzer, *Meletemata e disciplina antiquitatis* I, Leipzig, 1819

——, 'Five unedited Greek Scholia of Pseudo-Nonnos', ed. José Declerck, *L'Antiquité Classique* 45 (1976), pp. 181–89

——, 'Les Commentaires Mythologiques du Ps.-Nonnus sur l'homélie XLIII de Grégoire de Nazianze. Essai d'édition critique', ed. José Declerck, *Byz.* 47 (1977), pp. 92–112

——, *The Syriac Version of the Pseudo-Nonnos Mythological Scholia*, ed. with Eng. trans. Sebastian Brock, Cambridge, 1971

Novum Testamentum, The Greek New Testament, ed. K. Aland, M. Black, C.M. Martini, B.M. Metzger and A. Wikgren, Stuttgart, 1968

Olympiodorus, *The Greek Commentaries on Plato's Phaedo. 1. Olympiodorus*, ed. and Eng. trans. L.G. Westerink, Amsterdam, Oxford, New York, 1976

Origen, *Contra Celsum*, ed. and Fr. trans. M. Borret, *Origène. Contre Celse*, SC 132, 136, 147, 150, 4 vols, Paris, 1967–69; Eng. trans. H. Chadwick, *Contra Celsum*, Cambridge 1953, 3rd repr., Oxford, 1979

——, *Philocalia* or *Ecloga de operibus Origenis a Basilio et Gregorio Nazianzeno facta*, ed. J.A. Robinson, *The philocalia of Origen*, Cambridge, 1893; Eng. trans. George Lewis, *The Philocalia of Origen: a compilation of selected passages from Origen's works made by St. Gregory of Nazianzus and St. Basil of Caesarea translated into English*, Edinburgh, 1911

Ovid, *Metamorphoses*, Eng. trans. Frank J. Miller, 2 vols, 1916; rev. edn G.P. Gould, 1984

Palaephatus, *De Incredibilis: Palaephati Περὶ Ἀπίστων*, ed. N. Festa (*Mythographi Graeci* 3.2), Leipzig, 1902; Eng. trans. Jacob Stern, with Teubner Greek text, ed. N. Festa, *Palaephatus ΠΕΡΙ ΑΠΙΣΤΩΝ On Unbelievable Tales*, Wauconda, IL, 1996

Pausanias, *Description of Greece*, Eng. trans. W.H.S. Jones and H.A. Omerod (vols 1–4), index, maps, etc., R.E. Wycherley (vol. 5), 5 vols, 1918–35

Philostratus, *Life of Apollonius*, Eng. trans. F.C. Conybeare, 2 vols, 1912

Photius, *Library*, ed. and Fr. trans. R. Henry, *Photius. Bibliothèque*, 8 vols, Paris, 1959–77. Selections from the *Library*, Eng. trans. N.G. Wilson, *Photius: The Bibliotheca*, London, 1994

Pindar, *Olympia, Pythia, Nemea, Isthmia: Pindari carmina cum fragmentis*, ed. H. Maehler (post B. Snell), 2 vols, Leipzig, 1971; Eng. trans. William H. Race, 2 vols, 1997

——, *Scholia in Pindarum* (scholia vetera), ed. A.B. Drachmann, *Scholia vetera in Pindari carmina*, 3 vols, Leipzig, 1903 (repr. Amsterdam, 1969), 1910 (repr. Amsterdam, 1967), 1927 (repr. Amsterdam, 1966)

Plato, *Works*, Eng. trans. H.N. Fowler (vols 1, 4, 7–8), W.R.M. Lamb (vols

2–3, 12), Paul Shorey (vols 5–6), R.G. Bury (vols 9–11), 12 vols, 1914–29
——, *Epistle* 7, Eng. trans. Walter Hamilton, *Phaedrus and the Seventh and Eighth Letters*, Harmondsworth, 1973
——, *Scholia in Platonem: Scholia Platonica*, ed. W.C. Greene, Haverford, PA, 1938
Pliny, *Natural History*, Eng. trans. H. Rackham (vols 1–5, 9), H.S. Jones (vols 6–8), D.E. Eichholz (vol. 10), 10 vols, 1938–62
Plutarch, *Parallel Lives*, Eng. trans. B. Perrin, 11 vols, 1914–26
——, *Moral Essays*, Eng. trans. Frank C. Babitt et al., 15 vols, 1927–69
Polybius, *Histories*, Eng. trans. W.R. Paton, 6 vols, 1922–27
Procopius, *History of the Wars*, Eng. trans. H.B. Dewing, 5 vols, 1914–28
Septuaginta, ed. A. Ralphs, Stuttgart, 1935
Servius, *Commentarii in Virgilium Serviani*, ed. H. Albertus Lion, vols 1 and 2, Göttingen, 1826
Socrates, *Historia Ecclesiastica*, PG 67, ed. J.-P. Migne, Paris, 1864; Eng. trans. A.C. Zenos, in *A Select Library of the Nicene and Post-Nicene Fathers of the Christian Church*, 2nd series, vol. 2, repr. Grand Rapids, MI, 1996
Sophocles, *Plays*, Eng. trans. Hugh Lloyd-Jones, 3 vols, 1994–96
——, *Scholia in Sophoclem* (Scholia vetera), ed. P.N. Papageorgius, *Scholia in Sophoclis tragoedias vetera*, Leipzig, 1888
Souda Lexicon, ed. A. Adler, *Suidae lexicon* (*Lexocographi Graeci* 1.1–1.4), 4 vols, Leipzig, 1928 (repr. Stuttgart, 1971), 1931 (repr. Stuttgart, 1967), 1933 (repr. Stuttgart, 1967), 1935 (repr. Stuttgart, 1971)
Sozomen, *Historia ecclesiastica*, PG 67, ed. J.-P. Migne, Paris, 1864; Eng. trans. C.O. Hartran, in *A Select Library of the Nicene and Post-Nicene Fathers of the Christian Church*, 2nd series, vol 2, repr. Grand Rapids, MI, 1996
Stephanus Byzantinus, *Ethnica* (epitome), ed. A. Meineke, *Stephan von Byzanz. Ethnika*, Berlin, 1849, repr. Graz, 1958
Strabo, *Geography*, Eng. trans. Horace L. Jones, 8 vols, 1917–32
Theocritus, *Idyllia*, ed. A.S.F. Gow, *Theocritus*, vol. 1, Cambridge, 1952, repr. 1965; Eng. trans. J.M. Edmonds, *Greek Bucolic Poets* (*Theocritus, Bion, Moschus*), 1912
——, *Scholia in Theocritum* (scholia vetera), ed. K. Wendel, *Scholia in Theocritum vetera*, Leipzig, 1914, repr. Stuttgart, 1967
Thucydides, *Histories*, Eng. trans. C.F. Smith, 4 vols, 1919–23
Tzetzes, John, *Chiliades*, ed. P.A.M. Leone, *Ioannis Tzetzae historiae*, Naples, 1968

Xenophon, *Works*, Eng. trans. Walter Miller (vols 5–6), C.L. Brownson (vols 1–3), E.C. Marchant and O.J. Todd (vol. 4), E.C. Marchant and Glen W. Bowersock (vol. 7), 7 vols, 1914, 1918–1922, 1923, 1925

Zacharias of Mitylene, *Life of Severus* (*Vie de Sévère par Zacharie le Scoliastique*), Syriac text ed. and Fr. trans. M.-A. Kugener, *PO* 2.1, Paris, 1907, pp. 7–115

——, *On the Creation of the World* (*De mundi opificio*), Greek text with Latin translation, *PG* 85 1011–1144. The text is edited under the title *Ammonio* by M.M. Colonna, Naples, 1973, with an Italian translation by M.M. Colonna.

Zenobius, *Epitome collectionum Lucilli Tarhaei et Didymi*, ed. E.L. von Leutsch and F.G. Schneidewin, *Corpus paroemiographorum Graecorum*, I, Göttingen, 1839, repr. Hildesheim, 1965

OTHER WORKS

Works cited in full in the notes are not included.

Ariès, P. and Duby, G., *A History of Private Life*. I. *From Pagan Rome to Byzantium*, Cambridge, MA, and London, 1987

Barton, Tamsyn, *Ancient Astrology*, London, 1994

Bernardi, J., *Grégoire de Nazianze. Le Théologien et son temps*, Paris, 1995

Burkert, Walter, *Homo Necans*, trans. Peter Bing, Berkeley, 1983

——, *Greek Religion*, trans. John Raffan, Cambridge, MA, 1985

——, *Ancient Mystery Cults. Carl Newell Jackson Lectures*, Cambridge, MA, 1987

Cameron, Averil, *Procopius and the Sixth Century*, London, 1996 [1985]

——, *Christianity and the Rhetoric of Empire. The Development of Christian Discourse*, Sather Classical Lectures, vol. 55, Berkeley, 1991

Chadwick, H., *Early Christian Thought and the Classical Tradition. Studies in Justin, Clement and Origen*, Oxford, 1966

Chionides, N.P. and Lilla, S., *La brachygraphia italo-bizantina. Studi e testi 290*, The Vatican, 1981

Constantinides, Costas N., Panagiotakes, Nikolaos M., Jeffreys, Elizabeth and Angelou, Athanasios D. (eds), ΦΙΛΕΛΛΗΝ *Studies in Honour of Robert Browning*, Venice, 1996

Coulie, B., Nimmo Smith, J. and CETEDOC, *Thesaurus Pseudo-Nonni. Commentarii in IV Orationes Gregorii Nazianzeni. Thesaurus Patrum Graecorum*, Louvain-la-Neuve, 1992

de Jong, Albert, *Traditions of the Magi: Zoroastrianism in Greek and Latin Literature*, Leiden, 1997

Demoen, C., *Pagan and Biblical Exempla in Gregory Nazianzen. A Study in Rhetoric and Hermeneutics*, Corpus Christianorum Lingua Patrum II, Brepols, 1996

Fontenrose, J., *The Delphic Oracle: its responses and operations; with a catalogue of responses*, Berkeley, 1978

Gager, J.G., *Curse Tablets and Binding Spells from the Ancient World*, Oxford, 1992

Gantz, T., *Early Greek Myth. A Guide to Literary and Artistic Sources*, 2 vols, Baltimore and London, 1993

Guthrie, W.K.C., *A History of Greek Philosophy* 3, Cambridge, 1969

Jeffreys, E., with Croke, B. and Scott, R., *Studies in John Malalas, Australian Association for Byzantine Studies* Byzantina Australiensia 6, Sydney, 1990

Kaster, R.A., *Guardians of Language: The Grammarian and Society in Late Antiquity*, Berkeley, 1988

Kennedy, G.A., *Greek Rhetoric under Christian Emperors*, Princeton, NJ, 1983

Kraut, R. (ed.), *The Cambridge Companion to Plato*, Oxford, 1992

Laistner, M.L.W., *Christianity and Pagan Culture in the Later Roman Empire, together with an English translation of John Chrysostom's Address on Vainglory and the Right Way for Parents to Bring up their Children*, New York, 1951

Laks, André and Most, Glenn W. (eds), *Studies on the Derveni Papyrus*, Oxford, 1997

Lefherz, F., 'Studien zu Gregor von Nazianz. Mythologie, Ueberlieferung, Scholiasten', PhD thesis, Bonn, 1958

Lemerle, P., *Byzantine Humanism. Notes and remarks on education and culture in Byzantium from its origins until the 10th century*, trans. Helen Lindsay and Ann Moffatt, *Australian Association for Byzantine Studies* Byzantinia Australiensia 3, Canberra, 1986

Lietzmann, H., *A History of the Early Church*, vols 3 and 4, London, 3rd impression, 1967

MacMullen, Ramsay, *Christianity and Paganism in the Fourth to Eighth Centuries*, New Haven, CT, 1997

Marrou, H.I., *A History of Education in Antiquity*, trans. G. Lamb, New York, 1956

Meredith, Anthony, *The Cappadocians*, New York, 1995

——, *Gregory of Nyssa*, New York, 1999

Momigliano, A. (ed.), *The Conflict between Paganism and Christianity in the Fourth Century*, Oxford, 1963

Mossay, J. (ed.), *II Symposium Nazianzenum, Louvain-la-Neuve 25–28 août 1981*, Paderborn, 1983

Nimmo Smith, J., 'The Early Scholia on the Sermons of Gregory of Nazianzus', in *Studia Nazianzenica* I, ed. B. Coulie, Corpus Christianorum Series Graeca 41, Corpus Nazianzenum 8, Brepols, 2000, pp. 69–146

——, 'Nonnus and Pseudo-Nonnos: the Poet and the Commentator', in Constantinides et al. (eds), ΦΙΛΕΛΛΗΝ *Studies in Honour of Robert Browning*, pp. 281–99

Nimmo Smith, J. and Otkh'mezuri, T., 'The Georgian Versions of the Pseudo-Nonnos *Commentaries* and their Greek originals', *Le Muséon* 106 (1993), pp. 289–308

Parke, H.W., *The Oracles of Zeus*, Cambridge, MA, 1967

Pelikan, Jaroslav, *Christianity and Classical Culture. The Metamorphosis of Natural Theology in the Christian Encounter with Hellenism*, Gifford Lectures at Aberdeen 1992–1993, New Haven, CT, 1993

Pinch, Geraldine, *Magic in Ancient Egypt*, London, 1994

Reynolds, L.D and Wilson, N.G., *Scribes and Scholars. A Guide to the Transmission of Greek & Latin Literature*, 3rd edn, Oxford, 1991

Ruether, Rosemary Radford, *Gregory of Nazianzus, Rhetor and Philosopher*, Oxford, 1969

Sorabji, R. (ed.), *Philoponus and the Rejection of Aristotelian Science*, New York, 1987

Stead, C., *Philosophy in Christian Antiquity*, Cambridge, 1994, repr. 1995

Trisoglio, F., 'Mentalità ed attegiamenti degli scoliasti di fronte agli scritti di S. Gregorio de Nazianzo', in Mossay (ed.), *II Symposium Nazianzenum*, pp. 187–251

Trombley, F., *Hellenic Religion and Christianization c.370–529*, vols 1 and 2, Leiden, 1993

Weitzmann, K., *Greek Mythology in Byzantine Art* (*Studies in Manuscript Illumination* 4), Princeton, NJ, 1951

Weitzmann, K. (ed.), *Age of Spirituality. Late Antique and Early Christian Art. Third to Seventh Century*, catalogue of the exhibition at the Metropolitan Museum of Art, November 19 1977 through February 12 1978, Princeton, NJ, 1978

West, M.L., *The Orphic Poems*, Oxford, 1983

INDICES TO THE *COMMENTARIES*

INDEX OF ANCIENT AUTHORS, GENERAL SOURCES AND PROVERBS

Numbers denote *Commentary* and story number. Asterisks denote stories from the Appendix.

Apollonius Rhodius 43.17 (app. crit.)
Apollonius of Tyana 4.70 (utterances)
Arcadian riddle 4.33, 34
Aristaenetus the Historian 5.27
Aristophanes 4.90
Aristotle (Peripatetic School) 4.24
Beware of the Black-buttocked 4.39
(According to the divinely taught) Christians ... 4.68
Christian account 5.8
Christians say ... 43.18
Consulting Trophonius 4.1
Croesus and the Halys 4.95
Crow and borrowed feathers 4.63
Dius the Commentator 4.39
Drop of Luck 4.26
Euripus (tides) 4.34; 5.7
Fox (cunning) 4.44
Gregory 4 title, 4.7, 23, 24, 25, 26, 43, 44, 55, 67, 74, 76, 77; 5 title; 39; title, 39.1; 43 title, 43.1, 8, 13, 18
Helenus 4.72
Hellenica by Xenophon 5.4
Herodotus 5.3, 5, 27; 39.7; 43.5, 7, 18
Hesiod 4.65, 76

Histories by Herodotus 5.3 (Book 3), 5 (Book 6); 43. 7 (Book 4)
Homer 4.20, 33, 34, 53, 54, 61, 79, 83, 84, 85; 5.21; 43.16
Isaiah 5.38*
Lacedaemonian women 4.74
Lycurgus 43.7
Lydian chariots 43.10
(*Against*) *Menesaechmus* by Lycurgus 43.7
Minos (just man) 4.44
No story ... 5.30
Orphic poems 4.77; 5.13
Others relate ... 43.6
Phaedo by Plato 4.16; 5.31
Philosophers 4.27
Pig (Boeotian) 39.4
Plato 4.16, 22, 55, 75; 5.9, 31; 43.5, 14
Poets (Homer) 4.80; 43.14
Polles 4.72
Popular story 39.1
Posidonius 4.72
Present-day interpreters of Plato 4.23
Present-day interpreters of the philosophers 4.27
Republic by Plato 4.55, 75; 43.5
Rhapsode 5 Homer, *Iliad* 5 4.85

INDEX OF ETYMOLOGIES

Numbers denote *Commentary* and story number.

INDEX OF HISTORICAL FIGURES

Numbers denote *Commentary* and story number. Asterisks denote stories from the Appendix.

INDEX OF CONSTELLATIONS, MYTHOLOGICAL DEITIES, HEROES AND MONSTERS, PAGAN CULTS AND SACRED ANIMALS

Numbers denote *Commentary* and story number. Asterisks denote stories from the Appendix.

INDEX OF PEOPLES AND PLACES

Numbers denote *Commentary* and story number. Asterisks denote stories from the Appendix.

INDEX OF PRINCIPAL THEMES

Numbers denote *Commentary* and story number. Asterisks denote stories from the Appendix

THE TOPOGRAPHY OF THE *COMMENTARIES*

I give three maps under the above title, because the *Commentaries* encompass a complex 'thought-world' of historical and literary allusion from the earliest times of Greek prehistory onwards which cannot be easily represented without such a division. The first, the 'World-view of the *Commentaries*' reflects the traditional Graeco-Roman concept of linked land-masses, surrounded by the Ocean. Ethiopia, the Hyperboreans, India, Persia and the Scythians appear on this map, with the Taurus Range of mountains. It is based on a drawing of the world in *A History of Greece to 322* BC by N.G.L. Hammond, Oxford 1959, p. 622, fig. 33, reproduced by kind permission of Oxford University Press. The second shows the regions, cities, towns, rivers, islands and mountains mentioned in the *Commentaries* for the Mediterranean (the 'Western Sea', *Comm.* 5.35) and its environs, except for Mainland Greece. This last appears in some detail in the third, although the region of 'Dryopis' within it, for example, represents an imaginary country to the south of Thessaly, once inhabited by the Dorians on their migration south (see the notes to *Comm.* 4.41).

154

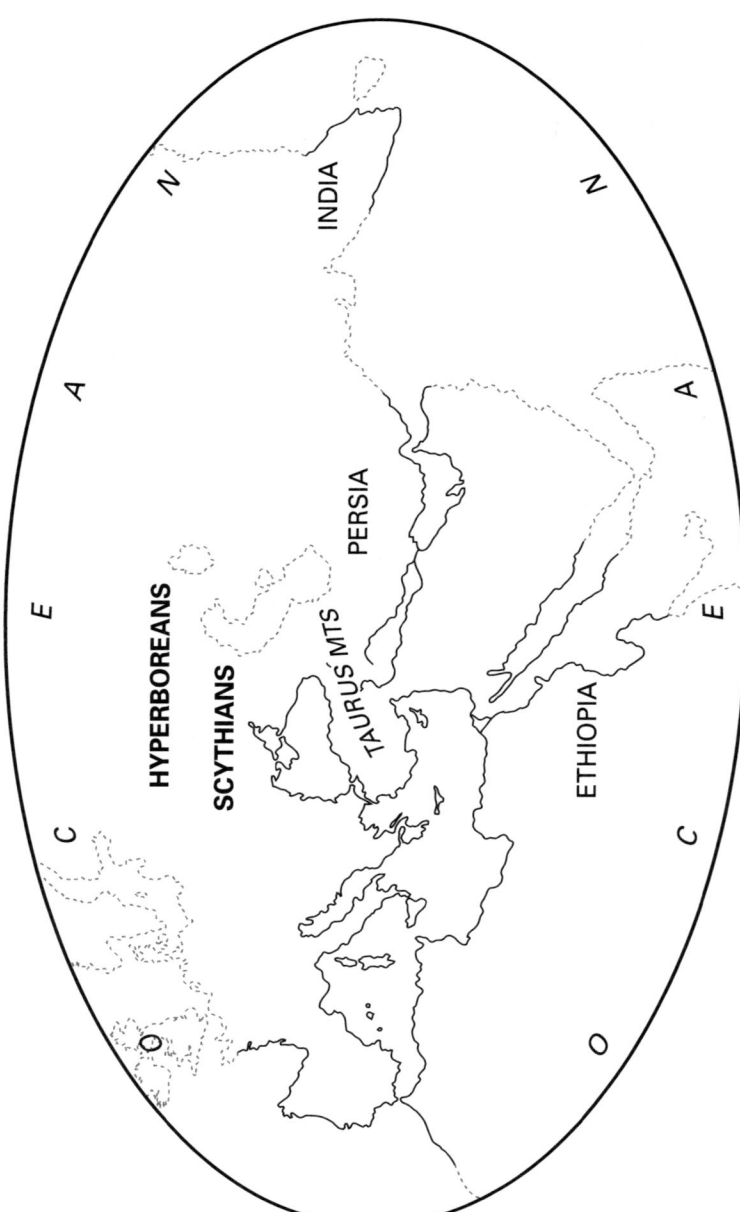

Map 1 The 'World-view' of the *Commentaries*

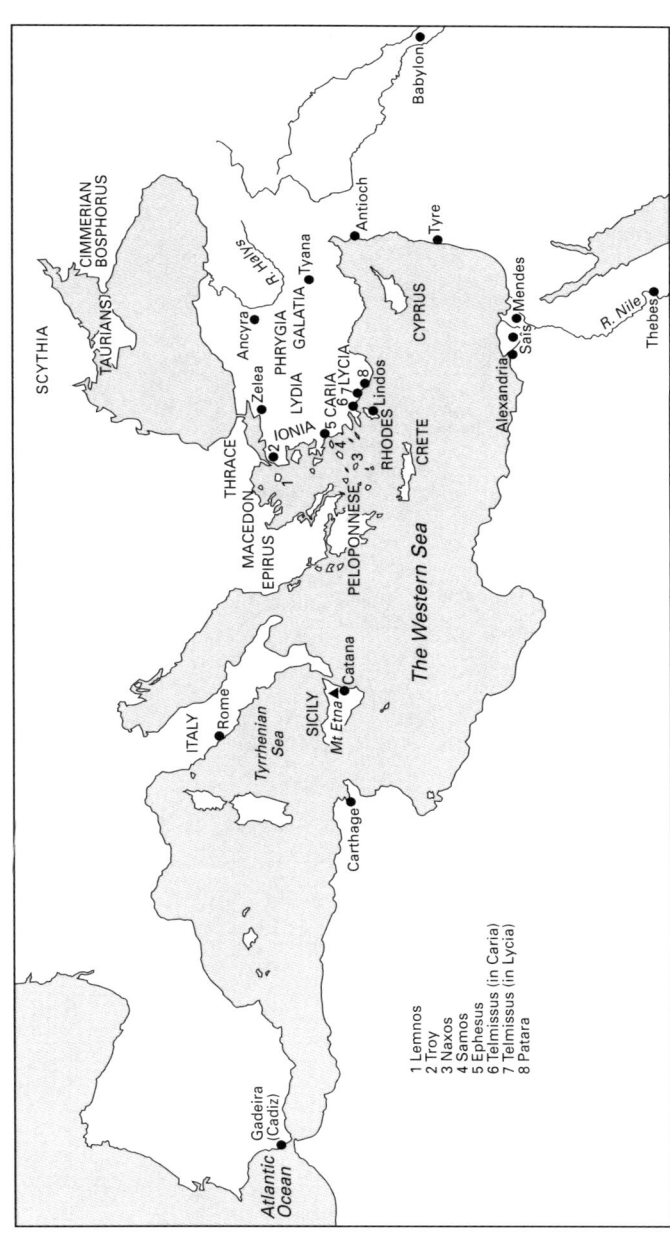

Map 2 The 'Western Sea' and its environs

Map 3 Mainland Greece